Computer Supported Cooperative Work

Springer
London
Berlin
Heidelberg
New York
Hong Kong
Milan
Paris
Tokyo

Also in this series

Gerold Riempp
Wide Area Workflow Management
3-540-76243-4

Celia T. Romm and Fay Sudweeks
(Eds)
Doing Business Electronically
3-540-76159-4

Fay Sudweeks and Celia T. Romm (Eds)
Doing Business on the Internet
1-85233-030-9

Elayne Coakes, Dianne Willis and
Raymond Lloyd-Jones (Eds)
The New SocioTech
1-85233-040-6

Elizabeth F. Churchill, David N.
Snowdon and Alan J. Munro (Eds)
Collaborative Virtual Environments
1-85233-244-1

Christine Steeples and Chris Jones
(Eds)
Networked Learning
1-85233-471-1

Barry Brown, Nicola Green and
Richard Harper (Eds)
Wireless World
1-85233-477-0

Reza Hazemi and Stephen Hailes (Eds)
The Digital University
1-85233-478-9

Elayne Coakes, Dianne Willis and
Steve Clark (Eds)
Knowledge Management in the
SocioTechnical World
1-85233-441-X

Ralph Schroeder (Ed.)
The Social Life of Avatars
1-85233-461-4

Kristina Höök, Alan J. Munro and
David Benyon (Eds)
Designing Information Spaces
Technologies in Industry
1-85233-661-7

Bjørn Erik Munkvold
Implementing Collaboration
Technologies in Industry
1-85233-418-5

Paul Kirschner, Chad Carr and Simon
Buckingham Shum (Eds)
Visualising Argumentation
1-85233-664-1

A list of out of print titles is available at the end of the book

J.H. Erik Andriessen

Working with Groupware

Understanding and Evaluating Collaboration Technology

With 24 Figures

 Springer

J.H. Erik Andriessen, PhD
Delft University of Technology, Faculty of Technology, Policy and Management, Department of Work and Organizational Psychology, Jaffalaan 5, 2628 BX Delft, The Netherlands

Series Editors

Dan Diaper, PhD, MBCS
Professor of Systems Science & Engineering, School of Design, Engineering & Computing, Bournemouth University, Talbot Campus, Fern Barrow, Poole, Dorset BH12 5BB, UK

Colston Sanger
Shottersley Research Limited, Little Shottersley, Farnham Lane
Haslemere, Surrey GU27 1HA, UK

British Library Cataloguing in Publication Data
Andriessen, J.H. Erik
 Working with groupware : understanding and evaluating
 collaboration technology. - (Computer supported cooperative
 work)
 1.Groupware (Computer software) 2.Teams in the workplace
 3.Teams in the workplace - Data processing
 I.Title
 658.4'02'0285
 ISBN 185233603X

Library of Congress Cataloging-in-Publication Data
Andriessen, Erik, 1941-
 Working with groupware : understanding and evaluating collaboration technology /
 Erik Andriessen.
  p. cm. -- (Computer supported cooperative work)
 Includes bibliographical references and index.
 ISBN 1-85233-603-X
  1. Human-computer interaction. 2. Groupware (Computer software) 3. Computer
 networks. I. Title. II. Series.
 QA76.9.H85 A65 2002
 004'.01'9--dc21   2002070460

Apart from any fair dealing for the purposes of research or private study, or criticism or review, as permitted under the Copyright, Designs and Patents Act 1988, this publication may only be reproduced, stored or transmitted, in any form or by any means, with the prior permission in writing of the publishers, or in the case of reprographic reproduction in accordance with the terms of licences issued by the Copyright Licensing Agency. Enquiries concerning reproduction outside those terms should be sent to the publishers.

CSCW ISSN 1431-1496

ISBN 1-85233-603-X Springer-Verlag London Berlin Heidelberg
a member of BertelsmannSpringer Science+Business Media GmbH
http://www.springer.co.uk

© Springer-Verlag London Limited 2003
Printed in Great Britain

The use of registered names, trademarks etc. in this publication does not imply, even in the absence of a specific statement, that such names are exempt from the relevant laws and regulations and therefore free for general use.

The publisher makes no representation, express or implied, with regard to the accuracy of the information contained in this book and cannot accept any legal responsibility or liability for any errors or omissions that may be made.

Typesetting: Camera ready by author
Printed and bound at the Athenæum Press Ltd., Gateshead, Tyne & Wear
34/3830-543210 Printed on acid-free paper SPIN 10868557

Preface

This publication has grown out of two frustrations. One is the experience that so many applications in the area of information and communication technology (ICT) are built without an eye to what the users can handle or need for their work, systematic user oriented evaluation of new tools is therefore limited. The video recorder provides a good general example of this phenomenon, but more worryingly so do many software tools designed for use in organisations. The other frustration arises from the fact that the people and the theories that can be used to provide this much needed user orientation are scattered over many disciplines and communities.

There is considerable knowledge available about task performance, human communication and group interaction and the way in which new ICT-tools can be used to support these processes, but scientists do not know each other, the studies, theories, journals and conferences are produced by different communities in isolation and little cross fertilisation takes place. In this book I have tried to bring together knowledge from various disciplines, as the basis for constructing a design oriented evaluation approach that hopefully contributes to providing a user orientation for new (technical) systems.

The two frustrations, user-unfriendliness, and disintegration of information are related to a third finding that ICT-applications often do not function according to expectations. To some extent this is a blessing; applications of information and communication technology have properties that may change the way we work and interact in unpredictable but very innovative and interesting ways. In many cases it is a curse, the tools in practice are often not used at all or only to a very limited degree. This is particularly true for applications that are designed to support interaction between people, in this book called *collaboration technology*. I do not consider these applications of ICT to be utopian hopes or hellish horrors (Kling, 1996). They are simply tools that still have many children's diseases and have to be honed much more than they are now. Solutions to problems and failures in this field, however, should be based on an approach stemming from the following perspectives:

- Computers (or any other technology) are not isolated objects, they form parts of social systems, that are evolving through time in reaction to societal, i.e. organisational and market, trends such as globalisation, virtualisation and efficiency drives. Design and evaluation should be directed at tools-in-context, or better even, to entire socio-technical systems. Technology and social systems are mutually shaped.
- The introduction of technology and new processes in organisations requires a careful approach and much attention to the conditions under which the introduction takes place.

- Socio-technical systems should be designed carefully. Nevertheless, such settings will evolve in new directions, often in unpredictable ways, through processes of "appropriation".
- The success of collaboration technology depends on the use(rs), not on the technology (garbage in, garbage out).
- The analysis of computer supported collaboration requires attention to various types of phenomena: human computer interaction, interpersonal communication, group co-operation, organisational functioning.
- So, adoption, use and the success or failure of collaboration technology depends largely on three main groups of factors:
    1. whether it is accepted by the users, and is suitable for their task,
    2. whether it fits and supports the social context, and
    3. whether it is introduced in a proper way and is tailorable to changing demands.

Therefore, to establish the value of information and communication technology in general and collaboration technology in particular, it is necessary to understand the processes of individual work, communication and group-interaction and its implications for support tools.

Objectives. The ultimate aim of this publication is to contribute to improvements in interaction amongst people, and between people and information sources. Central questions such as the following have to be answered. How can people co-operate successfully at a distance? Why is one collaboration tool more successful than another? What are the potential implications of the new technologies, both for effective work and interaction processes and for the quality of work and that of the life of users? How can we design new work settings using applications that conform to criteria of effectiveness and quality of work and life?

The book has three concrete objectives:

1. To analyse the *reasons for success and failure* of collaboration technology,
2. To provide *theoretical frameworks* for the systematic analysis of the conditions required for successful distributed collaboration and collaborative technology, and
3. To present an integrated approach, based upon the theoretical frameworks, for a systematic, *user oriented, design related, evaluation* of computer supported collaboration, i.e. of work arrangements where collaboration technology plays an important role.

Findings, concepts and theories will be presented that focus on individual and organisational behaviour with regard to new technologies, i.e:

- psychological theories concerning human computer interaction and work motivation,
- communication theories concerning mediated information exchange and media match,
- group dynamic theories concerning co-operation and team effectiveness,
- theories concerning implementation of technology and of adaptation processes.

Writing a book like this means for the largest part bringing together what others have discovered and for only a small part creative thinking by the writer. Bringing together the contributions of others has not only involved literature research, it has also meant listening to and digesting the ideas of people in my environment. Colleagues at the department of Work and Organisation Psychology of the Delft University of Technology in particular have contributed to this work in many ways. They have developed in co-operation concepts, models and evaluation methods of which some have become integrated in this volume. But equally valuable has been their support and their willingness to take over administrative, teaching or research obligations in certain periods. The exchange of views with colleagues from other institutes has also contributed much to this book. The integration of all these building blocks to achieve this publication and its models is my own responsibility, but I owe a depth of gratitude to these colleagues for providing the fine working climate and the intensive discussions that I enjoy so much. In this context I mention particularly Helen van der Horst, Laurens ten Horn, Albert Arnold, Jeroen van der Velden, Marion Wiethof and Miranda Aldham-Breary for their diverse but valuable ideas and help.

I dedicate this book to my wife, who just like me has struggled often with user-unfriendly computers, but particularly to my daughter Gemma. In ten years time she will probably work in situations where collaboration technology is seen as commonplace and she will require technical and organisational systems that are very user friendly and pertinent to the task at hand. I hope that this book may contribute to achieve these ends.

Overview

Part 1. Human Interaction and Collaboration Technology
The first three chapters present the basic technological tools and social psychological concepts concerning distributed and ICT supported work. It discusses major findings concerning the use and effects of using these tools and various perspectives on the interaction of tools and social contexts, i.e. on socio-technical settings.

Chapter 1. Social Processes and Support Tools
The first chapter starts with an exposé of the concepts "co-operative work" and "collaboration technology". Next it discusses major group interaction processes and the technical tools that are developed to support co-operative work.

Chapter 2. Implications of Collaboration Technology
This chapter contains a short overview of the major results of empirical research concerning the psychological and social implications of collaboration technology. It appears that collaboration technology can produce all kinds of positive consequences, related to the ubiquitous accessibility of information and people. Negative consequences can also be found. The major conclusion is that very few general conclusions can be drawn! The introduction of collaboration technology has some generic effects on communication but other effects depend on certain conditions. Three roads to success are distinguished, viz. user acceptance and motivation based on a psychological cost benefit analysis (Chapter 4), fit to task and social context (Chapters 5,6), adequate implementation and tailorability to emerging events (Chapter 7).

Chapter 3.The Role of Technology in Society
This chapter contains a discussion of various perspectives on the role of technology in society. A general theory of the relationship between human behaviour and societal institutions is presented i.e. Structuration Theory.

Part II. Theories for Understanding and Evaluation
The second part of the book discusses theories that are relevant for the explanation of acceptance of and working with collaborative tools. In the last chapter an integrated model, based on the various theories, will be presented that can be used as the basis for an overall evaluation of collaboration tools

Chapter 4. Technology Acceptance
In this chapter the focus is on the individual user. It deals with the question of how work performance is regulated and why people adopt and use certain tools. This question is answered by a discussion of theories concerning work motivation and technology acceptance.

Chapter 5. System Match Theories.
Many theories are based on the assumption that characteristics of various elements in systems have to match to be effective. In this case the focus is on the match between the characteristics of collaboration technology tools and the characteristics of the tasks, the users and the context. An example of this is the Media Richness Theory.

Chapter 6. Group Processes
Collaboration technology tools have to support interaction among people and that of people with computers. Proper design requires a knowledge of human task performance and of aspects of collaboration processes, i.e. of communication, co-operation, and co-ordination. Chapter 6 introduces basic theories with regard to these phenomena and the role of Collaboration Technology tools vis-à-vis these phenomena is discussed.

Chapter 7. Innovation and Implementation
The success of new systems is not only a matter of making tools that are appropriate for certain users or tasks. It is also a dynamic process of designing the system in a proper way, of diffusion of new technologies throughout society, of adoption by organisations and of adequate introduction and evaluation processes. Theories concerning technology introduction and of organisational change are discussed in this chapter.

Chapter 8. Integration for Evaluation
The implications of the theories discussed in the previous chapters are integrated into a framework (model) and an overview of relevant evaluation issues. This framework and overview form the basis for an *integrated, user oriented and design directed evaluation* approach. Whenever a (socio-)technical system is being developed this framework and overview can be used to provide a systematic analysis of (potential or actual) success criteria and side effects of the new system. The evaluation process contains three evaluation steps: concept evaluation, prototype evaluation and operational evaluation.

N.B. The major focus of this book is on interaction in organisations. Team effectiveness supported by collaboration technology is a central issue. Nevertheless, many findings and theories are also applicable to situations outside work organisations. Notions about media match or adoption of tools, about adaptation and computer usability are as relevant for systems to be used by the tele-shopping houseperson as for systems that are used by the organisational professional.

Erik Andriessen
Delft, August, 2002

Table of Contents

Part I. Human Interaction and Collaboration Technology

The first three chapters present the basic technological tools and social psychological concepts concerning distributed and ICT supported work. They discuss major findings concerning the use and effects of using these tools and various perspectives on the interaction of tools and social contexts, i.e. on socio-technical settings.

In the first chapter the concepts "co-operative work" and "collaboration technology" are introduced and analysed. Then the major group interaction processes are presented, which will be discussed in depth in later chapters. The technical tools, developed to support co-operative work, are inventoried and related to the group processes. Finally the various new types of work and organisation are considered, i.e. settings such as telework, virtual teams, and virtual organisations.

The second chapter discusses the various potential implications of collaboration technology, on the basis of a short overview of the major results of empirical research concerning the psychological and social aspects of collaboration technology. It appears that collaboration technology can produce all kinds of positive consequences, related to the ubiquitous accessibility of information and people. Negative consequences can also be found. The major conclusion is, however, that very few general conclusions can be drawn! The introduction of collaboration technology has some generic effects on communication but other effects depend on certain conditions. Three roads to successful introduction of groupware are distinguished, viz. user acceptance (see Chapter 4), fit to task and social context (Chapters 5 and 6) and adequate implementation (Chapter 7).

The third chapter contains a discussion of various perspectives on the role of technology in society, such as the technological and organisational imperative, the strategic choice perspective and the emergent structures perspective Structuration Theory is a general theory that combines some of these perspectives.

Chapter 1. Social Processes and Support Tools

1.1 The Changing World of Work

The world of work is changing. The type of work itself, the workers and their tools are becoming radically different. Three primary drivers can be distinguished (see Figure 1.1):

a. Technological changes, particularly the developments in information and communication technologies,
b. Market changes, particularly globalisation and liberalisation, with world wide competition,
c. Social changes, such as growing educational levels and individualisation.

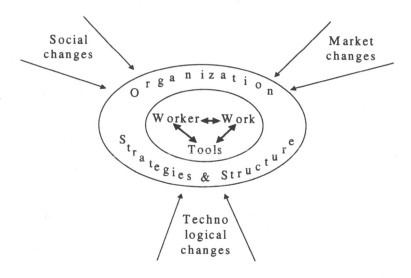

Figure 1.1 The changing world of work (Source: Howard, A. *The changing nature of work.* © by Jossey-Bass, 1995. Reprinted with permission of John Wiley & Sons)

The market side together with the technological changes stimulate the demand side, i.e. what needs to be done and how. Demographic and social changes influence the supply side, i.e. the kind of workers available. The impacts of the three major changing forces on the world of work are mediated by (inter)organisational structures and strategies; and the interaction between all these forces takes place in a larger political-economic-societal context.

The majority of employees in western societies consists of information or knowledge workers who produce or process information in one way or another. Employment in the service sectors, both private and public, is growing, which means that the number of information workers or knowledge workers, i.e. professional, managerial and clerical personnel, is rising at the cost of blue-collar workers.

Information work can be viewed as consisting of six types of processes, i.e. communication and information collection, processing, production, management (including storing and retrieving) and distribution. Information exchange and communication between individuals are becoming increasingly essential to organisations as vehicles for transactions, co-ordination and control. Particularly the categories Collection, Distribution and Interactive Communication contain many activities related to interpersonal interaction. The categories Collection and File Management refer partly to (remote) consultation of information sources. These processes play a large role in the working life of managers, professionals and other knowledge workers. A large part of their task has always consisted of communication activities. A survey in the USA (Porter, 1987) showed the large role of information exchanging and communication processes in major professional categories (Table 1.1). It appeared that, for example, management spend 35% on intake of information, and 50 % on distributing information and interactive communication. For professional staff these figures were 20% and 42%, while secretaries spend respectively 27% and 20% on these activities.

Other studies may give slightly different figures, because they focus on different target groups, but the general picture is the same (see Luthans, 1992, for extensive analysis of leadership behaviour). According to Panko's meta-analysis (1992), the average of managers' time spent in oral communication is 60%, of which about half is in face-to-face meetings, the majority in formal conference rooms with a quarter in dyadic conversations (Kinney & Panko, 1998). Another 25% of time is devoted to written communication. For top managers the total oral communication time is even more: about 75%. For other knowledge workers the figures are 35% for oral and 25% for written communication. A wide variety of means are used, from face-to-face meetings, to telephone calls, e-mail usage and writing or reading documents. With all this the use of ICT-tools is increasing. According to a 1998 survey among managers of 1500 large European companies the following figures regarding usage were found: e-mail 87%, mobile phones 84%, (portable) PC 85%, while 40% had used videoconferencing (Harris International, 1989).

Information processing is also related to the enormous hunger for information and the growth of information storage that our society is confronted with. Interaction between knowledge workers always involves the use of (large quantities of) stored information, in letters, documents, and in archives and libraries. Information and communication technology makes world-wide stores of information available to anybody with access to the Internet.

Another important trend is the one towards geographically distributed (and virtual) enterprising, towards networking of organisations and towards more teamwork. The increase in *geographical dispersion of activities* is due to the fact that more and more human activities such as international commerce and transport require interaction and communication over large distances. Information exchange does not necessarily imply teamwork or co-operative work. Probably even the majority of communication between people takes place in superficial and loosely coupled interactions. However, (virtual) teamwork is also growing in importance. Guzzo and Dickson (1996, p329) conclude that 80% of organisations with 100 or more employees use teams in some way and that 50% of employees in these organisations are members of at least one team at work. Virtual teamwork is much less widespread. Nevertheless, one can expect that this trend will continue. The main reasons why virtual teams and virtual organisations arise are the following (Hutchinson (1999):

- *cost-reduction*: teleworking and flexible workplaces require fewer costs per employee than the traditional one-employee-one-desk strategy.
- *globalisation*: bringing new products efficiently to global markets implies dispersing the organisation, but nevertheless bringing together the best expertise in project teams.
- *flexibility*: co-operation of (geographically distributed) employees from one or from several organisations in a temporary project team makes the organisation much more flexible and responsive to market requirements.
- *enabling technologies*: information and communication technology enables team members to access each other easily and also to access distributed information.
- *information capturing*: information and communication technology enables capturing, organising, storing and reusing the information developed by teams even - or perhaps particularly - when they are distributed geographically.
- *organisational consequences*: virtual teams are putting networks of expertise at the centre of productive work, instead of the traditional bureaucratic hierarchies.

Distributed work however forms a barrier for communication. The frequency of communication appears to decrease sharply with geographical distance. In fact, several researchers have found that working apart more than 30 meters implies about the same low level of interaction as being separated by several miles (see Allen, 1977, for engineers and Kraut, et al., 1990, for researchers).

Global and virtual interaction can be supported by the *development of certain sophisticated ICT applications and infrastructures*. Collaboration technology refers to a special type of ICT application aimed at supporting co-operative work. The world of ICT has already gone through several major stages of development. In the sixties and seventies information technology was developed to support the routine processing of standard data, resulting in separate (island) systems for production automatisation and administrative automatisation. Management information systems were very popular although their effectiveness was not always very high. Later the evolution of telecommunication infrastructures and networks allowed the integration of separate systems and the extension of facilities over large distances. This resulted in systems for Electronic Data Interchange between companies, and teleshopping and telebanking facilities for the consumer. More recently this development has resulted in the appearance of organisational Intranets, Extranets and electronic commerce.

Forty years ago Doug Engelbart, the father of groupware, envisioned *co-operation tools*. In the sixties he developed a demonstration system with shared data files, a shared screen and a video-conferencing tool. Yet it took until the eighties before this type of ICT application became widely operational, allowing not only for the massive exchange of remote data, but also for the support of co-operation between people at a distance. Barriers of distance and time differences today are becoming less and less important for communication. People from various parts of the world interact and co-operate almost as easily as if they were living and working in the same building. Note that the "almost" here means that in actual practice the utopian promises of some designers, companies and futurists have often not come true.

Technological developments are related to the *trend towards more teamwork* within and co-operation between organisations. Teamwork is considered to be essential to effective modern organisations. Certain problems can best be dealt with in teams; but teams also form the co-ordinating mechanisms that decentralised organisations need. Teamwork and co-operation require communication and information exchange and it is not by chance that at the same time tools for the support of interpersonal communication and information exchange were developed, tools such as e-mail, mobile telephones, video-conferencing, and co-authoring systems. These tools are sometimes collectively indicated with the term "groupware". The Internet, providing access to world wide information bases, is extending these groupware facilities to the whole world.

In this book I use the general term *collaboration technology* for all the applications of ICT that claim to support work interaction in and between organisations. A major role of collaboration technology is to co-ordinate people working at a distance and to allow them to interact with distant data-sources. Terms like virtual workplace, virtual work team and virtual organisations/enterprises, concepts such as teleworking, teleteaching and electronic commerce are not only indications of hypes, they also indicate real developments.

1.2 Interaction, Collaboration and Group Work

The concepts of group or of co-operative work are not very easy to define. Of course one can define co-operative work as the work done by a team, but this definition does not help much. Many activities in teams are done by individual members and therefore not carried out in a co-operative manner. Although many tasks, from washing dishes to writing an article, are often performed by one person, some of these tasks can also be performed in co-operation with other people. Other tasks, e.g. organising a conference, are impossible to do in isolation. In recent literature there may be found a kind of ideology about co-operation: close co-operation is supposed to be common in many groups; it should also be promoted, because it is supposed to be the ideal way of performing tasks. The truth is that even in tightly knit task-teams *the members perform the majority of activities separately*. Moreover, not all teamwork is better than individual task performance. As the saying goes, isn't a camel a horse designed by a committee?

The transition between individual and co-operative work can be very fluid, as well as between task-and-non-task activities or between several tasks (e.g. Robinson, 1993). Various in-depth studies have shown how seemingly separately working people co-operate now and then in a very subtle way (see Section 6.1). The conclusion is that although the term "collaborative work" generally refers to situations where two or more people act together to achieve a common goal, the actual extent of "togetherness" can vary substantially.

A similar phenomenon can be found around the concept of "group". McGrath (1984), a well known social psychologist, defines a group as *"an intact social system that carries out multiple functions, while partially nested in and loosely coupled to surrounding systems"*. This definition can comprise many types of collections of people, such as workgroups, friendship groups, professional colleagues or people interested in a certain subject. I distinguish four types of social interaction structures in organisations (see section 6.4.1):

- *Collections*, e.g. the many employees of a company who exchange work related information through e-mail or have informal interaction through a chat box.
- *Knowledge sharing communities*, e.g. a group of experts on 3D modelling of oil wells in an oil company, each working at a different location, exchanging information and views concerning their area of expertise, to keep up with the latest developments.
- *Teams* who co-operate for a certain period, e.g. a team of geographically distributed designers, working for several months on an assignment.

All these interaction types can be distributed geographically and many collaboration technology tools are used for the communication between the widely distributed members of those groups. Collaboration technology appears to make it possible for groups of a large size to co-operate as a group. Where face-to-face teams should not consist of more than about ten members, virtual teams may consist of thirty or more members. One of the major effects of the introduction of collaboration technology seems to be that certain types of meetings can now be held with a large number of participants.

In Chapter 6 it will be argued that the major activities in co-operative settings can be ordered into *five basic categories of interaction processes*. These basic interaction processes are the following:

Interpersonal exchange processes
- Communication i.e. using communication tools and exchanging signals. Communication has a special status in that it is basic to the other task and group oriented processes.

Task-oriented processes
- Co-operation, i.e. working together, decision making, co-editing etc.
- Co-ordination, i.e. adjusting the work of the group members; this includes leadership.
- Information sharing and learning, i.e. exchanging (sharing) and developing information, views, knowledge.

Group-oriented processes
- Social interaction, i.e. group maintenance activities, developing trust, cohesion, conflict handling, reflection.

This classification is not final and exhaustive, and the categories cannot always be distinguished neatly. Certain behaviours can serve several of these functions simultaneously. The classification is meant as a heuristic device for analysing group processes. In work teams all of these activities will be found; also in meetings but in a more superficial way. In loosely connected communities co-operation, co-ordination and social interaction may be absent entirely.

1.3 What is Collaboration Technology?

1.3.1 Setting the Scene

The term Information and Communication Technology (ICT, in Europe also called Telematics) refers to a mixture of hardware and software, of equipment and services:

- The telecommunication infrastructures, e.g. networks of cable or mobile systems, relay centres, satellites, ISDN.
- Data-transport services, e.g. telephone net, data net, and telematic services, i.e. value adding services, such as World Wide Web, videotext.
- Terminals, more or less intelligent: telephone, monitor, computer.
- Applications, both for stand-alone and for interactive purposes, such as word processors, electronic mail applications, video-conferencing or an information service.

Technical developments in these areas are proceeding at an ever-increasing rate and in each of the areas new inventions are continuously being announced. The law of Moore states that computing chips double their capacity every 18 months. The capacity of networks is increasing steadily. New interfaces, such as touch screens and voice interaction have made their first appearance. Miniature computers, embedded systems, are found in most forms of electrical equipment. Household apparatus such as the TV, telephone and computer are being integrated. The software applications used to support business, banking, health care and entertainment are becoming more refined by the day; and the Internet providers are offering more and more services, with the help of sophisticated tools such as joint web-browsers.

Computers can be made to be very intelligent and complicated by including a wide variety of applications and by connecting them to world wide nets and data sources. This is making computers more and more universal, and they can now incorporate services that until recently required separate provisions, such as letter delivery, telephone, telex, fax, and TV-viewing. Computers can therefore be used to support all kinds of interactions.

The term "interaction" in relation to information and communication technology can be applied to four phenomena:

1. *Human-system interaction.* Whether in stand-alone systems or in networked systems, users have to interact through an interface, with computers (human computer interaction) or with other terminals. The success of a technical system can be strongly limited by bad human interfaces, which may result in non-use, errors and frustration.

2. *Human-database interaction.* Human database interaction can take two forms, depending on who takes the initiative:

a. *tele-consultation,* i.e. the consultation of large databases at a distance, such as over the Internet; tele-consultation systems provide general information and can also give personalised advice. A mortgage system, for instance, may actually contain a model that customers use to calculate their particular mortgage level.

b. *tele-registration,* whereby a central database gathers information from humans or from non-human sources: tele-ordering, automated polling, but also for example monitoring air pollution.

3. *Mediated human to human interaction: tele-conversation.* To support social interaction, many (combinations of) systems have been developed and marketed. Johansen's (1988) four-cell classification is based on a combination of two dimensions, i.e. systems for communication at the same *time*, i.e. synchronous, or on-line, or different time, i.e. asynchronous or off-line, and systems for interaction at the same, co-located, or different, distributed, *place*. The category "same place - different time" refers for example to a teamroom where a message is left on a computer for persons who come later. Since this does not imply specific tools, it is left out in the following discussions, which are limited to the other three categories. The categories refer to systems for the support of the following types of communication:

- *different places, same time,* i.e. systems to support on line meetings of geographically distributed people: e.g. telephone, video, chat;
- *different places, different time,* i.e. systems to support information exchange off-line: e.g. e-mail, document storage systems, workflow management systems;
- *same place, same time,* i.e. systems to support face-to-face meetings: e.g. group decision support systems.

There is a fourth category: *computer to computer interaction.* This category refers to electronic exchange of standardised administrative data between computers, for internal data transfer or for transactions between organisations. The latter is sometimes called Electronic Data Interchange (EDI). Standardised information systems, however, are beyond the scope of this book.

Category 1, human system interaction, is an element in categories 2 and 3. These latter categories often go together in specific composite systems, often called *Groupware.* This concept is defined in various ways. A very clear and concrete definition is the following: "*Groupware technologies provide electronic networks that support communication, co-ordination and collaboration through facilities such as information exchange, shared repositories, discussion forums and messaging*" (Orlikowski and Hofman, 1997). However, the concept and definition suggest limitation to teamwork situations, where members have a common goal. I prefer to use the wider term *collaboration technology*, which refers to *those ICT applications that support communication, co-ordination, co-operation, learning and/or social encounters through facilities such as information exchange, shared repositories, discussion forums and messaging.*

Various research communities study the area of collaboration technology. Communication scientists usually use the term "computer mediated communication". Another community, consisting of computer scientists, anthropologists and sociologists, is referred to by the name of Computer Supported Co-operative Work (CSCW). The term CSCW has a dual nature, indicating, firstly, a type of work, and secondly a scientific (sub)discipline or community. The term was coined by Irene Greif (1988), who described it as *"an identifiable research field focused on the role of the computer in group work"*. This definition is quite limited in that it focuses very much on the computer. Bannon & Schmidt (1989) presented the following definition: *"an endeavour to understand the nature and characteristics of co-operative work with the objective of designing adequate computer-based technologies"*. The two definitions reflect the much discussed questions of whether CSCW is a new research field and whether it is dealing primarily with computer applications or with new forms of work. The relevant CSCW literature shows that the field is very fruitful, particularly due to its attempts to integrate both aspects, i.e. co-operative work and technology.

The term CSCW however, does not allow us to fully understand the content of the concept. Greenberg (1991) has noted that CSCW studies deal with

- computer support, but also with video or telephone applications.
- showing that group work is more often hindered by computers than supported.
- co-operative tasks but also with negotiation or even conflicts
- work but also with other social interactions e.g. teleshopping;

Nevertheless, the term has taken root and stands for a very successful scientific community.

1.3.2 A Classification of Tools

The traditional four cell classification of groupware tools, presented by Johansen (1988, see above) has been succeeded by several others in an attempt to take into account the growing sophistication and complexity of CT-tools (e.g. Coleman, 1997, p 8). In Table 1.1 Johansen's classification is combined with the five-fold classification of group processes.

The five functions. ICT in general, but collaboration technology in particular, appears to serve the five functions presented at the end of Section 1.2. The tools discussed below may be parts of complex groupware systems. Nevertheless, for evaluation and design purposes it is worthwhile to distinguish the various components.

- *Communication tools.* These systems make the communication between geographically distributed people easy, fast and cheap. In this way separate environments become more like a single face-to-face environment by overcoming space and time separations. Both *asynchronous message systems* and *synchronous communication systems* serve this function. The characteristics that make asynchronous message systems attractive are their asynchronicity, the distribution list facility, systematic storage and processing facilities.

- *Information sharing and consulting tools.* These tools make the storage and retrieval of large amounts of information quick, reliable and inexpensive; making access to remote data sources easy and fast. This function is served by shared *data-bases* for teams, and by a multitude of information sources connected by the Internet.

- *Collaboration tools.* These are tools to improve teamwork by providing document-sharing or co-authoring facilities. A subgroup consists of *Group decision support systems,* to support brainstorming, evaluating ideas and decision making.

- *Co-ordination tools.* These tools support the co-ordination of distributed teamwork by providing *synchronisers* i.e. tools to synchronise the work processes of a team (Ellis & Wainer; 1994). Group calendars and workflow management systems are the best known tools of this type. So-called "team-topology" tools also belong to this category. They contain information on the group and its members, such as location, activities, preferred group role, expertise, friendship networks, mentoring relationship or previous work associations.

- *Workflow management systems* are systems that manage the sequencing of a series of routine tasks. Their purpose is to provide information or documents at the right moment to the right persons and they control the adequate performance of certain work processes. Khoshafian and Buckiewicz (1995) distinguish three types of workflow systems, production, administrative and ad hoc workflow systems. The first two are generally large scale formal systems, handling day to day routine tasks with well defined procedural steps. These systems can be distinguished from groupware applications in that they focus mainly on large scale task allocation, instead of on communication between people and remote consultation. They are primarily applied to well-structured and repetitive work procedures, while CSCW is predominantly focused on small scale, irregular and less structured interaction processes. Nevertheless, group calendars are also categorised as groupware, while the third type of workflow systems, ad hoc systems, has a low level of routinisation. Ad hoc systems are much less standardised and have perhaps only goals and deliverables and certain time frames to consider. So, the differences between groupware and workflow systems are not very sharp. Nurcan (1998) presents a model that incorporates the two domains.

- *Tools to support social encounters.* Using permanently available cameras, monitors and other devices, people at geographically distant places can meet each other unintentionally, such as near the coffee machine. Systems have been developed to make socialising possible at a distance. One of these systems is the Media Space at EuroParc, where people meet colleagues at coffee bars 400 miles apart, connected through video walls (Bly, Harrison & Irwin, 1993).

Combining Johansen's categories with the five types mentioned above, results in the taxonomy given in Table 1.1.

Table 1.1 Types of Collaboration Technology

	Support between encounters: asynchronous communication different place / different time	Support for synchronous electronic encounters different place / same time	Support for synchronous face-to-face meetings: same place / same time.
Communication Systems	• fax • e-mail • voice-mail • video-mail	• telephone / mobile • audio systems • video systems • chat system	
Information sharing systems	• document sharing systems • message boards	• tele-consultation systems • co-browser	• presentation systems
Co-operation systems	• document co-authoring	• shared CAD, whiteboard, word-processor, spread-sheet	• group decision support systems (meeting support systems)
Co-ordination systems	• group-calendar • shared planning • shared workflow management systems • event manager • subgroup spaces	• notification systems, e.g. active batch	• command and control centre support systems
Social encounter systems		• media spaces • virtual reality	

Short description of specific tools
(Mobile)Telephone. Although communication via telephone is the most common form of mediated communication, there has been relatively little research on the use and implication of this medium in organisations. In recent years the use of mobile phones has increased immensely.

Video-connections. Video systems have a respectable history. The first commercial videophone AT&T's picture-phone was available in the mid sixties, but appeared to be a costly failure. According to a survey by Dutton, Fulk and Steinfield in 1982, AT&T had at that time video-studios in twelve cities, used by hundreds of firms, although only a few reported regular use.
        Four video-based systems can be found:

• *videophone*, i.e. a telephone with a little screen to see the other person.
• *camera* for showing objects to a person at another location.

- *studio conferencing system* for meetings of groups. Special studios are used with high capacity audio and video equipment, connected over a TV line. These facilities are also available on a portable basis, which makes it possible to provide an organisation with a temporary video unit.

- *desktop video system* for communication between two or more people. This requires PCs with a camera and some hardware or software application to support the video-link. The software usually combines the videolink with other applications such as a shared whiteboard, teleregistration of for instance traffic, and also to show new products to potential customers. A very popular application at present is the webcam that shows (continuous) images of people's homes or commercial exhibitions.

Complex E-mail and Multimedia systems. Originally electronic mail systems were quite simple. Gradually they are becoming more complex through the addition of various features, such as filtering and ordering messages and the addition of media for voice and images.

Message boards. When electronic mail messages are not, or not only, sent to specific addressees but remain stored centrally and are accessible to a large number of users, the terms *message board*, or *electronic bulletin board* are used. This feature is developed one step further in *computer conferencing*, in which specified groups of users participate in electronic discussions on certain topics.

Complex groupware systems. Commercial products such as Lotus Notes or NetMeeting are based on the client-server architecture, whereby the server is organisation specific. A less well-known composite system Basic Support for Co-operative Work (BSCW) is freely available over the Internet. A server is provided by the German company where it was developed. These types of web based applications may provide functionalities for communication, information sharing, co-operation and co-ordination, such as the following:

- Storing and sharing files; features for subfiling, uploading and downloading of these files. A shared workspace can contain different kinds of information such as documents, discussions, pictures, sound or video.
- Co-editing documents by a particular group, whose members have access to the data.
- Awareness support, e.g. through (asynchronous) *event managers* who provide information on recent changes in files, the arrival of new messages or who has consulted, down- or uploaded certain files. Some products provide data showing that users are using the system and that (synchronous) chat is possible.

Recently systems of this type, such as Groove, have been developed on the basis of the person-to-person architecture, which does not require a large central server.

Group (Decision) Support Systems (Meeting Support Systems) are developed to make face-to-face meetings more creative and effective. Via a network of computers in a meeting room (or even in a distributed setting) software tools for idea creation or alternative voting support the synchronous interaction of a group (e.g. Nunamaker et al. 1997). Group support systems have been defined as "*systems that combine communication, computer and decision technologies to support problem formulation and solution in group meetings*" (DeSancties & Gallupe, 1987). The systems usually have the following dimensions (Zigurs and Buckland, 1998):

- *Communication support*: simultaneous and anonymous input of ideas and comments by group members, input feedback, group display.
- *Process structuring*: agenda setting and enforcement, facilitation, record of group interaction.
- *Information processing*: gathering, aggregating, evaluating and structuring of information.

The term G(D)SS is in a way confusing. It refers to systems that support ad hoc meetings, not to systems that support continuously co-operating groups. Moreover, the idea generation support is often used much more than the decision support. Analyses of GDSS systems in practice show that team building activities or cohesion hardly play a role in this context, since the participants convene only for the short duration of the meeting (Herik, 1998). Therefore these systems should rather be called *Meeting Support systems*.

Virtual spaces. The first type are the Media spaces, video-based systems for social purposes. Here people meet colleagues at distant coffee bars or at other social areas, connected via traditional camera-with-monitor systems. Advanced systems with large video screens can give the impression that people are actually sitting at the same table. Various systems have been developed at major research centres, such as Portholes, the system that connects Rank Xerox PARC and EuroPARC (Bly, Harrison & Irwin, 1993). Even more advanced are spaces in *virtual reality*, where (symbols of) people can meet (symbols of) other people in virtual spaces (e.g. Schroeder, 2002).

General support functions. Many tools have *security* provisions, such as checking the identity of users through passwords, which at the same time may provide *privacy* to the users files. Another general support function is the possibility to customise various aspects of the system such as notifying the user of new messages, filtering messages, or even the complete user interface.

Although the classification in Table 1.1 suggests a sharp distinction between systems, in practice many applications become integrated and accessible from the same workstation. Actually many advanced systems are sets of more or less integrated modules and functionalities, that can be tailored to specific usage (see also Box 1.1).

New technical developments are responsible for substantial advances in groupware applications concerning web based techniques, increasing bandwidths, wireless (mobile) multi media communication, new interfaces such as gaze tracking and speech and gesture recognition, information search and selection and application sharing (e.g. Mills, 1999).

Box 1.1

On the basis of an empirical analysis of the various types of informal communication Bismarck, et al. (2000) distinguish several scenarios for informal communication:

In an office:

- Dyadic office conversation: of two co-workers in their office, on ad hoc exchange of short work related information
- To all present: i.e. work and non-work related remarks to anyone present in the office
- Joining conversation: spontaneous joining discussion amongst colleagues

Visiting:

- Visiting a colleague in another office
- Colleague in other office is not present, asking where he is
- Meetings in communal areas
- Chance meetings: very spontaneous, often discussing non-work related topics
- Conversations during breaks: both work and non-work related

The authors discuss the implications for virtual teams and requirements for systems that support these informal communications. They speak of cybureau's, cybervisits and cyberooms, to cover various of the above mentioned scenarios, and they present a prototype groupware system that is being developed at the University of Mannheim. The systems have the following characteristics:

For *Cybureau:*

- Status icons with information about activities of persons
- Filtered and modified acoustic and visual cues
- Presentation of keywords from a conversation
- Application sharing and whiteboards
- Knowledge profile of colleague

For *Cybervisit*:

- Possibilities for contacting groups of similar functions and shared competencies
- Leaving electronic stick-up notes on screen

For *Cyberooms*

- Notification when working on the same document as support of awareness
- Split text-window for establishing context
- Chatrooms and newsgroups for certain topics

To summarise, collaboration technology tools form a large group of widely different systems to support social interaction of various kinds. They have very different characteristics, but they can be combined into composite systems. Modern users can have a wide set of support tools available on their desk, and perhaps soon on their hand-held digital assistant (Hofte, 1998).

1.4 Organisational Imbedding

To most people collaboration technology tools are only interesting in so far as they are used to support certain interactions. Several organisational arrangements can be found where some or all of the above mentioned systems and interaction forms are combined, such as telework, virtual teams, and virtual organisations / enterprises.

Telework. Telework has been defined as *"Organisational work performed outside of the normal organisational limits of space and time, augmented by computer and communications technology"* (Olson, 1989, p.77). However, the term 'telework', although quite clear at first sight, appears to be used in a number of very different ways. The enthusiasm with which telework is discussed in journals and at conferences suggests that it might be identified as a phenomenon in its own worth. On closer scrutiny there are grave doubts about the usefulness of the concept. This becomes clear when one considers the various forms of telework that have been distinguished:

- *Tele-Homeworking*, i.e. paid employment undertaken by a person working entirely or for the most part at home, with visits to the site of the employer or client. Homeworkers can be divided rather clearly into low paid administrative employees, mainly women, who perform simple word processing or data processing activities, and high paid professionals, such as programmers.
- *Satellite office*, or *Neighbourhood office*. The first is an office of an enterprise, located at or near the place where groups of employees live. The second is a work centre, equipped with various electronic facilities, used by a number of people, working in different companies. The reason for working in a neighbourhood office is often a combination of reducing large travel distances, desiring social contacts and not having sufficient facilities at home.
- *Mobile work*, various types of employees such as sales representatives, service engineers or consultants, who work in more than one place and communicate with the head-office by the use of portable communication facilities.

Teleworkers originally formed a neatly distinguishable group. Both technological and organisational developments, however, have blurred the boundaries with other work arrangements. The forms of telework are just three of the many organisational arrangements that vary along the following dimensions. The first is the extent to which work is performed outside organisational premises. Secondly, the nature of task and the level of expertise required can vary from professional to simple clerical work. The third dimension is that of contractual relationship: full employment, semi-permanent contracts or freelance. Fourthly the level of ICT support can diverge substantially.

It is clear that work arrangements can no longer be classified as either telework or normal. Some writers nevertheless make a plea for retaining the concept of telework. *"Despite its lack of precision, the word telework has acquired a potent symbolic value.... The idea of the teleworker has become a representation of what the future of work might be"* (Huws, 1988).

Virtual teams. The developments in globally distributed commerce and science, and the availability of communication technology have encouraged the growth of virtual geographically distributed teams (see special issue of Communications of the ACM, dec. 2001 on Global virtual teams and collaborative technologies). Virtual teams can be defined as groups of geographically and/or organisationally dispersed co-workers that are assembled using a combination of communication and information technologies to accomplish an organisational task (Townsend et al., 1998). Hutchinson (1999) distinguishes three types of virtual teams: the *intra-organisational teams* of geographically distributed members, *inter-organisational distributed (project) teams* that co-operate, over a certain period, for a common goal, e.g. freelance or organisation bound experts that work together to provide a certain service, and *inter-organisational teams* in which the co-operation is sequential and each participating organisation is responsible for particular tasks. The second and third forms are very close to the virtual organisation discussed in the following section.

Virtual teams have to cope with the same problems as co-located teams, and above that they face special problems concerning mediated communication and information exchange. They have the same responsibility for adequately performing the five basic processes of groups (discussed in Section 2.1): *Communication, information sharing and learning, co-operation, co-ordination, and social interaction*, but have to execute these processes under quite special circumstances such as inadequate ICT tools and infrastructures, incompatibility of technology, missing non-verbal cues in communication and missing unplanned social encounters. These circumstances make co-ordination, co-operation and team- and trust building relatively difficult. *Global* virtual teams may have to deal with the additional issues of time zone, language and cultural differences (e.g. Dubé and Paré, 2001). Nevertheless these global teams can provide a challenge and an opportunity that is not based on the degree of technical sophistication but on the way the available tools are used and the interaction is managed (e.g. Qureshi and Zigurs, 2001).

Certain rules of thumb can be formulated to support effective functioning of (global) virtual teams:

- Where possible groups should start with face-to-face meetings and be alert to organise such meetings whenever needed.
- Group members should learn about each other's background.
- Special attention should be given to information (document) exchange and storage.
- Synchronous meetings have to be well prepared and structured.
- Minutes of meetings help assuring that all members understand the same conclusions.
- Information about the progress of the project and the activities of the project members should be provided.
- Extra attention to the development of trust and cohesion is required.

These rules suggest the following groupware support:

- Information storage and exchange tools.
- Information on background and expertise of the group members (*yellow pages*).
- Tools for synchronous communication: chat features, where possible video links.

- Tools for providing information regarding the progress of the project and activities of group members.
- The tools have to be easy to use and equally accessible to all members.
- Group members should be sufficiently trained in using the technology.
- *Globally* distributed teams should pay attention to training in intercultural differences, and give sufficient time and attention to express oneself for group members who do not talk the common language fluently.

Virtual organisation or enterprise. The concepts of v*irtual organisation* and *virtual enterprise* are not yet sharply defined, but refer generally to *a temporary and voluntary co-operation between a number of legally independent organisations.* These organisations may be very small, such as one-person consultancies (see Box 1.2). To customers and other stakeholders a virtual organisation has the appearance of a single identifiable organisation. In reality there is a network of owners that work together for the production of certain goods or services.

Box 1.2
Example: Terranova (pseudonym) provides training and consultation in the area of computers and software use and development. It is a network of about 60 mainly independent consultants and trainers, based in the Netherlands. The members co-operate in teams to work on projects. The distributed organisation members have their own office at home, and they co-ordinate much of their work through fax and telephone. On top of these means of communication they use a groupware system that supports a common document database, e-mail, a bulletin board system and the co-ordination of the work of project teams.

Virtual enterprises have a long history, such as in the co-operation between organisations for maintenance or research. Using collaboration technology tools the co-ordination of activities and exchange of information about customers, projects, markets and services can be organised very efficiently and effectively.

In this chapter the basic concepts and types in the area of group work and collaboration technology tools have been presented. In the next chapter the impact of these tools on communication and co-operation on work and organisation will be discussed.

Chapter 2. Implications of Collaboration Technology

2.1 Introduction

To what degree are new tools adopted and used in organisations and, if adopted, what effects do they have on an organisation? Is it possible to make general conclusions concerning the implications of collaboration technology for interaction and for work? Findings of empirical research concerning the adoption, use and effects of collaboration technology are presented in this chapter, based on overviews and meta-analyses such as those of Kraemer & Pinsonneault (1990), Andriessen (1991) and McGrath and Hollingshead (1994). Recent dissertations give reviews concerning specific applications such as e-mail (Hooff, 1997) or Lotus Notes (Hinssen, 1998).

The above mentioned studies focus on different kinds of collaboration technology, from simple e-mail to complex groupware systems, and on widely divergent organisational settings. They represent various types of studies, such as laboratory studies, field case studies and surveys. Many findings are still based on laboratory experiments, which makes generalisations difficult. Laboratory groups exist only for one session, perform one single task using a tool with which they have little experience. This may give valuable insights into basic processes of mediated communication and the efficacy of new software, however, it generally provides very limited evidence with regard to the effectiveness and usefulness of new systems for teams in companies, particularly with regard to adaptation and learning behaviour. Nevertheless, as studies of the introduction and operational use of collaboration technology in organisations become available, they show how the role of new tools and the structure of workgroups or organisational settings may radically change in these circumstances.

Despite all differences, some findings have emerged repeatedly, and have become part of the common knowledge of the domain. In this chapter only results of empirical studies are presented. In later chapters theories and concepts will be discussed that can explain the results. The findings are ordered in the following way:

- adoption and use (Section 2.2)

Effects of tool use on:
- task performance / quality of work (Section 2.3)

- interpersonal communication (Section 2.4)
- group interaction (Section 2.5)
- organisational processes (Section 2.6)
- societal processes (Section 2.7)

The chapter ends with a summary of the conclusions and with the realisation that effects are often contingent on certain conditions.

To speak of the impact of collaboration technology in general is not justified. Introducing a simple e-mail tool may have quite different effects from introducing a meeting support system or a complex groupware system with both synchronous and asynchronous tools. Wherever possible the implications of the specific tools will be discussed separately; the literature, however, is not always clear on this point, and making too many distinctions may be boring to read. Readers should therefore take care as they interpret the findings presented here.

2.2 Adoption and Use of Collaboration Technology

It has become quite clear that adoption of advanced information technology and particularly collaboration technology can have many favourable consequences:

- speeding up the exchange of information
- easy access to new information
- many people being able to receive information at the same time
- increased number of potential participants in discussions
- expanded horizontal and diagonal contacts
- easier to reach people

These characteristics can form the basis for strategic developments, they allow organisations to operate on a global scale, by using systems that provide information exchange and communication, teamwork and knowledge transfer over large distances. It might therefore be expected that the new tools are adopted and used on an enormous scale. Nevertheless it appears that technology acceptance is more limited than one might expect when considering these potential consequences. Is this a matter of individual preferences and intrinsic motivation or is it due to other factors?

As far as *simple e-mail applications* are concerned, they appear to be widely used and are sometimes supportive of strategic processes in organisations. The possibility to send and receive electronic messages thus overcoming time and distance constraints is considered to be of particular importance and a major improvement over traditional communications media.

Tele-Information systems, i.e. remote consultation of data sources, either through the Internet, other networks, or Intranets, is increasing rapidly in popularity and often fulfils strong needs for additional information, despite criticism concerning information overload or the difficulty of finding the right information.

Co-ordination systems, such as advanced groupware applications, *meeting support systems* (group decision support systems) and *synchronous communication systems*, such as video conferencing, appear to be highly promising for certain professional groups and situations. Their actual adoption however, is still very limited, and many failures with collaboration technology can be found (see Box 2.1).

Box 2.1 *Failures with collaboration technology*

Videophone. The first commercial videophone, AT&T's Picturephone, was available in the mid sixties, but appeared to be a costly failure. Since that time many companies have tried to promote the videophone for household or organisational use, without much success. It is not only image quality and costs that have prevented widespread adoption. Ideas about privacy, required correct behaviour and clothes, and lack of added value (seeing the other person is rarely functional) have also stalled adoption of this technology.

Groupware. Many studies have demonstrated the non-use or under-utilisation of complex group support systems such as Lotus Notes (e.g. Ciborra, 1996; Hinssen, 1998) or BSCW (see Section 1.3.2). These systems are used to store and share access to documents, but rarely for more sophisticated purposes such as co-authoring or team co-ordination. Reasons for this can be found in the complexity of the system, lack of user-friendliness, a limited advantage over other media and inadequate introduction of the media and training.

Telework. Although telework is not a tool but a work arrangement, it is a context in which many collaboration technology tools are used. Telework for office workers has been practised for many decades, but it has yet to reach the level of distribution that was predicted in the seventies and eighties. An important reason for this is that managers dislike loosing sight and control of their subordinates.

Knowledge systems. Many companies introduced shared document systems to support the work of for example departments for sales and servicing departments. Data about customers and service projects are entered in the system and every employee responsible for sales or service can consult that database. Standard customer data and experiences with and specifics about the customers are supposed to be entered in the database, however, many of these systems are rarely used as intended. The required motivation to enter data and expectations that useful information can be found in such a database are often lacking.

Breakdowns. It is a common experience that computer systems can go down. The magnitude of this problem was illustrated recently when a British study revealed that a quarter of all computer users experience some disturbances in their computer(network) each day!

Many barriers for widespread adoption can be found, such as market aspects, e.g. limited service and infrastructure provisions (see also Section 7.1), high costs, technical limitations, e.g. low video quality, not being suited to the task and resistance to having to learn a new system, particularly when there is low added value over existing systems. "*Unless there is a balance between the perceived effort required on the part of the user and the benefit delivered to that user, a person is not likely to employ the functionality present in a too*" (Bullen & Bennet, 1990, p297).

Even if there is relative advantage over the existing tools, it may take quite a while to discover and master the new possibilities. *"Even with prior coaching on the use of the software, instructors and students require experience to understand and exploit the features"* conclude White et al. (1998) after evaluating a complex tele-teaching system. Competence in using the new tools is not only a matter of technical instruction, but also of training and experience in new ways of working, communicating and teaching. Developing new competencies and motivation takes time. Experienced or anticipated user-friendliness of the tool, the requirements of the task, and the level of innovativeness of users also appear to influence adoption (Hooff, 1997).

The limited adoption of groupware-systems may be due to still other factors. Real co-operation requires a common goal and product, and an intensive mutual engagement. This implies a high level of non-verbal communication and a sharing of the same language and meanings, which is very difficult to achieve at a distance (e.g. Introna, 1998). Moreover, social factors as well, such as group cohesion, existing norms or critical mass appear to play an important role during adoption (see Box 2.2).

Box 2.2
Comparing adoption and use of two competing video telephone systems at a university campus, Kraut et al. (1994) concluded that group pressure and critical mass were the determining factors for the *adoption* of one system over another. Students choose the system that their friends used and that had the most important others connected. However, the complexity of the task and therefore the required media richness, predicted the frequency of *use* of various media. For sensitive discussions people used the video systems, while for more superficial contacts they used the telephone or e-mail.

Finally, there are clear indications that organisational factors can make a big difference. In a formalised organisation culture and a centralised structure e-mail is adopted less and is less effective in its use (e.g. Hooff, 1997). Management in such organisations is often not convinced of e-mail's added value or afraid of its effects on established lines of communication and control. E-mail and groupware thrives best in informal and decentralised organisations. Implementation is most effective when management and users are highly involved, but even then it takes time before the possibilities of new tools become realised. Hooff's study (1997) shows that users in large organisations start by using e-mail for simple information exchange, but when they become accustomed to its use, more and richer tasks such as intensive group discussions are also performed using this medium.

In summary, collaboration technology can bring about many advantages, but its acceptance and use in practice is often limited because of characteristics of the tools, the users and the (social) context. The role of these characteristics will be explored in more detail in the following sections. Theories concerning the mechanisms of tool acceptance and use will be discussed in Chapter 4.

2.3 Collaboration Technology, Task Content and Performance

Will the introduction of collaboration technology change the way people work, their task performance and the quality of their work? Collaboration technology is different from standard office automation technology. It is well known that the large-scale computerisation of administrative tasks has resulted in routinisation and de-skilling of jobs in certain sectors. Moreover, the introduction of automation in offices has resulted in task redistribution. Sometimes task enrichment and a blurring of boundaries between functions takes place, e.g. when professionals start typing their own documents, while secretarial work shifts to organising work conditions for the professionals: lay out of documents, arranging travels, organising workshops and archiving. Sometimes a polarisation takes place, for instance in insurance companies where clerical tasks become even more routine and only a few professionals handle the exceptional cases.

According to a European study (European Foundation, 1997) computerisation has resulted in stress, particularly for those who work with data input, e.g. in banks and postal services. This stress is attributed to high demands for accuracy and high work pace. Computerisation may also imply that people have less contact with each other, which makes them more susceptible to stressful situations, since social contacts help people to cope with stress. Finally, many people who work with computers become totally dependent on these machines and unexpected problems or downtimes are often extremely stressful.

In a review of studies concerning the psychosocial aspects of working with computers and the effects on employee physical and mental health (Smith, 1997), a mixed picture arises. It is concluded that, while *"computerised jobs are more sedentary, require more cognitive processing and mental attention, and require less physical energy expenditure than non-computerised jobs, the production demands of these jobs are often high, with constant work pressure and little decision making possibilities. Many jobs that require heavy daily computer use have been found to be stressful"*. The stress appears to be related particularly to work pressure, lack of control, fear for job security and poor supervisory relations. Work pressure and fear of job security are found in those cases where automatisation is introduced to increase productivity and decrease personnel costs. The correlation between automatisation and stress is therefore quite strong, but the stress is really an effect of competitive markets that result in work pressure and insecurity for "flexworkers" (temporary employees). ICT is thus not the basic cause of stress, although ICT enables this type of development.

The introduction of collaboration technology is not the same as the automatisation of routine administrative processes. The type of work that is supported by collaboration technology is generally the unstructured tasks of professionals and managers, of academicians and shop keepers, of consultants and service engineers. While in this sector routinisation of work is less common than in simple computer work, high complexity of tasks, intensive information processing and communication activities, and particularly irregular working hours and work pressure are quite common. ICT can be used very effectively to support the processes of accessing, collecting, processing and storing information. The great advantage of networks, including Internet and Intranets, is considered to be the way they provide fast and easy access to information.

Yet large-scale availability of information and easy access to all kinds of data sources may also be responsible for information overload. (Hiltz and Turoff, 1985; Rice, Grant, Schmitz and Torobin, 1990; Köhler, 1994). Moreover, computer breakdowns or slowdowns are also the curse of knowledge workers. Stress is therefore a common phenomenon. A survey in several countries showed that 30 to 65% of managers suffer from stress due to information overload, resulting in bad interpersonal relations, lack of decision making and illness. Information-overload can also be aggravated by lack of adequate feedback: Information systems provide too much information of a general nature and too little specific, work related, information. It is clear that much effort is needed to solve the pressing problem of how people can deal with the enormous flow of information. Fussel et al. (1998) argue that with proper presentation of information, increased document exchange may enhance co-ordination, without resulting in overload. Nevertheless, information-stress is a well-known phenomenon that seems to be on the increase all over the western world.

A quite different effect of collaboration technology is to be found in the case of telework. It may be that people lose the connection with their organisation, when they are a temporary worker or absent as teleworker or mobile worker. A lack of shared meanings, norms and knowledge of the organisation may lead to a general *lack of involvement* with the organisation.

2.4 Collaboration Technology and Interpersonal Communication

The questions addressed in this section are: To what extent does the *quality* of communication change when it is mediated electronically? And, secondly: To what extent does the *structure* of communication networks change in this situation.

Communication Quality. A distinction has to be made between asynchronous (off-line) communication and synchronous (real-time) communication. The impact of *asynchronous message systems* on the communication process can be summarised as follows (Andriessen 1991). It appears that mediated communication, even when using perfect video channels, constraints the exchange of certain signals such as non-verbal communication cues. It has been shown that lack of these cues limits the communication process, making it less easy going and more impersonal. This tends to have the following consequences:

- *Fewer contributions*: people talk and contribute less in mediated co-operation than in comparable face-to-face settings.
- *Task oriented communication*: the interaction tends to become more business-like and less personal than in comparable face-to-face settings. Users prefer to choose communication tools to exchange information but, if possible, not for intensive interpersonal contacts.

These effects may be limited to certain business settings, because it has also been found that electronic communication is sometimes used for very informal contacts. In asynchronous (e.g. e-mail) communication for personal use, people learn ways and means to substitute for non-verbal cues (see also Box 2.3). Typographic ways (emoticons) have been introduced to convey emotions, such as :-) to represent joy, and :-(to convey sorrow. Moreover, it is as yet unclear to what degree rich cues are really required for socio-emotional interaction, which is considered to be the most complex type of interaction.

Social chats and emotional communication appear to be used widely in private contacts over the Internet. Some contacts even appear to be very intimate, particularly with strangers, because people feel that they are anonymous and therefore not threatened. The concept of *electronic emotion* has been introduced by Rice and Love (1987). Rice suggests that the emotional *content* of electronic messages is even increased, precisely *because* non-verbal cues are filtered out.

Box 2.3 *Intimacy over the Internet.*
Stories of friendships that developed over the Internet have been documented widely, together with stories of the tricks and ruses being applied and the unhappy ends to many of the cyberrelationsships. According to a national survey (Katz and Aspden, 1997) 14% of a sample of Internet users reported having made friends over the Internet. A majority of those 14% later met their friends in person.

Video-channels. The arrival of video connections, i.e. videophones, video-studio's or desk-top video, has been heralded as a major improvement for distributed and mediated communication. Popular opinion holds that distributed meetings can now be almost the same as face-to-face meetings. The CSCW community and many others consider the presence of video-links in mediated co-operative situations to be of utmost importance. It has been estimated that 60% of normal interpersonal conversation implies gazing and 30% even mutual gazing (Sellen, 1992). Empirical studies however do not support the high expectations concerning video connections. Already in 1972 it was found that the voice mode makes the single most important contribution to task completion and that, at least in the experimental problem solving tasks used, adding high-quality video to an audio connection appeared to bring few extra benefits (Chapanis, Ochsman, Parrish and Weeks, 1972). Many other studies have confirmed this finding and have concluded that the added value of a video-link for the performance of distributed teamwork is often negligible. Egido (1988) concludes: "*Videoconferencing has been commercially available for over two decades, and despite consistently brilliant market forecasts, to date it has failed except in limited niche markets... Results of systematic research generally point to the dubious value of adding a visual channel... performance does not improve significantly*". The results of more recent studies (e.g. many contributions to Finn, Sellen and Wilbur, 1997) do not alter this conclusion significantly. So, good audio facilities are much more important for conferencing purposes, particularly in cases where video only adds the faces to the conversation, i.e. where video images are not crucial to the task at hand.

Sellen (1995) shows that the difference between face-to-face communication and video mediated communication is experienced as significantly greater than the difference between video mediated communication and audio mediated communication. This means that video communication is much more similar to a mediated communication setting such as a telephone conversation, than it is to a face-to-face meeting. Several explanations for this phenomenon can be given.

Firstly, *eye to eye contact is very difficult* in the case of desktop video. The common position for a camera is on top of the monitor; however this prevents direct eye to eye contact. Certain sophisticated equipment can give eye-contact, e.g. a semi-transparent mirror can be placed obliquely in front of the monitor, and the camera can be put over the mirror (Velden, 1992), but this is quite an unusual and costly solution.

Secondly, even in the most favourable situation, video conferencing via desktop is more tiring than expected, which can only be minimised by preparing and structuring the meeting quite carefully (see Box 2.4). Thirdly, meetings with more than three or four participants require *sophisticated camera settings* to accommodate adequate interaction (see Box 2.5).

Box 2.4

Teams of mechanical engineering students from Delft University, the Netherlands and Michigan State University, USA, co-operated for three months on a design project. Each team consisted of two to three students on both sides of the Atlantic. The team members interacted asynchronously through e-mail and fax, and synchronously through chat box and videoconferencing. They used a high capacity desktop video connection over ISDN-2. This resulted in a very good quality of video images. Nevertheless, the following effects were noted:

- even slight delays in sound or video make communication and particularly floor control quite effort-intensive.
- all sounds came from one speaker, so spatial orientation was difficult.
- the images of the partners on the monitor screen were quite small, so seeing facial expressions required much effort.
- participants felt compelled to look at the monitor, which prevented them from looking at documents or looking randomly at other parts of the room.
- additional people on the other side suddenly popped up on the screen, without any signal that they were approaching; this could be confusing.

Fourthly, even videoconferencing between two persons conveys *much fewer (non-verbal) information* and signals to the participants than face-to-face settings, and thus fewer cues for regulating the social interaction. Studies of videoconferencing have shown that as a result of this the structure of the users' communicative behaviour such as turn taking changes. Even in video-supported communication a rather formal style of communication has to be developed, with few interruptions and explicit handing over of turns of speaking. Other studies show differences in the length and content of the communication in video-mediated interactions (e.g. O'Conaill and Whittaker, 1997). It is true that in many cases the quality of the images and of the system as a whole are quite limited. Nevertheless the same effects have been found under more favourable circumstances.

It is clear that videoconferencing is not the dream it has often been promised to be. Very few organisations have introduced desktop videoconferencing facilities on a large scale, an exception is the firm analysed by Webster (1998), and in situations where it is installed it is infrequently used (Webster, 1998). Field experts are therefore quite sceptical about its future (*World News, 19-10-98: Still missing the big picture).*

Box 2.5

Radiologists in peripheral hospital X set up a weekly consultation meeting with an expert radiologist at an academic hospital in Y. The expert discusses a series of X-ray images with a group of six to twelve radiologists and physicians, that meet in a specially equipped room. The radiologists and physicians often view only the top of the expert's head on their monitor, since most of the time he is scrutinising the digitised X-ray images on his monitor. The video pictures of the radiologists' meeting are presented to him on a separate monitor, because he requires the full screen of the first monitor for the X-ray images. Consequently he does not often look at the screen with the video images of the medical group. In the peripheral hospital, one camera takes an overview of the room and the participants. This camera cannot therefore convey any facial details. A second camera can focus on a particular speaker, however, this requires the constant presence of a cameraman to focus the camera.

This does not prevent people from experiencing video as more pleasant and friendly than audio-conferencing and more effective for forming impressions of others (Wellens, 1989). There are also indications that bargaining or conflict solution in distributed settings may benefit substantially from a video link. The reason is to be found in the provision of background signals, i.e. context awareness.

The advantages of video appear to be much greater in situations where task-oriented data have to be exchanged over large distances: video-as-data (Nardi, 1996b). A video link is crucial for performance in these settings. This type of application can be found in an increasing number of situations (see Box 2.6).

Box 2.6

- A company in California shows pictures of their products to a potential South African buyer (Halper, 1998).
- A group of psychotherapists in Norway receives supervision via video (Gammon, et al. 1998).
- Civilians in Manchester receive visual information over public video screens (Strom et al. 1998).
- A company in photocopiers in the Netherlands is experimenting with maintenance-at-a-distance of complex copying machines by installing cameras at their client's office (Anker and Lichtveld, 1999).
- Ohio State has installed equipment in 20 jails, to make periodical first medical check-ups of prisoners.

Summarising, the role of a video-link for showing non-verbal signals in tele-meetings is rather limited, the function of providing situation awareness can be useful and only in situations where the exchange of object information is required does it really appear to have added value.

Loss of privacy. Behaviour registration systems and video cameras can be used to provide information about the activities of people. Advanced video systems may allow for a quick snapshot of other places to see whether a person is present (Webster, 1998). "Active batches" can also be used to provide information about the whereabouts of the person wearing one. And in some experimental settings, e.g. the Xerox PARC laboratories, camera's near coffee machines can facilitate unplanned communication. All these developments raise the issue of privacy (Stone and Stone, 1990). Webster (1998) has studied the introduction of a desktop video system in a large company (ca. 1000 employees). Privacy issues appeared to be quite extensive among a substantial subset of users. They reported a general worry about their privacy and particular resistance against the snapshot facility. These employees had the feeling that the system allowed management to monitor their performance. They opted strongly for a situation where they had control over the extent to which other people could see them. The fact that the technology already provided these controls had not sufficiently penetrated to the employees.

Empirical data are as yet scarce and the picture painted above is one that may go hand in hand with the positive effects presented in Section 2.2

Communication Structure. The introduction of tools for communication and collaboration almost by definition result in the growth of new communication channels. Although theoretically not necessary, in practice they appear also to result in an increase in the amount of information exchanged. This means that *message systems increase connectivity and interaction* (Garton and Wellman, 1995). Connectivity refers to the structure of existing communication channels. High connectivity implies a high potential for contact. Interaction refers to the actual frequency of use of the communication channels. The increase in this interaction is related to the fact that the barriers for communication are lowered. It appears to be much easier to make contacts with strangers in distributed settings than in face-to-face groups. The contacts may be superficial and the ties may be weak, nevertheless this will facilitate the social connections between members of large organisations. This may also result in an increased sense of connectedness with the organisation (Rice and Steinfield, 1994).

New communication media result in a heightening of the general interconnectedness with other employees, and also in the growth of new communities. Both within and outside organisational boundaries newsgroups and virtual communities abound. These groups appear to have the characteristics that are traditionally attributed only to face-to-face groups (Hildreth, Kimble and Wright, 2000).

Reduction of travel? Video conferencing is often introduced to reduce travel costs and the number of face-to-face meetings. In practice this is not always achieved, probably because the general trend towards (inter)national interaction in the field of commerce and other areas, increases the establishment of partnerships and co-operative activities. Some of the ensuing need for encounters may be fulfilled through mediated communication, but this has to be complemented by face-to-face meetings, resulting possibly in a net increase in physical mobility. Video conferencing is not equal to face-to-face meetings for developing group relations. Physical proximity is still the best way of establishing and maintaining good collaborative relationships (Bair, 1989). The example of the distributed student design teams (Box 2.4) shows that without collaboration technology some co-operation would never have been established. Once developed however, the co-operative arrangement required that project leaders visited each other now and then.

Substitution or complement. To what extent do new technologies substitute or only complement existing technologies? No general answers are possible. It appears that in few cases a *substitution* of existing media by new media takes place (see Box 2.7). The introduction, however, of new media is often initiated because there is a need to extend communication and information exchange, in which case it is complementary to the existing media, certainly in the beginning.

Box 2.7

The telex network between agencies all over the world of an international trading company was substituted completely by an e-mail system. This system became the backbone of the company's communication network and was widely used and appreciated (Veen, 1993).

Theories concerning communication processes are presented in Section 6.2

2.5 Collaboration Technology, Group Interaction and Performance

Two aspects of group interaction are distinguished in social psychology:

1) *task performance*, i.e. activities that are directly related to the goal of a group, such as decision making, problem solving and writing reports; when a group of people co-operate, a major task oriented activity is *co-ordination*.
2) *group maintenance*; i.e. activities that are related to issues such as building cohesion and trust, or struggling for power and status.

Both types of interaction occur in all groups, although the distribution varies, in relation to the task and situation at hand. Even in very task-oriented groups such as computer system design meetings, the bulk of time may be spent in group maintenance activities (60% according to a study by Olson, 1989).

Task performance. The effects of collaboration technology on group task performance have been studied for several types of tools. As far as (asynchronous) *message systems* and (synchronous) *audio/video systems* are concerned, several (meta-) analyses (Kraemer and Pinsonneault, 1990; McGrath and Hollingshead, 1994) have come to comparable conclusions. The tool supported groups show, in comparison to face-to-face groups, less co-operation, more time needed for task completion (e.g. decision making), lower satisfaction with the process and less confidence in the outcome.

    The final performance and quality of the products, however, seems not to depend on the use of mediated communication systems. Several authors (e.g. Wellens, 1989; Sellen, 1995; Velden, 1995) conclude that under certain conditions, video or even audio-only interaction can be as effective as face-to-face interaction for normal information-exchange, problem solving and decision making. This effect requires however that the communication strategy is adapted to the situation, i.e. that a more structured way of interaction is developed. This finding is quite generic. Communication patterns may change in mediated settings, but the final results do not have to be of less quality or quantity. The crucial factor is whether user(groups) adapt their interactions in such a way as to overcome the constraints of the situation.

The effect on real world workgroups has been studied by Hiltz (1988) on the basis of the results of a large-scale survey in the USA and Sweden. She concludes that the use of electronic message systems tends to result in an increase in productivity of workgroups. The earlier mentioned overview studies however contain much less evidence of productivity increase. Apparently the impact on productivity depends on situational aspects such as the type of task. Nevertheless one may expect that the faster communication and exchange of information can have a positive effect on the productivity of people and groups that depend on this exchange.

Achieving consensus is more difficult than in normal groups, because of the loss of social cues in mediated communication. The decrease in the explicit or implicit influence of dominating participants gives group members more freedom to keep to their own position, particularly in asynchronous computer conferencing. Moreover, it appears easier to misunderstand the meaning of certain messages in mediated communication (Steinfield, 1990). There are two ways to solve these problems. One is to introduce rules and roles in the group, i.e. to appoint a leader / facilitator and agree on certain procedures. The other way is to build these rules and procedures into the system. That is exactly what Meeting Support Systems and some asynchronous co-ordination systems do.

With regards to satisfaction with the (distributed) group or the meeting support, the results are very mixed. Several researchers present positive results, but McGrath and Hollingshead (1994) point out that participants in small group research are generally rather positive about the group. When non-supported control groups are used for systematic comparison, both more positive and more negative responses are found in mediated groups.

Meeting Support Systems (MSS) have been analysed quite intensively both in the laboratory and in the field. According to Kraemer and Pinsonneault's meta-analysis (1990) these systems tend to increase group task performance and decision quality, but fail to enhance group satisfaction or even decrease it, which is comparable to the earlier mentioned results concerning message systems and communication systems. Huang (1998) tried to delve deeper into the question how these results can be explained. He used the distinction between influence, i.e. having influence through providing information, and normative influence, having influence because others desire to conform. The MSS appeared indeed to favour task interaction and informational influence, particularly in problem solving tasks, while its use dampened socio-emotional interaction and normative influence, even in consensus reaching tasks.

Herik (1998) studied the diverging effect of meeting support systems in problem solving versus consensus reaching groups in governmental departments. Under well-developed guidance and preparation, problem-solving meetings could benefit substantially by using the MSS to their full extent. In consensus achieving meetings, however, the applicability of the MSS was often considered to be very limited, because in this situation participants preferred open discussions over structured entry of ideas in a computer.

The effect of the introduction of *asynchronous co-ordination systems* such as group calendars on task performance is unclear, partly due to lack of empirical data. These tools may help groups to schedule and co-ordinate group activities better and to increase participation in group communication (Finholt, Sproull and Kiesler, 1990). In an experiment with students co-editing documents using ShrEdit (a group editor system), the task strategy used appeared to be different from that in face-to-face situations. The tool helped the group to remain more focused on the core issues and to devote less time on less important topics. It thereby induced a less extensive exploration of the design space (Olson et al., 1992). Substantial effects on the final product could not be established.

Summarising, group performance does not have to suffer in geographically dispersed groups after the introduction of collaboration technology, with the condition that the group adapts its co-operation strategy. This means that the technology allows groups to be widely distributed and to still co-operate successfully, through the co-ordination capacity provided by collaboration technology. Satisfaction with the interaction process, however, has often been reported to be lower in mediated than in face-to-face settings.

Group Maintenance. Status differences between group members appear to play a less dominant role in electronic groups than in normal groups. Both formal status, i.e. being director or professor and informal status, based on loud speaking and impressive personality, is more difficult to convey through electronic means, due to the lack of non-verbal cues. The result is that group members may participate more open and more equally (e.g. the extensive overview of McGrath and Hollingshead, 1994). Contributions to discussions, and influence on decision making thus appears to be based more on competence and the quality of ideas, than on formal position or personality. The reason for this phenomenon is again found in the absence of cues for social constraints, i.e. precisely because the relationship is less personal, people feel freer to speak out. It has been shown however, that this equalising effect is particularly strong in ad hoc and short living groups (Benbasat and Lim, 1993). In long-standing distributed groups their effect is less present, because the actual social status of the members is quite obvious. High status participants, knowing about the equalising effect, may emphasise their dominance through other means e.g. by explicitly referring to their status, or including their "signature" with indication of position in messages (Weisband et al., 1993). Nevertheless, seeing "Prof. Dr." under a message may make less impression than meeting a professor during a meeting.

Box 2.8

The teams of USA and Dutch students described in Box 2.4 (Section 2.4) could not meet face-to-face. However, since it was expected that cultural differences might disturb the co-operation, extensive training and instruction sessions on both sides of the Atlantic preceded the project. During the training a half-hour video was shown of the students on the other side, doing design work. In this way, the students could become familiar with their partners and could see the differences in design approach and in the general behaviour of their partners. During the project, short video shots were sufficient to close the social distance adequately, although the students expressed their need to meet each other personally.

Group climate. One would expect that communication via media might hinder the development of a good team climate, which to many people is crucial for co-operation. Some studies, however, have indicated that mediated communication does not hinder a good group climate if the group members know each other already personally or have face-to-face meetings now and then (Velden, 1995). So team members that co-operate at a distance for a long time, should meet each other now and then face-to-face, to overcome the (social) distance that exists. If this is not possible, video's of other team members can be a substitute (see Box 2.8).

Flaming. Some distributed groups are characterised by flaming i.e. the use of very strong negative emotional expressions (Kiesler, Siegel and McGuire, 1984; Siegel, Dubrovsky, Kiesler and McGuire, 1986). This has been attributed to a lack of social norms, of sufficient feedback and of structure in mediated conversations. It has been compared to behaviour in large masses of people and referred to by concepts such as de-individuation and anomie. Spears and Lea (1992; also Postmes, 1997), however, have contested this position convincingly (see Section 6.7.2).

Summarising, very few universal consequences of the introduction of collaboration technology on group processes have been found. Social pressure, task- or group-relevant information exchange, conflict level, leadership and personal relations do not depend directly and unconditionally on the presence of supporting technology. It appears that certain tasks can be performed via communication channels that do not seem to be very favourable. People can adapt quite well to new circumstances.

2.6 Collaboration Technology and Organisational Processes

The role of introducing information systems in organisational processes has received much attention. The role of collaboration technology concerning organisational functioning has been less intensively studied, since CT-tools have a much shorter history. There is also another reason for being very hesitant concerning conclusions about its impact on organisational aspects. CT-tools are often less central to primary production processes than large information systems, so the influence of collaboration technology is probably less direct and dominating. Nevertheless some indications of widespread organisational effects have been found. Generally speaking, organisations may become less bureaucratised and more flexible, which is reflected in phenomena such as "border crossing", changes in interaction and decision making, and in power redistribution.

Border crossing. Many studies have shown that accessibility and availability of people and information have increased considerably as an effect of the introduction and use of collaboration technology. This can result in all kinds of forms of border-crossing i.e. ways in which traditional boundaries disappear or become less important (e.g. Davis, 1995):

- Status differences and distinctions between functions become less sharp. In many organisations e-mail can be and is sent directly to higher management.
- Certain information is easily available to all organisation members or to certain groups who where excluded before. An example is provided by the case of the digitised X-ray images becoming available to physicians, described in Box 2.11.
- Borders between departments and organisations become less important when one can easily consult and co-operate with people in other countries. The

organisation of international scientific conferences is an example of a situation where organisers sometimes have much more interaction, through the Internet, with other organisers, than with colleagues in their own department.
- It has become almost impossible to prevent information exchange and communication between countries (see Box 2.9).

Box 2.9

Blockading information exchange by the governments of former Yugoslavia during the civil war (1995) and of China after the Tien An Min massacre, was quite ineffective because of e-mail contacts with other countries.

- The sharp distinction between home and office and between permanent and temporary employees disappears with telework.
- Suppliers and customers become integrated through the use of EDI based logistic systems see Box 2.10.

Box 2.10

Hydrotech, a medium sized producer of hydraulic systems for automobile companies, is connected via an EDI network to automobile companies for orders and billing and to its suppliers of small parts. The administrative systems and the production schedules of the companies involved are interconnected quite strongly as a result of this network. The development of detailed protocols and infrastructure took quite some time and co-operative effort, with the effect that the companies involved will not easily cancel this network (Andriessen, 1994b).

Organisational interaction and decision making. Huber (1990) has made a valuable attempt to combine many findings in a series of propositions concerning the effects of advanced information technologies (AIT), i.e. *computer assisted communication technologies* and *decision aiding technologies*, on organisational design, intelligence and decision making. Huber limits his approach to AIT, thereby excluding production technologies and transaction enacting technologies. Huber's model is based on a combination of empirical findings with expectations based on theory in a systematic way (see also Gardner and Peluchette, 1991). His conclusions are summarised in a series of propositions (see below), that are specifications of the general model presented in Figure 2.1 below.

Huber's conclusions/propositions are the following:

Effects for groups and meetings. Use of computer assisted communication technologies and decision support technologies leads:
- to a larger number and variety of people participating as information sources in the making of decisions.
- to a decrease in size and variety of face-to-face groups, since (some) experts can be consulted remotely or be replaced by expert systems.
- to less of the organisation's time being absorbed by decision related meetings, since information exchange can also been done remotely and since decision support systems make meetings more effective.

Effects on level and flexibility of decision making. Use of computer assisted communication technologies and decision support technologies leads:

- to a more uniform distribution across organisational levels of the probability that a particular organisational level will make a particular decision.
  Actually two mechanisms can be found. Since information for decision making is more widely available, decisions can be made at higher organisational levels (which conforms more to the power norm), and also at more lower levels (which is better for timely decision making). Together these mechanisms allow for a greater distribution of decision making levels, which means on the average that highly centralised organisations become more decentralised and highly decentralised organisations more centralised.
- to a greater variation in the levels at which a particular type of decision will be taken.
- to a reduction of the number of hierarchical levels involved in authorising proposed actions and therefore of the time required for authorising.
- to fewer intermediate human nodes within the organisational information processing network, i.e. from sensor units such as marketing, to decision makers, unless this implies information overload for the decision makers.

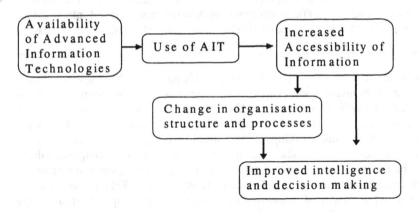

Figure 2.1 Organisational effects of advanced information technologies (figure constructed on the basis of text in Huber, 1990)

Effects for organisational memory. Use of computer assisted communication technologies and decision support technologies leads:

- to a more frequent development and use of computer resident databases as components of organisational memories; this can substitute for knowledge loss because of personnel turnover, for information not being stored, or for information not being shared.
- to more frequent development and use of in-house expert systems.

Effects on organisational learning, intelligence and decision making. Use of computer assisted communication technologies and decision support technologies leads:

- to more rapid and more accurate identification of problems and opportunities, implying better organisational learning.
- to organisational intelligence that is more accurate, comprehensive, timely and available, resulting in higher quality decisions and to a reduction of the time required to make decisions, although this may lead to lower quality decisions.

The relationships presented in the propositions are to some extent based on empirical studies. However, in other cases the findings have not been so clear. Huber's categorical statements have a flavour of the perspective of technological determinism (see Chapter 3), while other studies indicate that the effects depend on all kinds of conditions.

Power distribution. It has long been debated which changes in *influence and power distribution* and in structural *centralisation or decentralisation* are the effects of the introduction of ICT. Access to large databases can provide employees with resources, which may make them much more autonomous than before. The adage "knowledge is power" has been clearly demonstrated, since the introduction of new information networks can be an occasion for shifts in power and control, such as from higher-level managers to lower-level managers (e.g. Markus, 1983) or professionals to other professionals (Aydin and Rice, 1989; Andriessen, 1990, see Box 2.11).

Box 2.11

Introduction of an X-ray image network in a hospital can influence the power distribution of professionals (Andriessen, 1990). Digitising X-ray images and storing them in a central database makes them equally available to radiologists and medical specialists. In a traditional system hardcopy images are examined by radiologists, who then write a report and advise for the medical specialists. The specialists are dependent on the radiologist for the report and see the images only in exceptional cases. The medical specialists were enthusiastic about the new system because they could now draw their own conclusions on the basis of the available images, without having to wait for a report from the radiologists. The radiologists however considered the images to have too poor resolution for their fine-grained analysis. Moreover, the availability of the images to the specialists implied that the reports of the radiologists were in most cases no longer really needed, which might in due course lower the position, and possibly financial future, of the radiologists. In another hospital the X-ray information system had an extra feature. It provided a very easy to handle system for communication between radiologists and medical specialists. This system supported both audio contact and "application sharing" i.e. the possibility for the doctors to have the same X-ray picture on their screens, each with a pointer, to show the other person what part of the image they were referring to. This communication system supported co-operative behaviour.

Certain groups may perceive this equalising effect to be a challenge to their positions. Examples of organisations, where management has tried to prevent employees exchanging messages or accessing information sources can be found in the literature

(Zuboff, 1988; Ciborra and Lanzara, 1994) This reason for the lack of penetration of new technologies is also found in other contexts. The literature concerning telework comes to more or less the same conclusions, i.e. that management is not eager to lose its control over employees. Management information systems and behaviour registration systems can however be used to provide management with powerful tools to *control the behaviour* of employees (Björn-Andersen, Eason and Robey, 1986).

Various reviewers have attempted to define the direction in which the introduction of information systems actually changes the locus of control (Swanson, 1987; Peiro and Prieto, 1994). They conclude that both centralisation and decentralisation trends can be found in the literature reviewed. One reason for this seemingly contradictory finding is the fact that different systems can have different effects (Andriessen, 1990). A second reason is that the actual effect depends on a complex of interacting factors, i.e. on the organisational setting (see Section 2.7). A third reason is to be found in what George and King (1991) call the *ecological perspective*. This view holds that the (social, economic, legal etc.) environment provides the discretionary space for an organisation.

Organisational history provides further opportunities and constraints and it is only within these limits, that managerial choice in relation to other power centres determines the developments. In bureaucratic organisations computer technology is developed to make control stronger, while in organic organisations this same kind of technology serves horizontal information exchange and communication. This perspective substitutes the older perspectives of pure technological determinism, i.e. the introduction of technology has a general effect, or of pure strategic choice', i.e. management has all the freedom to centralise or decentralise decision-making (see also Chapter 3).

2.7 General Societal Effects

This book is not focused on general societal impacts of Information and Communication Technology. Nevertheless a few related issues will be touched upon, mainly to show how far-reaching the implications of ICT may be. Evidence of these effects is however still quite scarce. In the seventies great effects of new communications technology were expected, such as growth of the economy in general and improved opportunities for rural areas. Yet hand in hand with this optimism, the fear has grown that the new technology may contribute to undesirable developments.

The dual society. One fear is that of the *dual society*, i.e. a society with a large gap between those with and those without access to information and communication services. This phenomenon can be seen, at least to some degree, in the present distribution of ICT applications and services. There appears to be a strong relation between on the one hand income or education and on the other hand indicators of ICT access such as PC ownership and Internet use (Shneiderman, 2000). This raises the issue of *universal access*, i.e. adequate facilities should be available to everybody at reasonable prices. This should enable almost all citizens to access basic services. Guaranteeing universal access in itself may be sufficient to prevent a societal gap for simple technologies such as the telephone. In the case of more complex technologies such as computers and Internet, however, this is not sufficient to ensure successful usage. A plea is therefore made for *universal usability* (Shneiderman, 2000), i.e. for developing ICTechnology in such a way that all people can make use of the tools and the services provided without much difficulty.

Hage (1995) discusses the role of information technology in relation to the characteristics of post industrial society in general, and in particular in relation to the signs of role failures in the community and family, i.e. crimes, broken marriages, single parent raised children, poverty. Hage argues that the new demands of post industrial society have to be analysed intensively, such as the change towards mental rather than physical work activities, the intensity of interactions in all spheres of life, and the changes in work-, family- and leisure-roles. These changes imply that people must learn to live in complex role sets, with many contacts taking place mediated by communication technology. Furthermore people have to adjust to constant changes in society. To deal with these situations, complex and creative minds are required, that are adaptable, flexible and have the skill to understand symbolic, i.e. non-verbal, communications. Since not all individuals possess these characteristics to such a high degree, this may lead to another form of duality in society.

Is the present gap between societal groups regarding access to and use of ICT only a temporary or is it a structural phenomenon? Rogers (1995) concluded from his historical analyses that the introduction of a new technology in society at first often leads to social differentiation, but that later the benefits become more equally distributed. Whether this is true as a general trend has to be seen yet. Shneiderman (2000) reports that although *"the gap in Internet usage has been declining between men and women, and between old and young, the gap is growing between rich and poor and between well and poorly educated"*. Whatever the truth, the discussion about the threat of a dual society is active, and national governments as well as the European Community have substantial programmes designed to tackle this issue.

Social disintegration. Other analyses of trends in our culture have been made, such as regarding the issue of *quantity versus quality*. It has been suggested that an increase in information results in a belief of "the more information the better" and that interpersonal communication is the same as an exchange of information. Since communication and community depend much more on building understanding, on being together and developing trust than on exchanging correct information, these developments may contribute to a *fragmentation* of society. Turkle (1996) has claimed that use of the Internet leads to the destruction of meaningful community and of social integration.

Kraut et al. (1998) tried to study this phenomenon empirically. They analysed the effects of the introduction and use of Internet on the social relationships of 169 individuals from 73 families in Pittsburg, USA over a 2 years period. Diaries, questionnaires and interviews were used to provide the data. It appeared that heavy Internet use resulted in a decrease in time for communication in the home, a decrease of the number of people with whom one had contacts and increased feelings of loneliness, stress and depression.

These phenomena could be explained by the fact that Internet-use and Internet contacts are substituted for face-to-face social activities. This means that users spend more time on the Internet searching for superficial contacts and therefore have less time for direct communication and strong social ties. A counter argument could be that the Internet also allows for the development of new social contacts. The study showed, however, that only very few Internet contacts were realised. Moreover, such contacts can generally be characterised as "weak ties" (superficial contacts). Another explanation is also possible. Exposure to the Internet may have direct negative effects on behaviour and feelings, even when people keep spending the same amount of time on family relations. The data do not allow for the testing of these two explanations.

Kraut's study was limited to one locality and to a small number of people. The correlations, although significant, were very low (.10 to .15). During a panel discussion at the CSCW98 conference Wellman reported on a study in Toronto, Canada, where a community with many Internet users was compared with a community without Internet users. In the first community the people appeared not only to have more superficial contacts through the Internet but also more direct face-to-face contacts than in the second community. This may imply that Internet users are the people who have more contacts in general. According to a study by LaRose, Eastin and Gregg (2001) self-efficacy, i.e. belief in one's ability to perform a task successfully, and social support appeared to be important intervening factors which determined the actual presence or absence of stress and depression in conjunction with Internet use.

The Toronto results are confirmed by the results of a survey by Katz and Aspden (1997), who concluded that there was "...*no support for the pessimistic theories of the effects of cyberspace on community involvement. No differences were found in participation rates in religious, leisure and community organisations. The Internet appeared even to augment existing traditional social connectivity*".

It is clear that the impact of the Internet on social relations is far from obvious and it is equally clear that certain groups have at least benefited tremendously. Internet communities have been developed for chronically ill people, e.g. those suffering from arthritis, for handicapped or elderly people and have provided them with many previously undreamed of possibilities for social contacts.

Ubiquitous access and isolation. A third trend is related to *ubiquitous access.* Many people wish to be in touch with others frequently and to be reachable by others constantly. They want instantaneous communication, even if it is only to tell their partner that they are almost home. They do not want to wait, they do not accept postponement of the gratification of their communication needs. Therefore they have their mobile phone in their pockets and will take up and use the even more ubiquitous communication and information tools at present being developed. It is reported that some people who turn their mobile phone off have the eerie feeling that they are cutting themselves off from humanity. At the same time some society watchers suggest that the present, the "now" dominates our thinking much more than the past or the future. Are these technical and cultural trends related, and are they all-pervading or to be found only in certain cases, depending on certain conditions? Empirical findings about these developments and about to the degree to which continuing expansion of ICT may relate to it are still very scarce and difficult to find.

Can humanity deal with the information society? Such a general question is outside the scope of this book and probably cannot be answered. An analogy might illustrate the reason why both positive and negative answers are feasible. Imagine a farmer in a rural village, one hundred years ago. His main transport tool was a horse and cart. When confronted with automobiles, he may well have predicted that people would not be able to deal adequately with the interaction of many high speed cars. Actually, the first horseless carriages were obliged to drive with someone walking before them carrying a red flag. The farmer could never have dreamt that people would be able to drive in heavy traffic, processing enormous amounts of information and still being able to react with speed where needed. In the same way it may well be that we, or at least our children, will get used to all the ICT developments that will be introduced in the future and still be able to deal with it adequately. The analogy also shows the negative aspects of such an influx of new technology. Individually most of us can cope with dense traffic, however, loss of lives, of time and of money and destruction to our environment are the prices of development that we have forced ourselves to pay.

2.8 Conclusion

Collaboration technology has brought the possibilities of increased accessibility to and availability of people and information. Consultation of diverse often remote information sources and communication at a distance, with large groups of people is both possible and practised widely today, within work organisations and by the public at large. Thus the intended effects of collaboration technology, i.e. overcoming space and time constraints can indeed be found in practice.

Generic effects tend to be found in behaviour that is directly influenced by the use of new tools, such as communication behaviour, which has been changed by applications that support communication. Mediated task communication tends to be more formalised than face-to-face communication, since it has to compensate for the lack of social cues we take for granted in social meetings. Yet interpersonal communication e.g. over the Internet can also be very informal and even emotional. Another finding is that the general level of participation of group members may be less than in face-to-face teams, and this participation tends to be more equally distributed, partly because of a certain degree of anonymity. Whether this holds in permanent contacts is questionable.

For the rest, it all depends. Few generic effects on interpersonal communication, task performance, group processes, or organisational efficiency can be found. Adoption and use of a new system, and its effects on attitudes, behaviour, efficiency and effectiveness appear to be conditional. The discussions in this chapter have shown that the implications of collaboration technology tools appear to depend on the following major clusters of conditions, which are also relevant for design (Grudin, 1994):

Individual acceptance and choice of tools. The success of a tool depends on the ratio between on the one hand the need for certain activities, such as the need to consult people or databases, and on the other hand the existing barriers to support these activities. Tool use depends on a (subjective) assessment of costs and benefits. If the perceived usefulness is low even tools deemed to be fantastic by their developers will not be accepted. On the other hand, when distance is large and communication urgent, even badly functioning systems will be used. Video-conferencing may provide the benefit of seeing each other, but if this hardly adds to the task at hand and the effort of communication and the financial costs of the system are high, people are not motivated to adopt it. This cost benefit assessment is not just a matter of intra-person comparison, it also involves the interaction of many. Group calendars have failed, when only the project leaders really benefit from them, while the group members have to spend time and effort in keeping them up to date (Grudin, 1994). This problem has become even larger since the introduction of knowledge management systems, which require employees regularly to input data, e.g. about projects or customers, without seeing much profit in this activity themselves (Huysman and de Wit, 2002).

This individual cost-benefit analysis is however not (only) a rational process of calculations. Several examples have been given of user characteristics that condition the choice of ICT applications. People's perception of and attitude towards the technology, affects the way they use the technology. An individual-centred way of working may prevent fruitful use of group support systems. Innovative people adopt new tools much faster than others.

Match between tool and task, or between tool and other aspects of the context. In a previous section it was concluded that electronic message systems might be more suited to simple tasks than to complex tasks, while meeting support systems appear to be more effective for supporting problem solving tasks than consensus developing tasks.

Group and organisation characteristics. The role of group or organisational culture appears to be relevant. Certain organisations promote a competitive climate in which mutual trust and sharing of knowledge is perceived as "giving away power". In these situations a system that promotes knowledge sharing will probably not be used intensively. In a formalised organisation culture and a centralised structure e-mail appears to be used less effectively. Group size may be also significant. Small groups appear to benefit less from collaboration technology than large groups. Co-operating in large distributed groups is quite difficult and the introduction of group support systems in large groups may therefore result in greater increase in decision quality and satisfaction than when used in small groups (Benbasat and Lim, 1993).

Design and implementation. The design process and the way a new system is introduced and appropriated in an organisation appear to be crucial for acceptance. Intuitions of designers (or management) are especially poor for multi-user applications, resulting in an error-prone design process and bad management decisions. Moreover, groupware supported activities require a much more careful introduction in the workplace than product developers and management are accustomed to.

Appropriation, learning and innovation. Even if carefully introduced, technical tools may take up roles that are different from what was expected, due to the meaning a tool acquires in the eyes of the users. If adopted, a process of gradual adaptation of the technology takes place, which changes the original situation. This is sometimes called "appropriation" (see Section 7.3). Learning processes play an important role. New ways of interaction develop, partly as an unintended by-effect of the new socio-technical setting. People discover that the traditional way of working can be supplemented by new ways that are much more effective, efficient and pleasant. In a way this is the most fascinating process. The degree to which the introduction of collaboration technology enables and stimulates new ways of working and interaction is an indicator of its value.

Summarising. Collaboration technology may have some direct and therefore generalisable and predictable effects on communication behaviour, but its effects e.g. on task performance, organisational processes and effectiveness depend on other factors. This reflects the *law of logical distance:* The greater the logical distance, i.e. the greater the number of intervening variables, between a causal factor, such as the characteristics of a collaboration technology tool, and a dependent variable such as team effectiveness, the less the second can be predicted from the first, because of the potential interacting influence of other factors.

Technical tools become part of a socio-technical context. Their role depends on the functions they develop in a social context and on the way various forces direct their adoption and use. Technology interacts with all kinds of context factors and stakeholders' interests. The various aspects have to fit to be most effective. Change in one of the aspects of such a system will most likely result in changing the other aspects.

The concept of "fit" implies that the success of a new tool depends on the degree to which it matches the tasks, the users and the context it is designed for (see Chapter 6). This viewpoint suggests that ideally the configuration of tools and work context should be designed together. The fit however also appears to be a developmental issue: under certain circumstances people learn to use new systems, either by gradually and sometimes unintentionally moulding it to their own usage or by undertaking a systematic organisational change and implementation strategy (see Chapter 7). This dual mechanism will be encountered in many discussions concerning information and communication technology tools. New tools have to match the existing situation, and will be adapted during operational use.

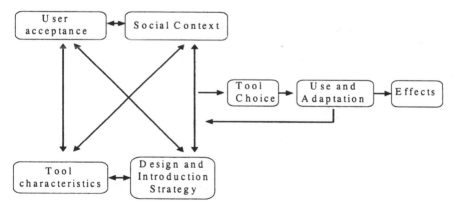

Figure 2.2 Interaction of factors determining impact of new tools and systems

These findings are illustrated in Figure 2.2. The elements in this figure will be explored further in the coming chapters and elaborated into a comprehensive model in Chapter 8.

It becomes clear from the model in figure 2.2 that choice, use and effects of collaboration technology have to be studied in the context of three types of domains and theories:

1. *Theories concerning match between tools and user or task* (Chapter 4 and 5), because success and failure of collaboration technology is partly a matter of individual acceptance and fit to the task.
2. *Theories concerning interaction processes* (Chapter 6), because success and failure of collaboration technology is partly related to the role it fulfils in support of social interaction and co-operation. If we want to develop teamwork-supporting systems, we need to know what teamwork is.
3. *Theories concerning design, introduction and adoption* of technology (Chapter 7), because success and failure of collaboration technology is partly a matter of the way the technology is designed, implemented and incorporated. Design and implementation should preferably not be focused on a specific tool, but on new configurations of technology, people, tasks and context. This "socio-technical" perspective is not new, but it is necessary to keep stressing its importance.

Theories concerning user acceptance, group context and implementation processes will be presented and discussed in Chapters 4 to 7. Many relevant models and theories can be found in the fields of Work Psychology and Social Psychology, of Organisational Behaviour, Communication Sciences and related disciplines: theories of individual motivation, work design, group dynamics, team-effectiveness, quality of work and organisational co-ordination. These traditional disciplines can however benefit from knowledge of and theories developed or adapted in the upcoming field of Computer Mediated Communication or Computer Supported Co-operative Work, theories such as Media Match Theories, Activity Theory, and Adaptive Structuration Theory.

In this publication I have set myself the task of analysing relevant theories in order to develop an overall integrated conceptual framework and to construct an approach for systematic design oriented evaluation of collaboration technology applications.

The evaluation approach has to have the following characteristics and must:

- focus on the usability and usefulness of both collaboration technology tools and co-operative work with collaboration technology.
- take into account the various nested levels of analysis: individual task performance, team interaction and organisational processes.
- intertwine with the design process, in that it provides guidelines and instruments to evaluate new systems before, during and after the design process.

Chapter 3. The Role of Technology in Society

3.1 Introduction

In this chapter I will elaborate further the general issue of technology's impact on society and organisation, before presenting theories and models concerning individual motivation, group processes and implementation. Having discussed the impact of collaboration technology in work situations, the conclusion was reached that very few general conclusions can be drawn. This leads us to the question: *Why is it that the results of impact-studies are so limited in generalisability?* Is the research of low quality, or are the questions about the impacts of technology perhaps wrongly phrased? The questions appear to be based on the assumption that technology in itself does have a general impact, i.e. that the introduction of certain tools must necessarily result in certain effects. This is called the "technological imperative" perspective and it has been challenged in several ways (George and King, 1991; Orlikowski, 1996). Firstly, by assuming that the effects of technology depend on certain conditions; this is called *the contingency perspective*. Secondly, by taking the perspective that people act purposefully to accomplish certain intended objectives and in this framework choose the technology they need.

This view may be called the *organisational imperative,* the *strategic choice* or the *planned change perspective*. A third view is called the *emergent perspective* or *situated change perspective*: changes emerge unpredictably from the interaction of people, technology and context (Markus and Robey, 1988; Orlikowski, 1996). These perspectives on social reality are given form in the following descriptions.

3.2 Four Perspectives

3.2.1 Technological and Organisational Imperative

The technological imperative view is the most extremely objectivist and functionalist. In this view, the introduction of technology in our society and in organisations is viewed as an independent and autonomous mechanism, with inevitable and determining influence on, or constraints for, human behaviour. It is viewed as an autonomous driver of organisational change. Leavitt and Whistler's seminal article (1958), predicting that IT would dramatically change organisations and the managerial function, is rooted squarely in this perspective.

In the ICT-field optimistic and neutral versions of this view can be found. An optimistic view holds that the existence of new communication technology will by itself result in free networking throughout the organisation, thereby causing the hierarchical chains of traditional organisations to be shed. Indeed it has been suggested that the introduction of much of the collaboration technology applications and the Internet will lead to more co-operation and equality in and outside of organisations. A neutral view holds that certain ICT applications (e.g. communication systems) will lead to more freedom and others (e.g. shared information systems) to more control.

The technological imperative view ignores the manner in which technology is designed and developed, and the role of humans in appropriating and interacting with it (Orlikowski, 1992). Moreover, the open-ended nature of many modern collaboration technology applications requires that end-users adapt the tool to their needs. This is called "tailorisation", i.e. users cannot just install a tool like the groupware system Lotus Notes and use it, but have to adapt it to their own work requirements. Of course the system allows for only certain applications, within clear constraints. Nevertheless, the system can be adapted to quite different purposes. Finally, in empirical research very few generic effects have been found (see Chapter 3). An open and one-sided technological perspective is therefore a rarity found in the literature today. But many reports still speak freely of the impact of information and communication technology on all aspects of society.

The perspective of the *organisational imperative* is as objectivist as that of the technology imperative but here the focus is on the determining force of organisational institutions in general instead of technology in particular. Evidence is taken from the fact that certain technologies are not adopted, while others are adapted to the organisational way of life. It seems to be the basic nature and logic of existing organisations that determine the development of technologies. This argument runs parallel to the results of Perrow's (1983) empirical studies of large, complex, technological systems, who has shown how the process of technological design encourages design engineers to create machine interfaces that reflect existing social structures and rationalistic assumptions about human action.

George and King (1991) in a review of the discussion on the relation between computerisation and organisational centralisation, take these arguments into account. According to their analysis the discretion for managerial choice is less than many expect. The organisational environment, including social and legal structures, provides the limits for organisational processes and the organisational history further shapes opportunities and constraints. Only within this space, can managerial choices and action determine the setting. The choices concerning information technology then tend to reinforce the decision authority status quo. George and King call this view the *ecology perspective* coupled with *reinforcement politics* and it explains the tendency in bureaucratic organisations for computer technology to be developed to make control stronger, while in organic organisations this same kind of technology serves to support horizontal information exchange and communication.

The technological and organisational perspectives differ as to the extent to which organisations are free to choose the technology, while the view of George and King falls in between. All perspectives are in agreement in the sense that they expect the introduction of certain technologies to have specific consequences.

3.2.2 Contingency Perspective

Since it is clear that the effects of technologies depend to a large extent on circumstances, fine tuned studies have been undertaken to model the various conditions that co-determine outcomes. The *Contingency Perspective* is central to major organisation theories and is related to General Systems Theory. The basic idea is that systems should match their environment to thrive and be effective. The major viewpoint in the area of organisational functioning is called the Structural Contingency Perspective (e.g. Gutek, 1990), which was developed to contrast with earlier theories concerning the one best way of organising (e.g. Donaldson, 1996; Pennings, 1998). The relevant contingencies for organisational structure are the turbulence of its environment (Lawrence and Lorsch, 1969), its production technologies (Woodward, 1965; Perrow, 1967), and its size (Blau, 1970). In the area of collaboration technology this is translated into the idea that the effectiveness of an application depends on its fit to the task, the user(groups) and the context (see Section 5.3).

The contingency principles can be made concrete into specific guidelines, such as the notion that large organisations should have more formalised and centralised and more differentiated (vertical and horizontal) structures than smaller ones, unless the organisation is subdivided into a multi-divisional form. Other guidelines refer to the turbulence or stability of the environment. Galbraith (1977) proposed that management should react to environmental turbulence and uncertainty by either reducing the required information processing, e.g. by making organisational sub-units more independent, or by increasing information processing capacity through the introduction of vertical information systems and/or lateral communication systems. Contingency models are widely used by consultants as a tool for analysing organisations and advising them on the way to salvation. A widely known model is that of McKinsey's 7-S model. According to this approach seven dimensions of organisations should match: Strategy, Structure, Systems, Style, Staff, Skills, and Superordinate goals.

Criticism of contingency theories focuses on two issues. Firstly, the central concepts, such as structure, technology, effectiveness and particularly fit, have been given widely divergent and sometimes quite diffuse meanings. Measuring the concepts has been difficult and the source of many disputes. The concept of fit or match is very central in contingency theories. The concepts have a long-standing tradition, supported by many empirical studies, not only concerning the fit between organisational structure and for example production technology, but also concerning the fit of task and media, users and work context (see Chapter 6). Nevertheless, although this concept is intuitively quite clear, is very difficult to measure it independently (Venkatraman, 1989). Secondly, the contingency perspective as such, leaves little room for the influence of change, of changing interpretations of reality and for appropriation processes. Theories in the tradition of organisational learning (Huysman, 1996), of emergent structures, or Giddens' Structuration perspective, are aimed at this wider view. The contingency perspective however has had a very high heuristic value. It has provided a fruitful basis for research in all kinds of fields. In the context of collaboration technology it has spawned several versions of the *Media Match* theories (see Chapter 6).

3.2.3 Strategic Choice Perspective

In the strategic choice perspective it is assumed that people have a free choice to adopt and control technological options and their consequences. Organisational change can be orchestrated in a very systematic and controlled way, through a strategy of *planned change*. This perspective lies behind the propagation of telecommunication to gain a competitive advantage (Keen, 1988): *"Telecommunications can be harnessed as a major new force for organisational design and redesign, and all large organisations need to exploit the opportunities it opens up"*.

It is, however, also the perspective of the Labour Process theorists, who consider modern management to be still basically tayloristic and warn for the degrading of jobs and for labour redundancies which often accompany the introduction of new technologies (e.g. Knights and Wilmott, 1988). In this view technology, and thus also ICT, is used by those in power to reinforce existing power structures.

The studies of Zuboff (1988) show how information technology can be designed for two radically different purposes, i.e. either to "informate" or to "automate" work, which will have either empowering or controlling and de-skilling consequences. In the strategic choice perspective it is probable that bureaucratic management will only introduce those applications of information and communication technology, that will strengthen the central control, while modern organic organisations will opt for applications which will enable creative networking.

3.2.4 Emergent Structures Perspective

The strategic choice approach views the conscious and rational choices of managers as all-determining, assuming insight into and unlimited choice over technological options and their effects. It ignores the role of other actors and of social and economic processes that make developments often very unclear, even for top management, particularly of smaller companies. The emergent structures perspective focuses on evolving and unpredicted processes and on the creative forces of users to interpret and use tools in novel ways. These theories emphasise adaptation, learning and appropriation processes. They hold that the uses and consequences of information technology emerge rather unpredictably from complex social interactions. The influence of unexpected external influences, the interaction of people with different backgrounds, interests and interpretations, the discovery of possibilities to use a tool in unintended ways, all make the outcome of the introduction of a new technology unpredictable. The development of new technology unpredictable. The development of new technologies and of new social structures is therefore not a matter of grand strategies of planned change but rather a series of actions in reaction to unplanned developments (see Box 3.1). Orlikowski (1996) speaks of *situated change* (see Section 8.2), Hutchins (1991, 1995) of *local adaptation and local design.*

Box 3.1

A new technology was introduced in organisation Zeta, as a platform for tracking customer calls, and for collecting and making available the company experiences with its customers. Over a two year period the organisational processes and culture within Zeta were gradually changed, not by planned strategy but in a process characterised by improvisation and changes in everyday practice (Orlikowski, 1996)

In the same vein Barley (1986) regards the introduction of new technologies as "*occasions that trigger social dynamics which, in turn, modify or maintain an organisation's contours...by altering institutionalised roles and interaction patterns*". A powerful framework for explaining these social dynamics is provided by Giddens's Structuration Theory (see below), and it's daughter, Adaptive Structuration Theory, that was developed specifically in the area of collaboration technology (see Section 7.3).

Howard (1995) presents a similar view in her discussion of the evolution of organisation. Her approach is derived from Complexity Theory, which is related to Chaos Theory: "*Complex systems advance not gradually but through... punctuated equilibrium... i.e. a pattern of innovation which progresses in fits and starts rather than a steady stream... Complex systems evolve through self-organisation and selection to what is called the edge of chaos. It is a balance point... a point of maximal differentiation and integration*". She predicts that in future work organisations will be more and more like complex systems in this sense: fluid, uncertain, interconnected, invisible. The central question is, *how can equilibrium be maintained at the edge of chaos.* The answer is related to Ashby's Law: changing and fluid environments require workers who are differentiated, creative, adaptable, responsible, relational and growing; and work that is characterised by empowerment, learning and interdependence. In such a situation, many problems can surface: insecurity and uncertainty, stress and social friction. But work could also provide compensations: challenge, flexibility, control and inter-relatedness. To maximise these potential benefits and to prevent the problems from becoming destructive is a big challenge. Future organisational psychologists should play a major role in this endeavour.

3.3 A Combination: Structuration Theory

3.3.1 The Theory in General

Although the various perspectives seem to exclude each other, they can be combined to a certain degree. They all reflect certain mechanisms that are visible in actual practice. Introduction of technology does have certain effects, but organisational traditions can be powerful constraints for the development of new structures. Certain conditions can make large differences in the impacts of new technologies and a major condition is the interaction of the people that happen to be involved and their way of dealing with new possibilities.

According to a model developed by van den Hooff (1997) two interaction processes are active at the same time, i.e. *organisational strategy making* which demands certain organisational structures, which in their turn demands certain communication practices, which then demand certain communication technology. and *communication technology developments*, which provide opportunities for communication processes, which provide in their turn opportunities for organisational processes, that then provide opportunities for strategic choices.

This model of the interaction of demands and opportunities is a specific example of a general view on the relation between people-in-action and institutional constraints, and this is elaborated in Structuration Theory. This theory was developed by Giddens (1984) in an attempt to overcome the antagonism between deterministic (objectivist) and voluntaristic (subjectivist) perspectives on social reality. Structuration Theory combines the focus on the structuring role of human action, with the focus on the constraining and enabling role of social structures. According to Giddens' view both perspectives are valid. Social reality is constituted both by the activities of human actors and by institutional properties, i.e. properties of "social structures". The concept of *social structure* refers to the rules and resources people use during action in a certain context. Human actions are enabled and constrained by structural properties of social systems, but these structures consist of the residues of previous human action, and are open to restructuring. Or, conversely, structures are created by human action, and then serve to shape future human action. This is called the principle of *duality of structure,* i.e. social structures are both the medium and the outcome of interaction. Structuration is the process of interaction between humans and social systems.

Structuration Theory (ST) acknowledges the important role of institutions, i.e. social structures such as an organisational structure, with its hierarchy and rules etc., group structure, with its role differentiation, values and norms, and individual characteristics, such as knowledge, skills, attitudes and dispositions. A technological system, with its hardware, software and procedures, or a society's legal system, also form a social structure. But ST emphasises the dynamic nature of social structures and of the human activities, by which the characteristics of the institutions are either confirmed (reproduced) or changed.

Actually there are three fundamental dimensions of structure and so three structuration processes, i.e. three domains in which the interaction between human action and institutional structures takes place: the domain of *meaning-constitution*, the domain of *power relations* and the domain of *norms and legitimisation* (see Figure 3.1). Actors give meaning, apply power and norms and thereby re-affirm or change the three structures. These structures in their turn provide schemes, resources and normative frames and in that way enable and constrain the behaviour of the actors.

Actors can thus under certain circumstances change the structure (i.e. produce new structures), both through intentionally changing them and by unintended consequences of their action. In the context of our discussion of co-operative groups this means that team structures and interdependence relations become institutionalised, but can also be changed, e.g. when new elements, such as new tools, become part of the setting.

Social Structures

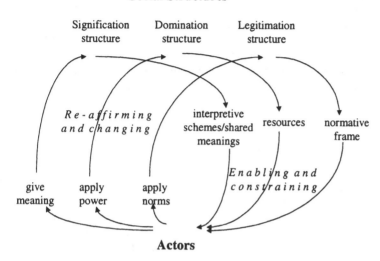

Figure 3.1 Structuration Theory. Three basic areas for structuration of human interaction (Figure constructed on the basis of text in Gibson, 1984)

Structures of signification are related to human communication and the common interpretation of events and things. These structures provide *interpretative schemes*: shared meaning and knowledge, used to interpret behaviour and events. A shared understanding of certain developments is necessary for adequate communication and action.

Structures of domination and power relations develop through the use of power and in their turn provide *resources*, i.e. the means through which goals are accomplished and power is exercised. Resources can be of two types, i.e. *authoritative resources*, knowledge and skills by which people can have command of others, and *allocative resources*, tools, money, etc and the means, i.e. knowledge and skills to use these. *"Structures of domination are evident when developers have to 'sell' the Intranet concepts to management to gain their support"* (Scheepers and Damsgaard, 1997, p11).

Box 3.2
Using Structuration Theory to analyse Intranet development in several organisations, Scheepers and Damsgaard (1997) show how the introduction of Intranets was hindered by the fact that users and management differed widely regarding the meaning and significance they attributed to their use.

Legitimisation-structures are formed by applying or developing *Rules* and *Norms*, including rights and obligations, governing appropriate conduct. For example, by referring to existing organisational directives, management can influence the development of certain technologies, thereby reproducing the existing normative frame and legitimisation structure.

Changes in structures are often the result of unplanned and unintended consequences of interactions. Changes in structures are generally quite gradual, i.e. evolutionary, although circumstances can also lead to radical, i.e. revolutionary changes. This is related to the distinction between what Giddens calls *discursive consciousness* and *practical consciousness*. Practical consciousness is the ability to act in a purposeful way, without being able to articulate this ability or knowledge ('tacit knowledge'). Discursive consciousness is the ability to describe and reflect explicitly on one's actions and motivations. Using discursive consciousness people can explicitly discuss and argue their use of a rule or tool and can decide to change this radically.

3.3.2 The Role of Technology

In the Structurational perspective technology and its specific applications are also social structures, with the same dual nature of social structures in general. Humans (designers) develop technical systems, with certain embedded rules, resources and meaning. The technical system shapes and constrains human behaviour in the setting where it is applied, and human actors in their turn shape the setting and the technical systems during and by their actions. The development of separate views on the role of technology has to some extent been caused by the fact that "...*the actions that constitute the technology are often separated in time and space from the actions that are constituted by the technology, with the former typically occurring in vendor or supplier organisations, and the latter occurring in customer sites...*" (Orlikowski and Robey, 1991).

The basic tenet of the structurationist perspective is that the relationships are not unidirectional and simply causal. Information Technology is an outcome of such human action as design and development, but also of appropriation and modification. But Information Technology also facilitates and constrains human action through the provision of interpretative schemes, facilities and norms. Thirdly, interaction with information technology influences the institutional properties of an organisation, through reinforcing or transforming the systems of signification, domination and legitimisation. And finally these institutional properties in their turn influence humans in their interaction with information technology; properties such as design standards, professional norms and available resources such as time and money. Summarising, the behaviour of human actors and the enabling or constraining role of the institutional realm interact. *"The specific institutional context and the intentions and actions of knowledgeable, self-reflexive humans always mediate the relationship between technology and organisations..."* (Orlikowski, 1992).

The introduction of technology in an organisation is viewed as an occasion for structuring the social processes, because its presence provokes human interactions that may subsequently effect revised social structures (Orlikowski and Robey, 1991). Attention should therefore be given to the reciprocal nature of the relation between the design, adoption and use of collaboration technology and to the effects this has on the user and his context.

Of course certain technologies are easier to revise and redesign than others. Large technological systems, such as factory production lines, are rather rigid and difficult to appropriate, i.e. make it 'their own', by individual users/operators. Pinch and Bijker (1987) use the term "interpretative flexibility" to indicate the extent to which users can and do engage in the development of a certain technology during design or operational use. Computer systems and particularly collaboration technology applications are quite open to such influences. Customer built organisational information systems and collaboration technology tools can be influenced during design and introduction, particularly when an evolutionary, participative design approach is used. Many collaboration technology tools rather require tailorisation and adaptation to local use (see Section 7.3).

Orlikowski characterises the role of technology with regard to the three domains of structuration as follows (Orlikowski and Robey, 1991, p.154):

1. Information technology *provides interpretative* schemes through which users come to understand and also structure their world. Example: the way a software program categorises data determines how users perceive social reality.
2. Information systems provide sources of information for actors, thereby *changing sometimes dramatically the power relations* between those actors (see the case of the radiologists and medical specialists in Section 3.6).
3. Information technology *conveys a set of norms* that indicate accepted actions, interests and practices in the workplace (see Box 3.3).

Box 3.3

Orlikowski (1992) describes a software development company Beta, where traditionally the designers constructed the user interfaces according to certain ergonomic principles. A design tool was introduced, which provided a standard format that prompted the designers to fill in certain information. The interface layout was then designed according to standard norms and rules. The tool enabled the designer in the sense that the design process was much faster than previously, but it constrained the design in that it had to adhere to standard rules. The consultants and also clients had to accept that this was the only way interfaces could be made up.

Structuration Theory states that actors can challenge and change the meanings, resources and norms, embedded in social structures. If they are powerful enough, they create new forms of interaction. Social structures, and thus also Information technology, will not always be used in ways envisioned by designers or intended by management. Social practices surrounding the development and use of information technology will therefore result in both intended and unintended consequences, and depend on anticipated and unanticipated conditions. So technology is neither all controlling, nor all empowering, but rather both, in varying intensities, depending on organisational conditions.

The structurational perspective points to the limits of participative design. Institutional conditions and strategic objectives of managers often determine the basic objectives and characteristics of a technological system. If the general thrust of the organisation is for the technology to increase efficiency, tighten controls and de-skill jobs, it is unlikely that users participating in certain design processes will be able to influence the design in the direction of user customisation, modification and experimentation during use.

Conclusion.

Structuration Theory provides a more general perspective on social reality than a testable theory. It has been used as a kind of sensitising framework for the explanation of barriers for certain ICT-applications and as a basis for deriving design guidelines for CSCW applications (Barley, 1986; Lyytinen and Ngwenyama, 1992; Scheepers and Damsgaard, 1997). Adaptive Structuration Theory (Poole and DeSanctis, 1990) is a specification of Structuration Theory specifically developed for the CSCW field to describe and explain appropriation processes in groups (see Section 7.3).

Box 3.4 *Central points of attention, derived from Structuration Theory*

1. Technological systems are part of a world in which there is a constant interaction between institutionalisation and individual action. Tools influence and are influenced by human behaviour.

2. This influence of and on technology is realised through the development of shared *meanings*, *norms* and *controls* that act as sources for structure, i.e. as constraints and guidance for human behaviour.

3. Attention is given to the fit between new tools and shared meanings, power structures, existing norms and rules, and the extent to which choice of systems is thereby determined.

Part II. Theories for Understanding and Evaluation

In the following chapters, concepts and theories will be presented that focus on specific aspects of our domain. The choice of the theories is not exhaustive but reflects partly the interests of the author and partly the popularity of certain theories in recent literature.

The focus in Chapter 4 is on the individual user and deals with the question of how work performance is regulated and why people adopt and use certain tools. This question is answered by a discussion of theories concerning work motivation and technology acceptance. System match theories, i.e. theories that are based on the assumption that characteristics of various elements in systems have to match to be effective, are discussed in Chapter 5. In this case the focus is on the match between characteristics of collaboration technology tools and characteristics of the tasks, the users and the context, for example the Media Richness Theory. The subject of attention in Chapter 6 is group interaction. Collaboration Technology tools have to support interaction among people and with computers. Proper design requires therefore knowledge of human task performance and of aspects of collaboration processes, i.e. of communication, co-operation, and co-ordination. Basic theories with regard to these phenomena are introduced and the role of collaboration technology tools vis-à-vis these phenomena is discussed in Chapter 6.

Finally, success of new systems is not just a matter of making tools that are appropriate for a certain users or tasks. It is also a dynamic process of designing the tool in a proper way, of diffusion of new technologies throughout society, of adoption by organisations and of adequate introduction and evaluation processes. Theories concerning technology introduction and organisational change are discussed in Chapter 7.

In Chapter 8 the theories discussed in the foregoing chapters are brought together in an integrated framework (model) and an overview of relevant evaluation issues is given. This framework and overview form the basis for an *integrated, user oriented and design directed evaluation* approach. Whenever a socio-technical system is developed this framework and overview can be used systematically to analyse the potential or actual success criteria and side effects of the new system. The evaluation process contains three evaluation steps: concept evaluation, prototype evaluation and operational evaluation.

Chapter 4. Technology Acceptance

4.1 Introduction

Why should people adopt and use certain tools? In previous chapters it has been shown that the optimistic expectations of designers concerning the faithful up-take of collaboration technology by potential users has been frustrated time and again. The seemingly obvious answer to the question why people should use a certain tool is that this tool is suited to perform a specific activity. Tools that are fit for a certain task are used and tools that do not fit the task are not used. You do not use a hammer to cut pieces of paper. This conclusion seems also to be trivial when discussing the functionality of certain IT tools: to produce text you use a word processor and not a spreadsheet; but even then, for certain texts you may prefer to use a spreadsheet program, while modern word processing programs may also perform calculations in matrices.

In the case of complex tasks, and particularly in the case of sophisticated collaboration technology tools, the assumption that tools are used when they are needed, is even less self-evident. Firstly, because of the *multipurpose character* of such tools: collaboration technology is not constructed for one specific purpose, but has many functions and is tailorable to various tasks (see Section 1.2). Often various comparable channels and tools are available, that can be used for different purposes. When you want to send some information urgently to a colleague, talking face-to-face, calling by telephone, sending a fax or an e-mail are all possible.

Secondly, because of the *motivation issue*: even if the system is well known, people do not always use the tools that seem to be the most effective. Human behaviour is also motivated by factors such as attitudes, beliefs, habits and dispositions. Sometimes people do not use effective tools simply because others do not, or because they feel uncomfortable with them. Moreover, these tools are often novel for potential users and the process of up-take is also determined by (sometimes mis-) expectations of what they can do and of resistance to changing old habits. Furthermore, the introduction of new tools will probably result in changing working conditions, an effect that may invite resistance. Together these factors influence intentions and behaviour, and this process does not always result in outcomes that are clear to others.

Thirdly because of the *user need* issue: tools are not always designed in accordance with what user really need. The concept of *user need* may at first glance be straightforward but appears to be difficult to operationalise. People often are unaware of their actual work behaviour and of the needs involved, and it is difficult to articulate needs in terms of tools or settings that have still to be developed and with which the person has no real experience.

The focus of this chapter is on the issue of motivation and on the potential determinants of this motivation. When discussing motivation a distinction has to be made between *the motivation to adopt and use* a new (socio-) technical system and the *motivation to work in a distributed way*. The basic issues concerning attitudes and motivation will be discussed in the next section.

4.2 Theories of Individual Performance

4.2.1 Action Theory and Cognitive Processes

Cognitive processes. Using certain tools and performing work is a form of human action. Several mechanisms regulate people's behaviour when trying to perform a certain task. Three mechanisms can be distinguished (Roe, 1998, see Figure 4.1):

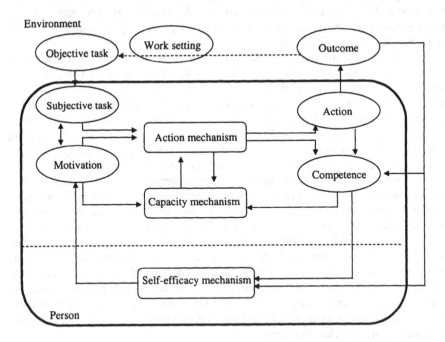

Figure 4.1 Model of individual performance (Source: Roe, R. A. (1998). Work Performance. In: P.J.D. Drenth, H. Thierry and C.J. de Wolff (Eds.), *Handbook of Work and Organizationa Psychology*. Second edition. © Hove, Sussex: Psychology Press. Reprinted with permission of Psychology Press)

1. The *action mechanism* regulates goal-directed activities in work settings. This includes cognitive processes such as perception, memorising, information

processing, and decision-making, and transfer of the results to muscular responses. Cognitive theories are used to model these processes, i.e. for constructing models that predict user performance (e.g. Howes, 1995). Through these processes external stimuli, such as tasks given, are translated into stimuli-as-interpreted by the subject, such as the definition of the subjective task and the motivation to go for it. This view is reflected in the Action Theory, discussed in the next section.

An important concept and criterion for proper usability of computer interfaces is *cognitive workload*. In the literature this concept is used in different ways. It refers either to the objective workload imposed by the task, or to the subjective judgement of the operator with regard to the demands of the task. In most cognitive workload theories workload refers to the information processing capacity of the operator, whereas it sometimes also encompasses emotional demands. *Mental effort* is a key concept related to cognitive workload. It is the effort needed to perform a task with a certain workload.

2. The *capacity mechanism* mobilises and allocates resources. Here the focus is on sources of psychic energy, on arousal (for perception), effort (for information processing activities) and activation (for response execution).

3. The *self-evaluation mechanism* cares for the maintenance of a positive self-image. In this process, factors such as expectations of success and general self-efficacy are responsible for the setting of performance norms. This results in the choice of proper action strategies.

This model points to the fact that when designing and evaluating ICT-tools from a user perspective, one has to take into account the question whether they fit the action mechanisms, the human motivation and the self-image of the potential users.

Guidelines can be derived from cognitive theories concerning the design of ICT applications. Such guidelines may refer to the way information should be presented on a computer screen or how a user should be guided through a software program in such a way that errors are minimal. The criteria for optimal cognitive functioning are often: the time it takes to perform a task, the number or types of errors and the feelings of ease and control of the users. The claim of cognitive theories is that they are able to predict human system interaction in terms of these criteria. A major reason why ICT applications may fail to function optimally is the fact that they do not support human cognitive processes. This is reflected in the term *user unfriendliness*. The International Standards Organisation has chosen to use the term *usability* as one of the major criteria for software program quality.

The *usability* of a system is the capability of a product to be used easily. It is one of the six main software quality characteristics presented in ISO standard 9126. The others are:

- *Functionalities*: the tool should provide the intended support functions.
- *Reliability / robustness:* degree of vulnerability against crashes, errors made etc.
- *Portability (technical compatibility)*: degree to which the tool fits to other technical systems, to different platforms such as the Internet environment.
- *Maintainability*, in view of the fact that new versions often follow immediately on older versions.

- *Infra-structural efficiency*: relatively low costs of infrastructure and other equipment needed for optimal performance of the tool.

In this ISO standard *usability* is defined as follows: Usability refers to *"a set of attributes of software which bear on the effort needed for use and on the individual assessment of such use by a stated or implied set of users"*.

This definition points to the fact that usability is situation and user dependent and not an objective and separate characteristic of a tool. A related standard, ISO 9241-11, stresses this fact again in stating that the assessment of usability is dependent on the context-of-use and that the level of usability obtained will depend on the specific circumstances in which the product is used.

According to the ISO 9221 standard the criteria for adequate usability are to be found in three types of indicators:

- *Effectiveness*, e.g. degree of goal achievement, errors and breakdowns.
- *Work efficiency*, e.g. time to complete tasks, speed of learning the system, memory and mental load.
- *User satisfaction*, e.g. satisfaction with the new system and with the control provided.

The six software quality characteristics form a set of criteria for the assessment of the value of particular tools (see Section 8.3).

Interfaces that do not conform to the usability standards appear to cause unnecessary errors and mental workload, but the causes are not uni-directional. It is generally assumed, and partially confirmed, that there are mutual influences, i.e. mental load may result in errors, but making errors may increase mental load. Together they may be responsible for low performance, which may affect the quality of products. Failing usability of interfaces may even be worse in the case of collaboration technology, where different users at different locations have to use different platforms, applications or application releases.

Although it seems to be quite obvious that designers should devote considerable attention to the usability of interfaces, in actual practice one often finds very badly designed systems. As an example, it is a common experience that users of overhead projectors often have to search for a long time to find the one button that turns the machine on, and then to find the knob that focuses the image on the screen. If even this simple interface can pose problems to casual users, the more one can expect that users find it difficult to deal with complex tools such as video-recorders, to understand presentations on a computer screen, or to navigate through a complex software program. This may be even more serious for users who are handicapped by manual or visual deficiencies.

Action (facilitation) Theory: A powerful perspective on human computer interaction is derived from Action Theory and the concept of action facilitation (Hacker, 1985; Roe, 1988; Frese and Zapf, 1994). The starting point of this approach is the assumption that work is a goal directed activity. The *objective goal*, or task, given to a person in a (work) situation is always interpreted by the person and "translated" into a *subjective perceived goal/task*. Performing a task proceeds on the basis of developed *cognitive plans*, so the first phase of a goal directed activity is *action preparation*, including orientation on the conditions and setting up an action plan.

The second phase consists of the *action execution*, step by step and checked on the basis of received feedback. This check may result in detecting and correcting errors, and in adapting the manner or the speed of acting, e.g. because the effort required to undertake the task is deemed too high and fatigue is setting in. In this case the original goal may then be changed. A central principle in the theory is that the tools used should provide sufficient feedback to allow adaptation of the execution of the task.

Action Theory makes a distinction between *acts, actions* and *operations*. Acts are complex sets of actions, aimed at realising intended goals. Actions are the smallest independent units of cognitive and sensory-motor processes that are still oriented towards conscious goals. Operations are components of actions, without independent goals.

The regulation of action can occur at several "levels". Action Theory at this point uses the theory of action regulation and information processing developed by Rasmussen, originally to explain various types of errors (Rasmussen, 1986, see also Reason, 1990). Figure 4.2 is a later version of the model (Rasmussen, 1987), which refers also to causes and reasons of action.

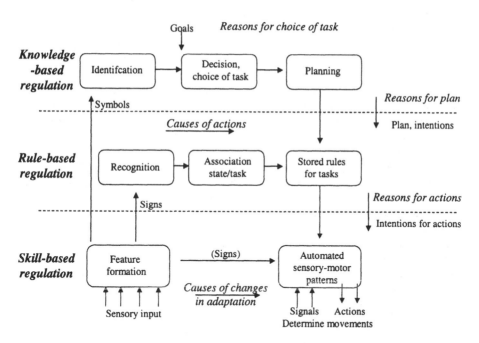

Figure 4.2 Levels of action regulation and mental functions involved (Source: Rasmussen, J. (1987). Reasons, Causes and Human Error. In: J.Rasmussen, K.Duncan and L Leplat (Eds.), *New Technology and Human Error.* London: John Wiley and Sons Limited. © 1997. Reproduced with permission)

The highest level of action regulation is that of consciously guiding every step one is taking, and checking every step against a goal. This is called *knowledge based* regulation of behaviour and occurs when a task is very complex or novel, like driving a car for the first time or solving a complex new problem. The second type of behaviour regulation, *rule based* regulation, happens by using well-known routines whenever they appear to be needed. Checking flight systems during flight is an example of such regulation, as is working with a PC and switching from word processor to spreadsheet program or e-mail program, whenever required. The third level of regulation is called *skill based*. It refers to completely automated behaviour, like cycling or typing for an experienced typist, which occurs with little conscious input.

When unexpected disturbances occur, e.g. when an aeroplane suddenly flies into bad weather, or when a typist is disturbed, people have to switch from automatic behaviour and find other rules for action. These in their turn may then become executed in a skill based way. When disturbances develop into a crisis, or when circumstances change drastically, knowledge based regulation may have to take over, i.e. a completely novel way of behaving has to be found (see also Section 6.2 on switching among levels of co-ordination). Various levels of behaviour regulation may occur together, e.g. when a person is typing and at the same time is holding a conversation with another person.

In any type of action regulation five types of mental functions are required, i.e. observation, identification, interpretation, task definition and procedure formation.

This theory is particularly relevant with regard to usability of applications. One principle of Action Theory is that *people tend to maximise the efficiency of their actions*, i.e. they prefer to "automate" their actions, because this decreases the level of conscious effort needed and therefore the mental load attached to the task. In terms of Regulation Theory this principle implies shifting the regulation level downwards to a rule and skill based level. In complex and exacting situations it is efficient to automate well known actions to allow sufficient capacity to deal with the more difficult aspects of a task. Learning and training are contributing to a downward shift in regulation.

When dealing with interaction with computers or media a distinction has to be made between primary tasks, e.g. text editing, and secondary tasks, e.g. interacting with the interface. Interfaces should be transparent, i.e. enable the user to operate the system at a minimum of "psychological cost", so that sufficient attention can be directed to the primary task. The concept of *"Action facilitation"* has been developed in this context. Action facilitation refers to the degree to which (technical) support for work activities helps the development and the execution of plans at all stages of a work process and makes it possible to automate action, i.e. shift the action regulation to the rule and skill based levels.

Box 4.1 *Evaluation criteria and design principles based on Action Facilitation Theory*

The following evaluation criteria can easily be translated into design principles:

- degree of adaptation to the user's language, work procedures and individual capabilities
- extent to which the program allows for action preparation
- degree to which adequate feedback is given
- room for modification of action programs
- degree to which supervision of action execution is supported
- existence of support for optimisation of action efficiency, by allowing changes of regulation level

Action Theory, similar to other cognitive theories, is particularly relevant for understanding the mental processes that take place in information processing for planned task performance. Interaction with a computer is interesting in so far as it facilitates this performance. Action Theory has led to the formulation of several evaluation and design principles (see Box 4.1). The validity of these design guidelines has been supported in various studies (Arnold and Velden, 1992; Frese and Zapf, 1994; Arnold, 1998).

4.2.2 Situated Action Theory

The very rationalistic view of cognitive theories on human behaviour has been criticised strongly. There is ample evidence that people's actions are not always derived from explicit goal setting and expectancy formulation. Behaviour may be regulated systematically, but may also be influenced by sudden incidents and local circumstances. According to several authors (e.g. Weick, 1979) persons often justify their behaviour *after the fact* by formulating the goals they think they pursued and the expectations they think they had.

The central focus of Situated Action Theory (SAT, Suchman, 1987) is the concrete activities of people in specific settings. SAT does not dispute that formal and generic characteristics of tools or social structures are relevant, but according to the theory researchers should also direct their attention to the situational determinants of individual action, to behaviour as a response to the environment and to the improvisational nature of human activities. The central issue is that all (inter) action is situated, i.e. it is a function of the intentions of the actor and also of emerging characteristics of the situation.

Situated Action Theory is not elaborated in a detailed way, with specified dimensions or specific predictive hypotheses. It is rather a general perspective, with roots in ethnomethodology and constructivism (see also Structuration Theory, Section 2.5). This perspective is in opposition to the rationalistic and cognitive science view that human behaviour is related to the precise execution of developed plans. SAT's essential framework can be represented in the following principles (Suchman, 1987, p50):

Plans are representations of situated actions
Plans are general guidelines for situated actions, but do not in any strong sense determine their course. They are best viewed as a weak resource for what is primarily ad hoc activity. In many cases it is only after we encounter some desirable state of affairs, that we identify this state as the goal toward which our previous actions, in retrospect, were directed.

In the course of situated action, representation occurs when otherwise transparent activity becomes in some way problematic
When a disturbance occurs and action becomes problematic, rules and procedures are explicated for the purpose of deliberation. This principle is to a certain degree related to the notion that when skill based action is disturbed, shifts in regulation mechanisms occur, i.e. from skill-based to rule based and to knowledge based behaviour.

The objectivity of the situation for our action is achieved rather than given
Social facts and norms are constructed, and the question for social science is to discover how the objective grounding is accomplished. Objectivity and mutual intelligibility are a product of systematic practices.

Mutual intelligibility is achieved in actual interaction, rather than by being discharged once and for all by a stable body of shared meanings.
Conversations can result in all kinds of misunderstandings and proper regulation requires mutually accepted rules, which often arise from the interaction in hand.

Situated Action Theory has several strong points. It explicates the fact that task performance is always situated action, which may often not be a rational, step by step plan executing process, but rather an ongoing process of developing motives and increasing clarity about the course of actions to be taken. This view also has implications for understanding tool acceptance or tool use and for the design process. When tasks and artefacts are not approached in a purposeful and systematic way, tool acceptance and use may be very haphazard and playful. In activities such as browsing on the Internet one may encounter such behaviour, but also in the way task-dedicated tools such as word processors or groupware are used, when people navigate the system or use certain functionalities for ad hoc reasons.

The design of certain tools may be adjusted to this emerging behaviour, where the structure of activity does not precede action, but grows in the interaction with the environment. General goals may then be more important than detailed plans. This implies also that we often do not know specifically what future state we desire to bring about, although our European rationalistic culture induces us to make up post hoc rationalisations about our original motives. SAT emphasises the situated construction of objectivity and shared meanings through the role of conversational interaction. Empirical research based on SAT is therefore characterised by the minute study of conversations and speech acts.

Situated Action Theory is a sensitising perspective for analysing the situatedness of behaviour, and not a concrete model for designing or evaluating the impact of new tools or work settings. The approach seems to be particularly relevant for the analysis of unstructured tasks and free behaviour such as surfing the Internet. A major case in Suchman's 1987 book refers to the interaction of several persons with a complex (new) photocopier and the problems that were presented by its expert help system. On higher aggregation levels, plans and purposeful actions of major projects are constructed and followed more or less precisely. Suchman's example of planning for a canoe trip through rapids (p52) shows that she accepts plans in general but argues that these plans do not and cannot contain all the details of minute actions. The value of the theory is that it draws attention to the improvisations and emergent processes in human action at the level of detailed actions, and to the important role of the context.

Box 4.2 *Central points of attention stemming from Situated Action Theory*
1. Plans are general guidelines, action is situated action, determined by local events.
2. Facts and norms are socially constructed.
3. Breakdowns are opportunities for reconstruction.
4. Tools should not constrain adaptation to situational changes and structures.

4.3 Motivation Theories

4.3.1 Introduction

In the previous sections the discussion centred on the mental processes related to regulating behaviour in general. Some behaviour is more or less automatic or regulated by external events. Other behaviour is directed by intentions and motivation. In this section the focus is specifically on the issue of motivation for tool acceptance and use.

Motivation theories deal with the intentions of people to behave and perform in a certain way, and with the factors and mechanisms behind the intentions. Basically two kinds of motivation theories can be distinguished, i.e. reinforcement theories and cognition oriented theories. Skinner's behaviour modification theory, based on operant conditioning principles, is the best known example of a *reinforcement-oriented theory*. It does not imply any role of internal representations, of intentions or of interpretation processes. Behaviour is explained in terms of the connection of behavioural responses to stimuli. Other motivation theories are based on assumptions of internal processes such as goal setting, expectancies and need gratification. These cognition-oriented theories are presently by far the most popular. One can differentiate between two types of cognition oriented motivation theories, i.e. content and process oriented. *Content theories* focus on the kinds of needs and motives that lie at the basis of motivated behaviour, while *process theories* specify the processes by which needs and other factors, e.g. perceptions and expectations, result in motivated behaviour.

The Need Gratification Theory of Maslow (1968) is a well-known example of content theories. It points to the existence of many individual needs, which are clustered into five categories, ordered from low to high: physiological needs, need for security, for belongingness, for recognition, status and power and need for self-actualisation. The theory further contains a hierarchy principle: higher needs can only become motivational when lower needs are satisfied. Although its popularity is still high, both the five-cluster categorisation and the hierarchy principle have been challenged. Alderfer (1972) concluded on the basis of extensive studies that the five clusters should be folded into three: Existence, Relatedness and Growth. The theory states that people basically want (1) to safeguard their *existence*, through food, shelter, job and income, (2) to *relate* to other persons meaningfully through social contacts, friendship and recognition, and (3) to *grow* and develop their abilities, through achievement and self-actualisation. This theory seems to be useful concerning issues of new work settings, particularly mobile work, telework and flexwork. Collaboration technology should support or at least not hinder these three needs. Outdating of skills may frustrate the first cluster of needs, mediated communication or virtual organising may frustrate the second one, while the use of new tools may support the realisation of the third.

The *Expectancy Value Theory* (EV theory) is the essence of process theories. Originally related to the economic *utility theory*, it has been developed into various psychological versions, and to some degree validated in many empirical studies. In the context of work psychology it consists of three parts, i.e. a motivation part, a valence part and a performance part (Vroom, 1964; Thierry, 1998):

- The motivation part specifies that the intention to behave in a certain way depends on the interaction of:
  a. the *expectation* that this behaviour, e.g. high effort, will lead to certain outcomes, e.g. high performance.
  b. the *attractiveness*, i.e. valence, of these outcomes.
- The valence model specifies that the attractiveness of outcomes is determined by firstly the degree to which these outcomes are instrumental in achieving certain individual rewards, e.g. satisfy certain needs, and secondly the valence of these rewards, e.g. the strength of the needs. The link to the content theories becomes clear in this valence model, since the, Maslowian needs can determine the relevance and attractiveness of outcomes.
- The performance model implies that the actual performance is a function of people's intentions and also of their competence and of situational constraints.

In short, the actual behaviour is a function of situation, competencies and intentions, and the intentions are a function of expectation multiplied by the attractiveness of certain outcomes.

The Expectancy Value Theory and derived theories (see below) enjoy a high popularity and are supported in many empirical studies. Their very rationalistic view on human behaviour has however been criticised strongly. There is ample evidence that people's choices are not always derived from explicit goal setting and expectancy formulation. According to several authors (e.g. Weick, 1979) persons often justify their behaviour by formulating *after the fact* the goals they (think they) pursued and the expectations they (think they) had. This after-the-fact motivation is then reported when asked about expectations or outcomes. This perspective touches upon the discussion in Section 3.2.2 on Situated Action Theory.

Empirical studies concerning the Expectancy-Value Theory have resulted in the addition of extra factors to the model. Firstly, it was discovered that expectations and motives, i.e. the determinants of intentions, are influenced on the one hand by *experiences* with the actual outcomes of behaviour (=feedback loop) and on the other hand by *personal habits* and by *norms and values*. Secondly, the relation between intention, i.e. effort, and actual behaviour is influenced by *role perceptions*, i.e. perceptions of what is expected of the person, and by *problem solving strategies*.

Some of these additional factors are taken up in a more recent version of the theory called the Theory of Planned Behaviour.

Theory of Planned Behaviour (TPB). According to TPB (Ajzen, 1991) people's actual behaviour is determined by their behavioural intention and by *situational constraints*. The behavioural intentions are now conceptualised as depending on the person's attitude towards that behaviour, the subjective norms concerning the behaviour and perceived behavioural control (see Figure 4.3).

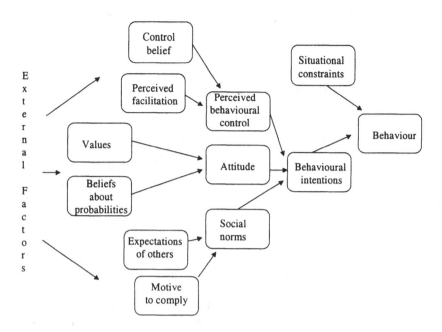

Figure 4.3 The Theory of Planned Behaviour (Figure constructed on the basis of text in Ajzen, 1991)

The theory has the following major elements:

- *Attitude* is based on (a) values of consequences of the behaviour and (b) beliefs about the possibilities (probability) to achieve these.
- The *Subjective Norm* is the perception of what behaviour is proper; this perception is determined by (a) perceptions concerning other people's expectations and (b) the motivation to comply with expectations of those others. A person is more inclined to use Internet if he or she feels that valued others (e.g. friends) consider the use of Internet a must.
- *Perceived Behavioural Control* is the perception of the presence or absence of requisite resources and opportunities necessary to perform the behaviour. This is determined by (a) *control belief*, i.e. the perception that one has the necessary skills, resources and opportunities(= *self-efficacy,* or *internal control)*; and (b) *perceived facilitation*, i.e. the person's idea concerning the importance of the resources for the achievement of outcomes.

External and internal factors such as system characteristics, individual dispositions and situational aspects are assumed to have effect by influencing attitude, norm and control belief.

Motivation for tool use. EV theory and TPB may explain tool choice and tool use. For some people, e.g. with high innovation attitudes, learning needs or social needs, the use of new collaboration technology tools will offer a fascinating experience of accessibility of information, of increased contacts or simply of fun. They will be motivated strongly to use and experiment with these tools and perhaps they can serve as a 'mediator' to help their environment master the tools. Other people are motivated to use a tool just because its usefulness for their work outweighs the disadvantages.

Expectancy-Valence Theory and TPB may also explain certain behaviours concerning social interaction. People engage in systematic interaction when they expect this interaction to result in attractive personal rewards. In this area of interpersonal interaction EV theory is similar to *social exchange theory* (e.g. Kelley and Thibaut, 1978). This approach points to the fact that people are only motivated to co-operate, if they can derive attractive personal outcomes from it, and/or avoid negative outcomes, such as embarrassment or effort. Success of distributed teamwork can only be attributed to the setting being sufficiently individually rewarding. Co-operative activities, whether mediated or not, may fail because these personal rewards are absent. This means that lack of success of distributed teamwork may therefore NOT be due to technical deficiencies, but simply to the participants not being motivated to co-operate, due to perceived lack of rewards. Yet technical aspects may well be detrimental to motivation. If needs of esteem or status are frustrated by the remoteness and impersonality of the mediated interactions, motivation may decline.

Attractive rewards should be available, yet unless people are aware of them and of the fact that these rewards are attainable, there will be little motivation to take up a task. If the expectation that spending much effort in finding valuable information over the Internet is probably worthless because it is so difficult to discover it, an individual's motivation for surfing the net will decline considerably.

In the following sections various other factors will be presented that could be included in a "balance sheet" of benefits and costs of new technologies.

4.3.2 Technology Acceptance Model

The well known Technology Acceptance Model (TAM) developed by Davis (1989) is an offspring of the above mentioned theories. Davis wanted to develop a theory that was focused on the use of IT-tools. He therefore uses the concepts of *perceived usefulness* to operationalise the value aspect and *perceived ease of use* to operationalise the expectancy aspect. All external and internal factors that are likely to influence decisions to use technological tools, do so via their impact on these two variables (see Figure 4.4).

Perceived usefulness (PU) is defined as *"the degree to which a person believes that using a particular system would enhance his or her job performance"* (Davis, 1989, p320). Davis distinguishes the following aspects of this construct: perceived usefulness for job effectiveness, usefulness for job efficiency, e.g. savings in productivity and time, and usefulness for the job as a whole. Note however that this formulation says nothing about the way in which these effectiveness and efficiency outcomes may be achieved. Whether it is via a changed and better way of working or via other means is not explicated. This issue is taken up in further sections.

Perceived ease of use (PEOU) is *"the degree to which the person believes that using a particular system would be free of effort"*. It has three aspects, physical effort, mental effort and ease of learning the system.

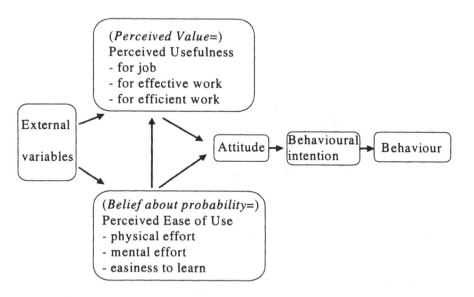

Figure 4.4 Technology Acceptance Model (Figure constructed on the basis of text in Davis, 1989)

The perceived usefulness of a system is supposed to be greater if the system is easy to use so PEOU influences PU. According to Davis' own empirical studies PU has a substantial effect on intention to use, while the effect of PEOU is smaller and disappears in combined regression analysis. He concluded therefore that indeed PEOU operates through PU. Many studies have supported these findings and Davis' conclusions. In Davis' own study he found that the theory predicted reasonably well the use of an office automation package, a text editor and two graphics packages.

Feedback from past usage. Feedback about past usage may positively affect ease of use (Bajaj and Nidumolu, 1998). This idea is related to concepts about learning of skills and routinisation of human action (see Section 3.2). With repeated usage a tool may require less effort to use. The positive effect of feedback works only if and when the use of a tool reinforces certain positive feelings about it. If use of an ICT tool becomes an integrated part of one's habits and general working style the ICT application becomes a real tool. If not, it remains a burden and constraint to normal activities, which may lead to negative attitudes towards a specific tool and perhaps to ICT applications in general.

The TAModel seems to be inferior to the TPB model, since it contains far less variables to explain attitude and behaviour. Mathieson (1991) compared TAM and TPB in detail and performed an empirical study to test the value of the two models in predicting students' intention to use two software packages. The predictive power of the two models did not differ much. TAM is even superior in the sense that it is easier to apply, since it makes use of general attitude scales. But

TPB appeared to provide specific information that could be better used to guide system development.

4.4 External Variables

In the above mentioned models for technology acceptance, people's perceptions, beliefs and attitudes are determined by external variables. In the next sections the following external variables will be discussed: personal characteristics, task characteristics, situational constraints and innovation characteristics. Group characteristics will be discussed in Chapter 6.

4.4.1 Individual Characteristics

Personal characteristics and psychological processes form an important category of external variables that determine the motivation to adopt and use certain tools. Three types of personal characteristics can be distinguished:

1. Stable dispositions: personality, cognitive styles and innate abilities.
2. Acquired characteristics, acquired through experience and education:

   - *Knowledge*, both formal, explicit knowledge and implicit, tact knowledge.
   - *Skills*, on the basis of explicit training or implicit experience. Skills for handling the tools, for performing the task, for co-operating with team-members, and for communicating in the general environment, i.e. communication competence are all relevant.
   - *Attitudes, norms and values*, e.g. attitudes concerning technology in general, such as innovation-orientation or resentment against new technologies (e.g. Cannon-Bowers et al., 1995).

   The acquired characteristics may be strongly dependent on cultural background, i.e. on national, organisational and group membership. Particularly in international co-operative teams differences in attitudes and values, educational level, professional discipline, language competence, and co-operation skill can be an important barrier to optimal (mediated) communication.
3. Demographical characteristics: Position/role in an organisation, age, formal education, and background.

Self efficacy and cognitive dissonance. Two stable dispositions deserve particular mention. One is *Self-efficacy or Internal Control,* i.e. the degree to which one believes that one can execute courses of action required to deal with prospective situations. This characteristic has been mentioned as an important personality variable in the context of ICT use. According to Davis's (1989) interpretation it is similar to perceived ease of use. Others have operationalised self-efficacy separately from PEOU and found that it improved the explanatory power of the TAModel substantially (Fenech, 1998).

Some people are more tolerant than others concerning cognitive dissonance. The theory of Cognitive Dissonance may explain negative attitudes toward ICT-tools. This theory holds that cognitions can be consonant, unrelated or dissonant. Consonant cognitions refer to knowledge and attitudes that fit together, that are in line with each other. Dissonant cognitions are those that are felt to be incompatible. Being addicted to smoking, and at the same time hearing or knowing that smoking can cause cancer, is dissonant. Being very interested in computers or the Internet, but not having the money to afford to use it is also dissonant. Dissonance is assumed to be psychologically uncomfortable. The theory poses that people will try to reduce the dissonance. Dissonance reduction may take several forms, i.e. not only the form of changing the behaviour, e.g. stop smoking or working hard to be able to buy the computer. Another psychological mechanism for dissonance reduction is to change attitude or belief. Smoking may be believed to be less damaging than is advertised and the attraction of Internet use on a computer may be changed into the belief that computers are unimportant and actually detrimental to social life. This same process may be responsible for the fact that after trying out a potentially useful but difficult to learn computer program, people may develop the belief that it does not really have much advantage over existing systems, and stop working with the program, reverting to one that is more familiar to them.

4.4.2 Job and Task Characteristics

In the Technology Acceptance Model perceived usefulness is operationalised as usefulness for job effectiveness, for productivity and time saving, and for the job (Davis, 1989), i.e. for end products of the work. The theory however does not explicitly explain why the use of a tool should lead to more effectiveness or efficiency. Two theoretical domains can be found that may fill this gap, i.e. *system match theories* and *job design theories*. *System match theories* deal with the principle that systems and tools should fit the situation and task in a particular way, to be effective. People are likely to search for matching tools. Perceived usefulness of a tool may therefore refer to the fact that the person perceives the tool as fitting to the task at hand. This view is discussed in the next chapter.

Job design theories point to certain characteristics a job should have to be motivating for people. The introduction of new systems and tools may make a better *match* with the task, but may also result in more attractive ways of performing that task, i.e. a higher quality of work. Perceived usefulness may then refer to the fact that the new tool is improving or expected to improve the quality of work. It appears that people are indeed more inclined to use a system if it has enriching effects on their work. From an extensive literature review Gill (1996) concluded that new technologies could have substantial motivational effects on work and job characteristics. He distinguished three basic categories of jobs, i.e. having *Control* over task activities (implying autonomy, choice, self-determination), being *Aroused* by interesting activities (such as stimulating, complex, variable tasks), and being able to *Achieve* attractive goals (implying meaningfulness, significance and responsibility). The relation between control or achievement and motivation is linear, the relation between arousal and motivation is an inverted-U shape: a low level of arousal is not motivating, a very high level may be stressful.

The above-presented concepts between brackets are derived fr om the Job Characteristics Model of Hackman and Oldham (1976, 1980), which provides a coherent theoretical framework for Gill's findings. This model is based on sound psychological theory and empirical studies. It provides a strong basis for modern job design. Gill combined the Job Characteristics Theory with the TAM model and found that the expected changes in job characteristics predicted very well the adoption and long term usage of expert systems.

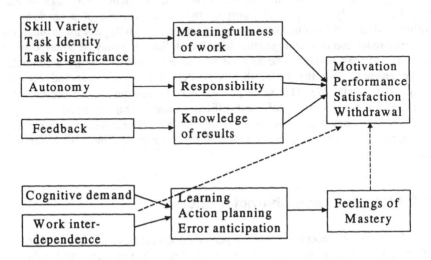

Figure 4.5 Traditional and modern dimensions of quality of work (Source of upper part: Hackman, J. R., and Oldham, G. R. Motivation through the design of work. *Organizational Behaviour and Human Performance, 16*, p250-279 © 1976, Elsevier Science (USA). Reproduced with permission. Lower part is constructed on the basis of text in Wall and Jackson, 1995)

The following principles are essential in this Job Characteristics Theory (see Figure 4.5):

- Five *job characteristics* can be identified as of major importance: skill variety, task identity and task significance, autonomy and task feedback.
- Job characteristics are responsible for *critical psychological states*: skill variety, task identity and task significance result in meaningfulness of work, autonomy to feelings of responsibility, task feedback to knowledge of results.
- Positive critical states lead to four general *outcomes*, i.e. internal work motivation, high work performance, satisfaction with work and less absenteeism and turnover.

The model holds particularly for those individuals that have high *"growth needs"* (Maslow, 1968). Employees with low growth need prefer routine jobs with low autonomy.

Wall and Jackson (1995) convincingly argue that *cognitive demand* and *work-interdependence* may become at least as important as the work motivators identified by Hackman and Oldham as design parameters for jobs (see Figure 4.5). Particularly work-interdependence points to the increasing importance of co-operative work, in addition to individual task performance. The two factors not only determine motivation in a direct way, but also are relevant for learning, action planning and error anticipation, which increase the feeling of mastery and thereby influence motivation. This feeling of being in control makes the individual more resistant to the stressful demands of modern jobs. The two theories visualised in Figure 4.5 illustrate the change in perspective, due to changes in work.

The foregoing implies that on the one hand effects of introducing collaboration technology depend on the task it is supporting, and on the other hand that the implementation of collaboration technology changes the tasks and quality of work.

4.4.3 Situational Constraints

According to TPB both subjective control-belief and objective situational constraints are important for system use. This is related to the issue of *freedom of choice*. Attitudes cannot influence behaviour when people are not, or do not feel, free to act according to their intentions. When clerks in a bank have to work with certain information systems there is no question of choice, so attitudes and cost benefit arguments about using the tool will hardly play a role. Collaboration technology tools however are often used by professionals, who do have a considerable discretion about the way they perform their activities. Winter, Chudoba and Gutek (1998) have expanded this notion. They found that attitudes predict the number of tasks for which one uses the computer, not only for those who have real freedom of choice, but also for those who have *knowledge about the system*. The interaction with *knowledge about the technology* is interesting. People may be very attracted to use a collaboration technology tool, but when they do not have the knowledge and skills to use it they will not be able to work with it. So *individual competencies* influence both attitudes and the constraints that are found in the situation.

Situational constraint and freedom of choice are related to physical or financial *accessibility* of PCs or other tools. Perceived usefulness may be related to this accessibility. Physical accessibility is relevant in organisations where certain terminals may only be available to a limited number of people. Research has shown that the easier terminals are to access, the more they will be used (Culnan, 1985; Rice and Shook, 1988). Availability of PCs may be ubiquitous at the turn of the millennium, but this does not yet apply to certain sophisticated collaboration technology tools. Moreover, for many people the personal computer and the Internet are not available at home, for financial or other reasons. Although libraries in the local community and Internet cafes may provide some access, this is far from the freedom of choice that others enjoy.

Finally *Critical mass of users* appears to be a situational constraint for use. Perceived usefulness of media is only adequate if a certain minimum number of relevant users is involved. (Culnan, 1985; Markus, 1987; Rice and Shook, 1988; Rice, Grant, Schmitz and Torobin, 1990). When few people are accessible others are not so interested in using a certain medium. This argument is less and less valid for common media such as email, but may be relevant in other cases.

4.4.4 Innovation Characteristics

The *Theory of Innovation Diffusion* of Rogers (1995) points to the role of certain characteristics of innovations that explain the adoption of new technological applications (see also Section 7.1). In the context of this chapter their role may be conceptualised as external variables influencing the perceived usefulness and perceived ease of use of innovations.

- *Relative advantage*: the degree to which using an innovation is perceived as better than using an existing alternative. This contributes to 'perceived usefulness', but points explicitly to a trade off with existing tools.
- *Complexity*: the degree to which an innovation is perceived as difficult to understand and to use. This contributes to perceived ease of use.
- *Compatibility*: the degree to which using an innovation is perceived as being consistent with existing values, needs and past experiences of potential adopters. This is to some extent related to the norms in the TPB model, but has wider connotations.

The following external variables have not been mentioned as yet:

- *Triability*: the degree to which an innovation may be experimented with before adoption.
- *Observability*: the degree to which the results of an innovation are visible to others.

A final external constraint is represented by the *financial costs*. Many studies are focused on adoption of innovations in organisations, where cost aspects may not be so relevant. Adoption of ICT applications by consumers and by managers, however, will certainly be determined also by perceived and relative costs.

Many of these variables are not only relevant for determining the adoption of a novel system, but also for determining the use or choice of existing systems. Triability, observability and visibility, however, appear to be specific to very novel tools. After incorporation the role of these factors probably soon disappears.

Moore and Benbasat (1991) developed and tested reliable scales for the measurement of these and related constructs. Ortt (1998) tested the role and relevance of these variables to predict the intended use and perceived effects of the use of CASE tools, i.e. tools to support the software development process (Iivari) and fax, PC with modem and videophone (Ortt). Generally speaking the relevance of certain of the variables mentioned was confirmed.

4.5 Summarising the Technology Acceptance Models

It is the interaction of two sets of factors, the context-of-use and the user, which forms the determinants of individual action (see Figure 4.6).

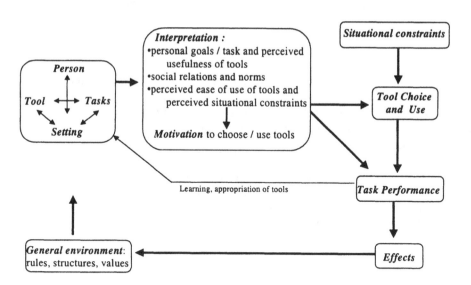

Figure 4.6 Integrated model of tool adoption and task motivation

Individual acceptance, adoption and use of ICT-tools and media appear to be the result of the interplay of two clusters of factors, situational and personal. The *situation* consists of a physical and a social (organisational) environment, the goals to be achieved and tools and artefacts, with which the goals may be reached. Together they form the *context-of-use*. The *user* has certain properties, i.e. knowledge, skills, attitudes, based on dispositions and roles. People perceive and interpret settings in their own way as a product of general dispositions and attitudes, and based on knowledge and skills. They define the tasks in a certain way, interpret the social roles, norms and constraints, and adapt the tools and artefacts in use.

Attitudes, beliefs and goals determine intentions, i.e. motivations of a person, while situational constraints determine to what extent the intentions can be realised in behaviour. Several types of behaviour have to be distinguished in the ICT field in general and the collaboration technology field in particular: whether or not to buy a certain tool, whether or not to try it out and whether or not to use it continually. These behaviours depend to a large extent on the relative perceived usefulness, ease of use and enjoyment to be had when using the tools in question and these three factors are influenced by individual characteristics such as computer knowledge and efficacy and by the social norms concerning usage.

Finally there is a feedback-effect on these factors caused by the frequency of usage of the tools in the past and by the actual effects this has had.

Box 4.3 *Central points of attention from motivation theories and technology acceptance theories*

1. Distinction between motivation to adopt tools, motivation to choose/use tools and motivation to work.

2.   The importance of *perceived usefulness* i.e. the degree to which new tools or systems are expected help achieve attractive outcomes, e.g. higher quality of work.
3.   The importance of perceived ease of use concerning new tools and systems.
4.   The role of the innovation characteristics for adoption and for use of new tools.
5.   The role of social norms and control beliefs for acceptance and motivation to use new tools.
6.   The role of freedom of choice, accessibility, critical mass.
7.   The role of individual characteristics in determining motivation and acceptance.

In this chapter the spotlight has been on the processes of individual motivation, attitudes and beliefs concerning collaboration technology tools. The characteristics of these tools and the degree to which these characteristics match the goals and tasks of the user, are the object of attention in the next chapter.

Chapter 5. System Match Theories

5.1 Introduction

The idea that the characteristics of collaboration technology should match the requirements of task and context seems to be very basic and plausible. Many empirical studies and much theorising have been devoted to the question of precisely which factors determine this match. The idea of "match" or "fit" implies a relation between two sets of characteristics, i.e. those of the tools and those of the context, i.e. of the users, the tasks and the groups. Many properties of CT-tools have been identified (see Section 5.2). The concept of media richness in particular has drawn attention and stimulated many studies (see Section 5.3).

Empirical analysis has shown, however, that media choice and interaction effectiveness is only to a limited extent predicted by the media richness of the tools. Some people perform quite complex activities using a simple tool, e.g. bargaining over an e-mail link, or use complex tools for very simple tasks, e.g. desktop video for rather simple exchange of information (Webster, 1998). More complex models have been constructed, illustrating the fact that tool choice and effectiveness are determined by other characteristics of the tools, such as media synchronicity, by situational factors such as distance and access to computers (see previous section) and by social pressure (see Section 5.3). This last aspect forms a bridge to the next chapter.

5.2 Characteristics of Collaboration Technology

The central claim of system match theories (characteristics of the tool have to match the characteristics of the context) requires that characteristics of the tool can be ascertained. Many classifications of properties have been presented. The properties can be defined in terms of objective and subjective characteristics of the systems. A first indication of objective properties can be deduced from Table 1.1, i.e. whether a system supports asynchronous or synchronous processes, and co-located or distributed processes. Clark and Brennan (1991) have defined characteristics of relatively simple communication systems, while others (e.g. Rice, 1987) refer to characteristics of complex systems (see Box 5.1).

The list in Box 5.1 is not exhaustive but a collection of characteristics that have had major attention in the literature.

Box 5.1 *Characteristics of collaboration technology*

According to Clark and Brennan (1991)

1. *Copresence:* Degree to which communicators are in the same physical location
2. *Visibility:* degree to which communicators can see each other.
3. *Audibility:* degree to which communicators can hear each other
4. *Contemporality:* message is received at roughly the same time as sent.
5. *Simultaneity:* A and B can send and receive at the same time. 5 and 6 together are also called *Synchronicity, Interaction,* or *Feedback*: the extent to which the medium allows immediate response.
6. *Sequentiality:* turns cannot get out of sequence.
7. *Reviewability:* the degree to which communication yields a physical result to be (re)considered and possibly edited or deleted later.
8. *Revisability:* the degree to which A can revise messages for B.

According to Rice (1987) and others

9. *Bandwidth:* the extent to which the medium allows the representation of different communication modes to be integrated, such as text, auditory and visual signals, smells, gestures and other non-verbal signals (see next section). 5 and 9 together provide the degree of *media richness* (see next section).
10. *Awareness:* the extent to which the system allows the communicators to be aware of the context, activities and intentions of each other (e.g. Totter et al., 1998).
11. *Structuring:* the degree to which the system structures and thereby limits free interaction.
12. *Control:* degree of member control over the system.
13. *Integration/compatibility/portability:* the degree to which the results of one application are directly available to other applications and vice versa.
14. *Comprehensiveness*: the number and variety of functions offered to users (DeSanctis and Poole, 1994).
15. *Critical mass:* the extent to which multiple interacting users are necessary for the system to have value.
16. *Access:* the extent to which the user has access to the medium and can store, retrieve and process data, e.g. in relation to security measures.
17. *Spirit:* the general intent concerning the tool and its use, as defined by the designers (see Section 7.3).

Communication costs

Clark and Brennan (1991) define another characteristic of complex media, i.e. communication costs. In their theory the choice of a medium appears to be related to the purpose of the communication, the *required grounding*, which is low for exchange of factual information and high for ambiguous discussions, and the *costs of communication*. They identify several types of costs, such as the following:

- production costs: e.g. speaking takes less effort than writing
- reception costs: listening is easier than reading
- start-up costs: starting a telephone call is generally easier than setting up a video conference
- delay costs: stopping to talk during a conversation may cause much confusion, while a delay in sending an e-mail reply has practically no costs attached

- display costs: indicating an object or showing attention by looking at the speaker, costs much less during face-to-face conversation that in a video supported conversation

The difference in communication costs between media can often account for their differential use: face-to-face contact for negotiating or reprimanding, which requires high costs such as perception of non-verbal signals for signs of understanding, and e-mail for co-ordinating schedules, which may only require reviewability of the agreements.

Characteristics of the system – user relation
The characteristics presented above can be determined in a more or less objective way. The innovation characteristics of Section 4.4.4 can be characterised as relational properties, since they are characteristics of the relation between the system and the user. Robinson (1989) pointed out other relational characteristics of complex collaboration technology systems that he deemed crucial for successful use:

- *Equality*: In terms of who benefits from, and who does the work for, the application. Examples are electronic calendar or project management systems. Most of them fail because of a disparity between those who will benefit, e.g. the project leaders, and those who must do the work, e.g. team members or secretaries.
- *Mutuality*: Participants should be able to change their input in the light of views and feelings expressed by others. "Bad systems freeze viewpoints".
- *New competence*: Complex systems are only attractive if they add new possibilities to existing communication and decision procedures instead of only enhancing existing abilities. This is related to the "added value" aspect (see Section 4.4.4.)
- *Double level language*: Some systems contain only a set of formal procedures to structure group interaction. Besides this *formal level*, being the structure for the primary task, a second channel, the *cultural level'* should be present to allow participants to talk about the formalised procedures in the case of ambiguities, questions and comments.

The media characteristic that has attracted the most attention is *media richness.* This is discussed in the following section.

5.3 Media Choice and Media Richness Theory

For numerous purposes face-to-face interaction is the most attractive way of interacting. Shopping, getting to know a person, finding answers to very unclear questions and conflict solving are preferably done in a situation of direct personal contact. If this is not possible the telephone is, under certain conditions, an acceptable substitute. Using an e-mail for such purposes is even less attractive, although if it is the only way to arrange things quickly, people will accept this. The web may be interesting when questions are clear and a person is trying to find specific information. Doing business over the Internet, however, is still very limited, particularly when it requires special expertise.

Organisation Theory points to the fact that tasks may differ in complexity and analysability (Perrow, 1983), uncertainty (Galbraith, 1973), or ambiguity (Weick, 1979). Uncertainty implies that more information is required, ambiguity (equivocality) means that the meaning of certain information is not apparent and people therefore require help in the interpretation of the information. According to Perrow, the less clear, analysable and structured a task is, the more discretion a person should have to perform the task, and according to Galbraith, the less clear and structured the information is the less co-ordination should be done by formal rules and systems, or by precise planning. Direct contact, mutual adjustment, meetings and other liaison mechanisms (see also Section 6.6) should be used to provide co-ordination in this situation.

The organisation-theoretical notions of complexity in tasks and organisational tools, are "translated" to the area of mediated communication in terms of the Media Richness Theory, and the concept of social presence. Common to these approaches are two arguments. The *first argument* holds that media differ in experienced "nearness" of the person one communicates with. This concept is called *social presence* or *social distance* by Short, Williams and Christie (1976). Others, referring to mass communication theories about media and channel characteristics, used the terms *bandwidth, channel capacity* (Fulk and Steinfield, 1990) or *media richness*. *Media richness* is the extent to which a medium is capable of sending rich information, i.e. providing several kinds of information, i.e. text, pictures, smell, noise etc., and immediate feedback (Daft and Lengel, 1984). As one moves from the informationally rich face-to-face situation to informationally lean written bulletins or memos, the number and types of sensory channels available for information exchange are reduced and people are assumed to feel a greater 'social distance'. Two-way video is assumed to come close to face-to-face situations in 'social presence', telephone communication comes next, while electronic mail is experienced as quite limited and felt to be at the level of memos. This sequence has been found in many studies of experienced social distance of media (e.g. Short, Williams and Christie, 1976; Thomas and Trevino, 1989).

The *second argument* of the theory is that media use is most adequate if the medium is matched to the complexity of the task at hand: information-lean media best support tasks such as simple information exchange, because other media are unnecessarily rich and therefore inefficient. Visiting a person only to give them a literature reference may be a waste of time, however, for tasks involving complex interpersonal communication such as bargaining or getting to know each other, information rich channels such as face-to-face meetings or video conferencing are better suited.

Both uncertainty and ambiguity can play a role. Gathering more information, even through simple media can often reduce uncertainty. Ambiguity-reduction however requires rich information exchange, i.e. intensive communication of ideas and opinions. In such contacts, both information content and non-verbal signals, i.e. the way people sit, dress and gesture, and context awareness, may play a role. The media should allow rich information exchange for such communication.

McGrath and Hollingshead (1993) have summarised the practical side of this theory in Figure 5.1. They order the media in a straightforward and frequently used way. The tasks are defined and ordered according to McGrath's theory of the group task circumplex (see Section 6.5).

Tasks of increasing info richness requirements	Media of increasing potential richness of information			
	Computer systems	Audio systems	Video systems	Face to face
Idea generating	good fit	marginal fit info too rich	poor fit info too rich	poor fit info too rich
Problem solving	marginal fit medium too constraint	good fit	good fit	poor fit info too rich
Judgement tasks	poor fit medium too constraint	good fit	good fit	marginal fit info too rich
negotiation tasks	poor fit medium too constraint	poor fit medium too constraint	marginal fit info too lean	good fit

Figure 5.1 Information richness and task medium fit (Source: McGrath, A.J.E., and Hollingshead, A.B. *Groups Interacting with Technology. Ideas, Evidence, Issues and an Agenda*, pp. 111, © 1994. Sage Publication. Reprinted with permission of Sage Publications, Inc.)

The figure illustrates the notions that performing a complex task, e.g. negotiating, through a simple medium such as e-mail is ineffective, while performing a simple task, e.g. sending some data through a rich medium such as video conferencing is inefficient. With practice, however, people can become so used to and versatile with lean media such as e-mail that they can interact quite well with others via such a tool. The intensive contacts that take place over the telephone or over the Internet, even virtual sex, are an illustration of this phenomenon. McGrath and Hollingshead (1994; Heeren, 1996) pose therefore that the fit between task and medium is not a one-to-one relation but should fall within quite a wide *band of good fit* (see the ovals in Figure 5.1). If outside the outer band, then indeed the medium is badly used. If the situation falls within this band, performance of the task through that medium is perhaps not very easy or fitting, but through with a more or less mental effort and adaptation processes one can compensate for the misfit.

This phenomenon is an example of the general *law of system-context adaptation*, a law that also holds for organisational change processes in general: *The less a new, technical and/or social, system matches the existing situation, i.e. the characteristics of people, tasks and/or context, the more effort and time it will costs to adapt the new system and the situation to each other.*

The adaptation can take place through various mechanisms, i.e. through changing the people involved via training, education or recruitment, through changing the tasks, the context or the tool. These changes can come about through systematic change programs, through self-regulation or through a combination of both. In the case of collaboration technology several ways are available to achieve this adaptation. The task may be redefined, the technology or its use may be redesigned or adapted, or common understanding and shared knowledge may be developed. In short, adaptation takes place through planned changes or through gradual appropriation.

Here we find a connection with the psychological concepts concerning mental effort for computer tasks and *action facilitation* (see Section 4.2.1 on Action Theory), and with notions from Adaptive Structuration Theory (Section 7.3). Where the Action (Facilitation) Theory points to the need for interfaces that require minimal effort, the band-of-good-fit notion warns that in certain cases extra effort is necessary to compensate for a medium that for very practical reasons may be less than optimal. The Adaptive Structuration Theory implies that such effort may in due time decrease through mutual adjustment of the user, the task and the system.

Several studies have tested various version of media match theory. (e.g. Rice and Williams, 1984; Steinfield and Fulk, 1987; Trevino, Lengel and Daft, 1987; Thomas and Trevino, 1989; Fulk and Ryu, 1990; Schmitz and Fulk, 1991; Menneke, Valacich and Wheeler, 2000). The theories are supported to some degree, but several studies also showed results which deviated from the predictions. The theory appears to be quite plausible and popular and the principle that systems should fit the task and situation at hand, is in many cases the major guiding principle for designers. This principle has also met with criticism, which corroborates with the fact that the empirical support is often rather limited. The reasons for this are given below:

Firstly, researchers do not always distinguish adequately between the objective channel capacity and the subjective social presence:

- *channel capacity*, or cuelessness, bandwidth, refers to the following dimensions of interaction: number and types of sensory channels available for information exchange, i.e. text, sound, images, the possibility of using natural language instead of codes, and direct feedback.
- *social presence* refers to the experienced psychological nearness of the person(s) one communicates with.

The two do not correlate completely. The rating of the social presence of certain media appears to vary substantially between users (Fulk and Ryu, 1990) depending for example on the experience the user has with the medium. Hooff (1997) has demonstrated that users in large organisations start using e-mail for simple information exchange, but when they become accustomed to its use, more and richer tasks may also be performed using this medium.

The *second* reason for a limited support of the media match theories is that media choice is also influenced by other factors. Elsewhere conditions are mentioned such as accessibility and freedom of choice (see Section 3.4.3), geographical distance (Trevino, Lengel and Daft, 1987; Webster, 1998), urgency (Steinfield and Fulk, 1986), symbolic value of the medium (Trevino, Lengel and Daft, 1987), and particularly social influence (see Section 5.5). This implies that people may choose a tool that seems to be too lean or too rich, when the situation provides good reasons for it. Moreover, the adaptation/appropriation argument (see above) implies that the choice and use of media may evolve, according to certain learning experiences.

The *third* reason is that the theory originated in the area of communication media, but is applied to all kinds of technologies and tasks. Zigurs and Buckland (1998) therefore developed a more specific task-technology theory that is assumed to be applicable to Group (Decision) Support Systems. They distinguish between five types of tasks (on the basis of increased complexity) and three dimensions of GSS (see also Section 1.8).

Tasks:	*Required support:*
simple tasks	communication support
problem tasks	information processing
decision tasks	information processing and process structuring
judgement tasks	communication support and information processing
fuzzy tasks	all three support functions

The authors provide precise definitions of central variables and the theory is in agreement with findings from many studies, however, it has yet to be tested empirically.

An alternative: Media Synchronicity Theory?

Menneke, Valacich and Wheeler (2000) tested McGrath's version of media richness theory (see Figure 5.1). It appeared that the theory was supported for negotiating tasks, but not for problem solving tasks. It was expected that for this type of task, simple media would be effective. This did not turn out to be the case. Qualitative data analysis showed that the seemingly simple problem solving tasks was actually quite complex. Before the group members could start with solving the problem, they had to go through a complex stage of finding out what information partners had and particularly to find an adequate strategy for solving the problem. This shows that tasks are often not as simple as they seem to be, but consist of subtasks, each with its own media requirements. The next section on task characteristics provides more insight in this issue.

In reaction to this finding the Media Synchronicity Theory was developed (Dennis et al. 1998). According to this theory all tasks are composed of two fundamental communication processes: *conveyance* of information and *convergence* of opinions. Communication effectiveness is thought to be influenced by matching media capabilities to the needs of these processes. Media synchronicity is *"the extent to which a communication environment encourages individuals to work together on the same activity, with the same information, at the same time"*. This implies two dimensions of communication, immediacy of feedback and concurrency, i.e. number of simultaneous information exchanges. *Low synchronicity* implies few feedback activities and strong concurrency, providing for intensive, fast, multiple information exchange, required for conveyance processes. *High synchronicity* implies direct feedback from all participants and discussions focusing on single issues (low concurrency), a communication mode that is suitable for *converging* communication activities. The theory was supported in a laboratory experiment. The discriminatory power vis-à-vis the Media Richness Theory, however, is not yet proven, since media richness theory would have predicted the same results in this experiment.

Media synchronicity may perhaps be a more useful concept than media richness. It does not solve, however, the problems of characterising tasks more precisely, or of discovering the role of other factors in media choice. The next section will be devoted to these questions.

5.4 System - Task Fit: Task Dimensions and Task Types

In the previous sections it has been argued that the role and effects of collaboration technology in team performance depend on the type of task the group has to perform. Indications were presented in Section 1.3 that collaboration technology is more effective for simple than complex tasks, more effective for problem solving than for consensus forming tasks. This section focuses more specifically on the task aspect. In what ways can team tasks differ? The Media Richness Theory and Zigurs' and Buckland's task-technology fit theory (previous section) have already been used to identify certain relevant task characteristics. What are the potential types of tasks that one must take into account when designing a collaboration technology application?

"Task" refers here to the goal that a person or group has been set to achieve, either by themselves or by others. A task is first a more or less formal goal that has been set, which is then to some extent redefined by the actors when actually performing the task. In the literature, however, the terms task and goal are not sharply defined. The problem with these concepts is that in some situations not only is the goal is prescribed, the actual actions that serve to achieve the goal are also prescribed. The task of a group of consultants may be defined in terms of the goal, e.g. the group's task is to develop a proposal for a reorganisation of a company. The task may however also be defined in terms of actions to reach that goal, i.e. the group's task is to consult with management and employees, and to organise workshops to reach consensus concerning a reorganisation process. Tasks and actions differ in the level of abstraction. The task of a committee is to come up with a proposal, its actions are in areas such as having meetings, writing notes and consulting other persons. These actions are not the goal the committee has been set, but the means to achieve the goal. The task of a flight crew is to bring a plane safely to its destination, e.g. the crew's actions are taking off and landing, controlling machine functions and consulting ground bases.

When distinguishing task types one has to take into account the level of aggregation of actions. Although sharp boundaries cannot be drawn, many authors distinguish three levels, e.g. the overall *project or job level*, the middle level, referring to *specific tasks*, and the level of *subtasks, activities or actions* (McGrath, 1990).

In Action Theory (Section 4.2.1) a task is the smallest set of behavioural actions with its own objective (Arnold, 1998). Activity Theory speaks of activities, consisting of actions, which consist of operations (see Section 6.3). This terminology is a bit confusing because in other contexts activities are part of actions.

Teams are more often defined in terms of their project, e.g. designing a new product, than in terms of more specific tasks, such as specification of user requirements or actions, e.g. drawing a work flow diagram. Teams exist over a relatively long time and have a whole set of tasks as part of their project. Some groups, however, such as committees, may be short-living and very task specific, i.e. they have only one specific goal and not an entire project. If all or most of the tasks of a team have to be supported by CT-tools several of these tools may be required. A relatively simple tool, e.g. e-mail, may be sufficient for a simple action such as sending a message.

Task-typologies: the project level
At this level of discussion task types are related to group type. Several typologies of groups and work teams can be found in the literature. Traditional distinctions are those between *membership group*, e.g. a football team, and reference *group*, e.g. medical professionals for a physician; or *formal* and *informal* groups. As far as workgroups are concerned, Sundstrom, DeMeuse, and Futrell (1990) distinguish four types which differ with regard to two very crucial characteristics i.e. *internal differentiation of expertise (ID)*, and *external integration (EI), i.e. with the environment.*

- *Production and Service* oriented teams: autonomous working groups in an automobile plant or in an insurance company, maintenance teams; low ID, high EI.
- *Projects and Development* oriented teams: design teams, research teams; high ID, low EI.
- *Action and Negotiation* oriented teams: flight crews, surgery teams; high ID, high EI.
- *Advice* oriented teams, often temporary: committees, task forces, management teams, quality circles; low ID, low EI.

Mohrman, Cohen and Mohrman (1995) present a categorisation that overlaps with that of Sundstrom et al., but explicitly mentions another category, i.e. *Integration-teams*, such as management teams, who co-ordinate the tasks of other units. Integration teams are also high ID and high EI.

When these groups want to use support tools, they will probably need to have both general collaboration technology tools and specialised tools that are tailor made for their tasks. The more their external integration, however, the more connectivity with the environment they need. The more internally and geographically differentiated they are, the more communication and co-ordination tools they need.

Task-typologies: the middle level
Tasks can be differentiated according to certain dimensions and according to their type. The former implies the identification of certain aspects in which all kinds of tasks can differ, the latter a taxonomy of different task types.

a. Task dimensions. In the previous sections the dimension of *task complexity* received central attention. *Level of interdependence* is also important for groupwork i.e. the degree to which group members must rely on one another to perform their tasks effectively given the design of their jobs. The higher the task interdependence, the higher the need for co-ordination. In this context the role of collaboration technology becomes clear. In the case of distributed groups, task interdependence implies that the group needs extensive technical support for communication and co-ordination between the group members (see Table 1.1).

Other major distinctions are whether a task is more or less *structured*, i.e. a fixed sequence of prescribed activities versus an open stream of unprearranged actions, and whether tasks are performed by the group members at the same time, i.e. *synchronously,* or at different times. i.e. *asynchronously.* Complex tasks can consist of a combination of activities and a combination of these dimensions. The type of tools required may be matched: support for structured or unstructured interaction, for synchronous or asynchronous interaction.

b. Task taxonomies

Some task taxonomies consist of specific and concrete co-operative tasks such as the one by Wilbur et al. (1993) who distinguish the following nine modes, when discussing the applicability of groupware:

- conferencing
- voting
- presentation
- socialising
- dialogue
- joint authorising/editing
- idea generation and evaluation
- planning/scheduling
- shared data administration and browsing

Specific applications are being developed for each of these activities. This classification is quite practical and geared to groupware support, but lacks any theoretical basis.

A more general major distinction is the one between problem solving and consensus forming tasks. For *problem solving tasks* the knowledge and expertise of the participants is all important, while in *consensus forming tasks* the viewpoints and interests of the participants play a large role. Herik (1998) shows that the role of meeting support systems is potentially much richer for problem solving than for consensus forming.

In studies concerning mediated communication (Short et al., 1976; Rice, 1987) the following more or less standard set of co-operative tasks is used, which also contains the above mentioned dichotomy:

> exchanging opinions (2.4); exchanging information (2.4); generating ideas (2.9); problem solving (3.5); resolving disagreements (3.9); bargaining (4.0); persuasion (4.0); getting to know someone (4.3)

The figures between brackets represent the average *dis*satisfaction (highest dissatisfaction is 5) of users with the usefulness of computer conferencing for that specific task (Rice and Love, 1987).

On the basis of social psychological theories, McGrath (1984) developed a well-known classification of *co-operative tasks*, which includes many of the above mentioned types. It is called the group task circumplex (see Section 6.5) and is based on the combination of two dimensions along which tasks can differ, i.e. *co-operation versus competition* and *cognitive versus behavioural activities*. The following tasks are distinguished: creative tasks (brainstorming), problem solving and decision making, conflict resolution, and execution of activities. All of these tasks can play a role when a team is realising its goal, but their relative importance may vary.

5.5   System - Context Fit: Social Influence Theory

Although the Theory of Planned Behaviour (Section 4.3.1) explicitly refers to social norms and compliance motivation as determinants of system choice and use, the focus of all the above mentioned theories has been on individual attitudes and characteristics, and on task dimensions. In the case of co-operative work however, social relations also determine technology choice. Perception of media and task-characteristics, such as required and provided richness, is actually a social process (Fulk, Steinfield, Schmitz and Power, 1987; Fulk, 1993). They have adapted the social information processing theory (Salancik and Pfeffer, 1978) to media use in organisations. They developed the *Social Influence Theory* of communication technology use "*to account for the consistent finding that the use of new media often depended not only on the characteristics of the media and the user, but also on the attitudes, norms, and behaviour of the people one works with and on the collective definition of the meaning of these tools*".

Social information, i.e. the perception of attitudes, statements and behaviour of salient others, is of prime influence for people's behaviour. The basic propositions of the theory are given below (see also Figure 5.2).

- Attitudes towards media are a function of the objective media characteristics, of media experience, of knowledge and of social influence.
- Attitudes towards tasks are a function of the task itself, of the individual's experience with the task and of social influence.
- An individual's media use is a function of the attitudes toward communication media (media perception), of perceived communication requirements (task perception), of social information and individual differences.

However, these relationships hold only in cases where the group is important and attractive for the person who uses the media.

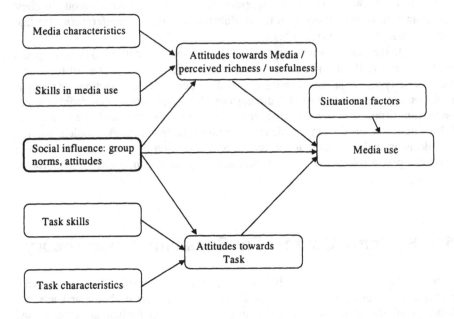

Figure 5.2 Social Influence Theory (Figure constructed on the basis of text in Fulk et al., 1987, Fulk, 1993)

The Theory overlaps to quite a degree with notions discussed in the previous sections on technology acceptance. Several studies have supported the Theory (e.g. Trevino, Lengel and Daft, 1987; Fulk and Ryu, 1990; Schmitz and Fulk, 1990). The social determinants of technology use is illustrated by the example of a group that can easily meet face-to-face, but where a message system is intensively used when people do not like each other but still have to co-operate. Aydin and Rice (1989) showed that attitudes towards the use of media were determined more by the social world of the department and the function of the users than by the media characteristics. The example given in Box 2.5 concerning the digital X-ray system in hospitals also shows that the success of the system depended on the fit to the *social setting*, in this case the relation between radiologists and medical specialists.

Of course social influence cannot predict all tool choice behaviour. Kraut et al. (1994) compared various theories by studying the determinants of media adoption and use of two video-conferencing systems. They found partial support for media richness and for Social Influence Theory, as well as for Critical Mass Theory. Supporting the Media Richness Theory it was found that the simpler and more analysable the job was, the less video was used, which implies a fit between task and medium. Media richness, however, could not explain why one video-system was adopted over the other. Adoption appeared to be related to critical mass and social influences: people choose that video-conferencing system that their friends recommended and by which they could talk to many friends. So their conclusion was that social norms and critical mass determine *adoption*, while task-requirements-fit determines the frequency of actual *use*.

The Social Influence Theory emphasises the fact that social processes influence media choice and media use. It is however a logical next step to inquire whether media should not only match individual tasks, but also group tasks, and not only the individual user but also characteristics of the group involved. A match to group dimensions is also relevant when designing and evaluating collaboration technology tools. This is the subject of the next chapter.

5.6 Conclusions Concerning Match-Models

The central question to the adherents of match-theories is: How to proceed in order to match the characteristics of a system and the setting for which it is constructed? Three different answers to this question are possible:

Analyse the setting very precisely and then make the new system as fitting as possible. This approach is basic to traditional information systems design and has proven its value. It assumes, however, a static, unchanging environment and ignores the fact that the introduction of a new tool changes the setting. In addition, collaboration technology tools are often constructed for widely different contexts.

A more flexible version of this approach is the iterative prototyping and/or participative design strategy (see Section 7.2). In this strategy early versions of a new system are tested and future users are involved in the design process.

Adapt the situation to the new system, by training the users and by adjusting the tasks. Or even better, *combine 1 and 2: Design a completely new socio-technical system*. This is suitable for situation specific design in which the tools are dedicated to the situation at hand. Yet in many cases a collaboration technology tool is used that is designed for a wide variety of settings.

Make the tool adaptable. Off the shelf systems such as word processors or standard groupware systems allow for, or even require, adaptation to the user organisation. This process is also called "tailorisation". In these cases the individual end-user can determine to a certain degree the characteristics of the actual application. The individual construction of macros in a word processing programme, or the shape of a data-file created in Lotus Notes are examples of this process.

This principle could be extended to all forms of collaboration technology. Eason and Harker (1994) make a plea for a three-level design approach, consisting of three design cycles: the basic design cycle by the vendor organisation, a first customisation by the buying organisation and a further tailorisation and adaptation by the user(group). Even better is the approach in which existing elements of collaboration technology systems are combined into a composite system that is optimally suited to the situation (Hofte, 1998).

Box 5.2 *Central points of attention from System Match Theory*
1. Fit between media richness and task complexity
2. The role of social processes in determining the perception of media richness and task complexity
3. Fit between implementation effort and novelty of new tools and new settings
4. The role of new tools / systems for co-operative tasks

Chapter 6. Group Processes

6.1 Introduction

The previous chapter ended with the conclusion that group norms can be a powerful determinant of acceptance and use of tools and media. This argument is developed further in this chapter. Use of Collaboration technology is part and parcel of social activities and group dynamics. It is assumed to make interaction processes easier and more effective. Its main focus is not to support individual work but to support co-operative work. This chapter is devoted to answering the following questions: What is the essence of co-operative work? What is effective co-operative work and what is the role of collaboration technology in distributed co-operative work? A major part of this chapter is therefore devoted to an analysis of group dynamics and team effectiveness.

Basic notions concerning individual and social activities are introduced in Section 6.2. A theory concerning the role of tools in social interaction, i.e. Activity Theory, is introduced in Section 6.3. This theory has become popular in the CSCW community. Concepts and theories concerning specific group processes such as communication and co-ordination are discussed in Sections 6.4 to 6.8.

6.2 From Individual to Group Work

The degree to which people co-operate, and the degree to which tasks require co-operation, vary substantially, not only between jobs but also within jobs over time. Many jobs, tasks or activities can be thought of as moving continually from being performed individually to co-operatively (see Box 6.1).

This applies to management teams, to groups of clinicians in hospitals, to design teams, flight crews or teams in automotive plants.

The transition between individual and co-operative work can be very fluid, as well as between task-oriented and non task-oriented activities or between several tasks (e.g. Robinson, 1993). Various in-depth studies have shown how seemingly separately working people co-operate now and then in a very subtle way (Heath and Luff, 1992; Schmidt, 1994). This applies to the work of many command and control operators, air flight controllers or stock market dealers whose activities can be characterised by concepts such as:

- being peripherally aware of each others behaviour and information
- sending *un*directed information to others, e.g. by talking loudly
- stepwise progression into collaborative activities, which last from a few seconds to minutes.

Box 6.1

In a study of the use of Lotus Notes (Hinssen, 1998) several small groups were described. Two of the groups, both four member groups, were developing software for external clients. Tasks were distributed, e.g. one person did the analysis of information flows and specified the requirements; another did the actual programming and testing, while one member was particularly responsible for user interface issues. The other groups in Hinssen's study consisted of two employees. In all cases the group members indicated that they worked quite independently. Active co-operation was quite rare. Some mutual adjustment (meetings) was required regularly, but the bulk of the work was done individually. Various forms of interdependence and therefore of co-ordination could be found in each group.

So, although the term *collaborative work* generally refers to situations where two or more people act together to achieve a common goal, the actual extent of 'togetherness' can vary substantially. Sometimes the co-operation is difficult to detect, although awareness of what the others do appears to be crucial for successful task-performance. Since co-operation may be very subtle and proceed through not more than being peripherally aware of other activities, supporting technology should be applied very carefully. It may have to accommodate this subtle communication, or at least should not distort it.

Box 6.2

Two London Underground operators work with several other employees in the same control room. One, the line controller, co-ordinates the running of the railway, the other, the divisional information assistant (DIA) provides information to passengers and to station managers. When the line controller communicates with train drivers and discusses e.g. stagnation, the DIA "overhears" this conversation, draws his own conclusions, and may announce this to passengers at the underground stations involved. This "co-operatio" takes place without formal task-prescription, and without any direct mutual conversation (Heath and Luff, 1992).

Designers of collaboration technology should therefore take account of the fact that all co-operative tasks are a combination of individual and co-operative activities and that co-operation may happen through ephemeral communication and *context awareness* (see also Section 6.3).

6.3 Activity Theory

Activity Theory (AT) is a comprehensive theory concerning human social interaction with tools, in the context of a community. Where Structuration Theory has been developed to explain societal institutionalisation processes, Activity

Theory has a background in individual and social psychology and claims to form a bridge between the two. It is related to the cognitive psychological Action Theory (see Section 4.2.1), e.g. in its focus on purposeful human action, but it has developed a rich idea of *context* in which these human actions take place, incorporating notions of the social construction of norms and artefacts. Activity Theory was developed in the beginning of the nineteenth century in Russia, not in reference to computer work but to education and interaction with human artefacts in general. Recently, however, it has received broad attention within the communities of human computer interaction (HCI) and of computer supported co-operative work (CSCW). This attention springs from the fact that HCI theories were being criticised for viewing human beings only as collections of cognitive actions. In AT human beings are viewed as actors with motives, being part of and influenced by communities with a rich context (Kuutti, 1996). The theory is illustrated by Figure 6.1, which is an adaptation of Engeström's visualisation (1990).

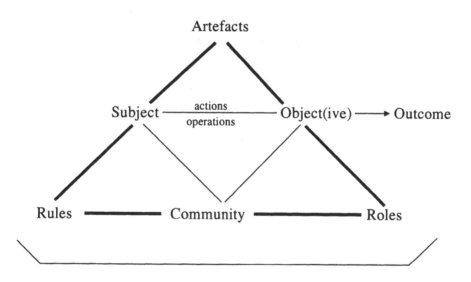

Figure 6.1 Activity Theory model (Source: Engeström, Y. (1990). *Learning by expanding.* Helsinki: Orienta-konsultit.Engeström, © 1990 Reproduced with permission by the author)

According to AT the fundamental unit of analysis is *human activity*. This concept is much more comprehensive than that used in common parlance. It consists of all the elements shown in Figure 6.1, i.e. it is a coherent system of mental processes and behaviours that are directed to achieve conscious goals, in the context of social structures. An activity always refers to a subject, i.e. an actor, that is motivated to perform a task, i.e. to direct actions towards an object(ive). This use of the concept *action* as part of an activity may be a bit confusing because in some other theories, activities are considered to be part of actions. Actions are conscious goal directed processes, performed through the use of artefacts and in a community with rules, including norms and culture, and roles, including division of labour. Through these actions the subject transforms the total setting, resulting in certain outcomes.

The term *object* refers to a goal that the subject wants to achieve, e.g. the object for a physician may be 'healing a patient'. Working towards this object, i.e. to heal the patient, is the objective of that physician. The subject's ideas and expectations about the object form the basis for his or her objective. Achieving the object is the reason, the *motive* for the actions.

The theory implies that activities are always object(ive)-directed, i.e. always motivated, although not necessarily all members of a community understand the motive. In this situation one speaks of *alienation*.

An activity can have a rather broad scope. Kuutti (1991) gives as examples of activities: building a house, completing a software project and carrying out research into a topic. It is important to note that the subject in an activity can both be one person or a group. An activity is hierarchically composed: it consists of (chains of) *actions*, while actions consist of (chains of) *operations*. Where activities have an *object*, actions are conscious and *goal*-oriented, in the service of the objective of an activity. Operations are oriented to *conditions*. The actions receive their meaning from the activity for which they are performed. The same action can serve different activities, while an activity may be realised through different actions, depending on the situation.

Box 6.3

The objective of diagnosing a patient can be realised in several ways by a clinical physician, i.e. through several actions: accepting the diagnosis of a trusted general practitioner, doing his own set of lab tests, or checking an existing record (Bardram, 1997).

In the same sense operations depend on the conditions for the actions. If the conditions change then the operations also change, although the goal of the action may remain the same. Similarly, actions may change while the object of the activity remains the same. Co-ordination may be needed to reorganise the operations towards the goal of the action or to reorganise the actions toward the objective of the activity (see section below on co-operation and co-ordination).

Actions are comparable to what in the HCI context is often referred to as tasks. The hierarchical structure of e.g. tasks, subtasks, and operations (or projects, tasks, subtasks according to McGrath, 1984, see Section 5.4), encountered in many models, is also found in Activity Theory, in terms of activities, actions and operations.

Actions are realised as chains of operations, which are well defined routines, used by the subject subconsciously as answers to conditions faced to the performing of the action. All operations are actions at the beginning, but when the corresponding model is good enough and the action has been practised long enough, the orientation phase will fade and the action will be collapsed into an operation, which is much more fluent. At the same time a new action is created which will have a broader scope and will

contain the recently formed new operation as a subpart of itself.
When conditions change, an operation can again 'unfold' and
return to the level of conscious action (Kuutti, 1991).

Basic notions of Action Theory (Hacker, 1985) and of Action Regulation Theory (Rasmussen, 1986, see Section 4.2) can be recognised in this quote: knowledge based, rule based and skill based regulation of behaviour. This is not remarkable, since Activity Theory has the same roots as Action Theory, i.e. in the work of Russian scientists such as Leontjev (1978). Activity Theory is distinguished from Action Theory in that it focuses on processes of a higher aggregation level than human-tool interaction, and also on the historically and culturally determined contextuality of actions and tools. This is reflected in the concept of *mediation*.

A central notion in AT is the idea of *mediated* action. The mediation of action means that it is structured and guided, on the one hand by artefacts and on the other by the community. Characteristics of the community are therefore an integral part of an activity, which means that human action, or interaction with technical systems, can never be studied without taking account of its context, and this context does not simply consist of a set of objective characteristics. A context has its historical development, but is again defined and given meaning by the subject. Its characteristics are therefore "in the eye of the beholder".

The concept of *artefact* refers both to material objects and to cultural entities such as signs and language. This notion is comparable to Giddens' (1984) structurational view on the role of both technology and language as media for social practices and having both restricting and enabling implications (see Section 3.5). It is not a strange idea that language is determined by the history of the community, and that language determines people's actions. Artefacts such as computers or video systems also incorporate the ideas developed in a culturally determined environment and in their turn govern human actions. *According to Activity Theory, technological developments and technological systems are fundamentally social interventions, developed in and for communities of practitioners.*

The *community* consists of those people who share the same objective of activity. This community can be very broad such as a hospital or a company, or a smaller subset such as a department or a team. Activity Theory is not very precise in its delineation of community. Or rather, the term is comparable to the term systems in General Systems Theory: a system can consist of subsystems and can in its turn be part of a larger system. What is called system, or in Activity Theory community, depends on the focus of attention. The lowest level of community is a group of which an individual is the acting subject. The community, however, can also be a department or organisation. The subject in this case may be a team. A specific type of community are the *communities of practice* or communities of interest discussed in Section 6.8.

The community's rules and roles mediate the relation of a subject to the objective. These concepts are comparable to what in group dynamics and social psychology is called the *culture* and *structure* of a social setting. The *rules* refer to norms and values, attitudes and traditions, formal and informal laws. The *roles* refer to the differentiation within a community based on division of labour.

Dynamics and change
The visualisation in Figure 6.1 may evoke the impression that Activity Theory is quite static, since it only contains elements and not processes. Actually, AT deals with several dynamic processes. The artefacts and community rules and roles constrain the actions of the subjects, but at the same time their actions can be the source for changes and adaptations of the setting. Central to this is the view that development is the result of overcoming *contradictions* between the elements within an activity. One source of contradiction is the difference between the goals of the subject, i.e. anticipated future results of the action, and the actual results. Contradictions may also result from conflicts between the values of various members of a community, or be the results of new objectives being introduced by outside forces, e.g. a research department having to shift from fundamental to applied research. Or by the characteristics of a new tool, e.g. a groupware application for sharing experiences, which does not match the existing individualistic and competitive way of working. Contradictions may be reflected in *breakdowns*, i.e. in moments when the relation between activity elements becomes the object of attention. Trying to fit the contradicting elements makes for the dynamics of an activity system (see also Box 6.4). The notions of the philosopher Hegel concerning historical development through the synthesis of thesis and antithesis may be recognised in this notion of development through overcoming contradiction.

The dynamics of mutual adaptation of contradictions, inconsistencies and mismatches results in changing tools, members, rules, roles or objectives or the introduction of new ones, and this gives an activity its dynamic and historical character. This idea of breakdowns leading towards adaptation in a new situation can be related to the process of appropriation, discussed in the section on (Adaptive) Structuration Theory (see Section 7.3). It also links AT to the ideas of tool - task fit in contingency theories (see 5.3), but gives it a much more dynamic character.

Box 6.4

Engeström et al. (1997, p.199) describe how in court-cases contradictions may exist between the object of solving a certain case in a flexible way and both the artefacts used (highly standardised forms) and an inflexible division of labour (the public defender and clerk not realising that the judge will need certain information). According to his analysis the contradiction could be repaired through collaborative action, i.e. a sidebar conference between judge, prosecutor and public defender.

Co-operation and co-ordination
Solving contradictions through collaborative action is an example of the view of Activity Theory on various functions of co-operation in work settings (Engeström, et al. 1997). Collaboration is in Bardram's (1998) study defined as an "... *activity with one objective but distributed onto several actors, each performing one or more actions according to the overall and shared objective of the work. The dynamics of collaborative work imply the constant shift between three levels of action, i.e. co-ordination, co-operation and co-construction. At the "lowest" level is co-ordination, i.e. the normal and routine flow of interaction ...where individuals are following their scripted roles ...where the script is coded in written rules, in plans, in schedules, or in tacitly assumed traditions and norms*" (see Figure 6.2).

Bardram uses the scheduling of operations in a hospital, together with requests for and booking of examinations at related departments such as radiology and laboratories as an example. These actions were supported by an information system called *Patient Scheduler*. When patients did not arrive or a staff member was ill, the schedule of that day could not be followed. This is a breakdown, which results in a second level of collaborative action, i.e. *co-operation*. Co-operation takes place when the normal means of achieving the object of an activity are not available and new means have to be established. In the case of the above mentioned hospital, certain staff members had to come together to find a solution to the problem, such as re-scheduling operations or re-allocating staff. The changes were then entered in the *Patient Scheduler*.

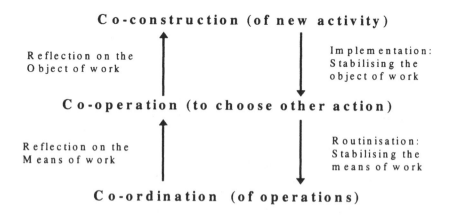

Figure 6.2 The dynamics of co-operative work (Figure constructed on the basis of text in Bardram, 1998)

The highest level of collaboration is called *co-construction*, i.e. interaction to reflect on the goals and organisation of the activity as such. In Bardram's study co-construction takes place to redistribute the available operation theatres to the various surgeons or to discuss the available resources with the radiologists. The *Patient Scheduler* did not support this level of collaboration, but the system collected data on operations and patients, and this data could be used to inform the decision making co-construction process.

So the dynamics of collaborative work are partly determined by the transitions between the three levels of collaboration (see Figure 6.2), i.e. changes to a higher level because of breakdowns and changes to lower levels to implement and to routinise the new rules and work arrangements.

The implication for groupware design is that the different levels of collaboration and the dynamics of the shift between the levels should be supported, or at least not hindered, by a technical system. Bardram notes that the design of a computer system for the support of work practices, is in itself a co-construction of that work practice, which *"...demands, as such, a concern for implementing and routinisation to be viewed as part of the same design effort"*.

The three levels of co-ordination are related to the levels of operations, actions and activities, presented earlier. Routinised operations are co-ordinated by formal or informal rules. When breakdowns occur the operations once again become actions, for which other rules have to be found through co-operation. When the rules appear not to be sufficient, a new activity has to be identified and formulated through co-construction. These concepts show a strong parallel to the levels of individual behaviour regulation, i.e. skill based, routine based and knowledge based, of Action Regulation Theory (see Section 4.2.1). Nevertheless, it should be born in mind that Regulation Theory is strictly oriented to individual behaviour. The three levels of behaviour regulation are theoretical constructs concerning processes that occur within the brain. Activity Theory expands the scope of these concepts, in relation to what in a particular case is the subject: an individual or a group. In the first case the reflection and routinisation processes are intra-individual cognitive processes. In the second case they are reflected in the social co-ordination and co-construction processes.

Activity Theory and information and communication technology
The point that makes AT interesting for the field of information and communication technology (ICT) is precisely the fact that it is not a theory about technology but a theory about human (inter)action and about work activities supported by artefacts. Collaboration technology tools are artefacts, they incorporate the values and ideas existing in a certain culturally determined environment. Technological systems are social creations that receive their meaning in a community of users. They are "...*invented, purchased, and put in use, they wear out, they are discarded and replaced by new ones. Thus there is an ongoing dialectic between what is taken to be structural and processual, stable and dynamic, representational or discursive forms in work practices*" (Engeström and Middleton, 1996). In AT artefacts, thus also technologies, mediate people's behaviour. The focus of study should therefore not be human computer interaction, but computer mediated activity (Kaptelinin, 1996).

Conclusions
Activity Theory is quite flexible and multi-interpretable in its concepts. This can be considered as both an advantage and a disadvantage. An example is the concept of an activity system. According to Kuutti and Arvonen (1992) a formal organisational department can be an activity system, but they state then that "...*in most traditional, hierarchical organisations the formal borders of an organisation do not necessarily fit together nicely with activities, because often only the managers of organisational units are 'active subjects', who use their units as tools to strive after their goals*". The concept, however, is quite fuzzy, if it is necessary to investigate whether units have more active subjects than the manager, before you can decide what your unit of analysis is.

The attractive aspects of AT (see also Blackler, 1995; Kuutti, 1991; 1996; Nardi, 1996b) are to be found firstly in its *integration of individual action and social context*. Secondly, its emphasis on *historical* and on *mediating* processes is very relevant e.g. to the HCI- and CSCW-areas where technical, cognitive and non-historical approaches prevail. "Mediating" in this context is more than mediated communication. AT relates this mediation concept to the general processes of action that are determined by the historically determined culture and structure of the social setting, and draws attention to the whole setting of collaborative work instead of only to specific communication issues. Finally, AT draws attention to notions of contradictions and conflicts in communities; contradictions which initiate breakdowns and thereby new developments, possibly due to conflicts between traditional settings and new collaboration technology.

Key concepts such as *rules* and *distribution of labour*, however, are much better specified in social psychological and sociological theories concerning (group) culture and (group) structure (see Sections 6.2 and 8.3.1). Other theories deal in greater depth with group processes such as communication or co-ordination. Each of the basic social processes will be discussed in turn in the following sections.

Box 6.5 *Central points of attention from Activity Theory*
1. Historically determined nature of artefacts and of community
2. Goal directed behaviour
3. Fit between new tools (systems) and the relevant community, with its rules (culture) and division of labour (structure)
4. Changes in activities, actions (tasks) and operations, and in objects and motives, goals and conditions as consequence of the introduction of tools
5. Three levels of co-ordination processes and the way new tools and systems support the switch between levels
6. Contradictions and breakdowns as catalysts for change and innovation

---

6.4 Groups and Teams

6.4.1 Groupness as a Variable

Co-operative work is performed in the context of a group or team. Teams are not just fashionable objects of study for the social scientist, they are increasingly found in the work place. Applebaum and Blatt (1994) examined several large surveys and 185 case studies of teams such as quality circles and autonomous work teams. They concluded that in the late eighties strong growth was found in autonomous work teams, with 47% of large US companies employing such teams in 1990.

The concepts of group and team require specification. McGrath (1984), a well known social psychologist, defines a group as "*...an intact social system that carries out multiple functions, while partially nested in and loosely coupled to surrounding systems*". This definition can comprise many types of collections of people. It refers to workgroups and to other collections of individuals such as friendship groups, to professional colleagues or to people interested in a certain subject. This is particularly important in the context of this publication, since many collaboration technology tools are used for the communication between widely distributed and only very loosely connected individuals, such as employees of a company or members of newsgroups. Collaboration technology appears to make it possible for groups of a great size to co-operate as a team.

When a number of people explicitly co-operate towards a common goal, they are often called a work group or team. Guzzo and Dickson (1996) define work groups as follows: "*A work group is made up of individuals who see themselves and who are seen by others as a social entity, who are interdependent because of the tasks they perform as members of a group, who are embedded in one or more larger social systems (e.g. community, organisation) and who perform tasks that affect others (such as customers or co-workers)."*

In this definition the concepts of *team* and *workgroup* become similar, but are differentiated from the general concept of group as defined above by McGrath.

The difference between close-knit teams and loosely coupled groups is not clear cut. All the above mentioned characteristics can vary substantially, resulting in a wide range of more or less coupled groups. *Groupness should be conceived as a (multi-dimensional) variable*: some collections have more characteristics of a team, others less so (see also Giddens, 1984, p377). The following characteristics may be used to define this groupness variable (e.g. McGrath, 1984; Busch et al. 1991; Hogg, 1992; Guzzo and Dickson, 1996):

- interdependence of goal and task performance
- intensity of interaction
- the duration of the interaction, i.e. single meeting, ad hoc task force or permanent team
- formality of team membership
- continuity of team membership
- number of people involved (size)

The more a collection of individuals have a common task, the longer and more often they interact, the longer and more formal their group membership and the smaller the number of members, the more a group is considered to be a real task oriented team. Air flight crews have a high groupness, while low groupness is found in many committees.

Box 6.6 *Beware of the term "team"*
Work groups may be called teams, but are not always very tightly knit. We studied a group of researchers that work together and called themselves a research team. This group had 16 members, but was divided into senior researchers/supervisors and junior researchers who did the main research. The members were working in four university departments. A groupware application was assumed to support the co-operation in the whole team, but in actual fact the separate research streams had few goals in common. Task interdependence appeared to be low and the junior researchers each had their own project. The groupness level was quite low and so the use of the groupware application was very limited (Egyedi and Andriessen, 1998).

Co-location is not required to speak of groups: some project teams are geographically widely distributed. Team membership may change. An upper limit to size is difficult to establish. Some groups are permanent and others are established on an ad hoc basis, such as a task force or crisis team. The time horizon may be very short, i.e. a few hours. We tend to refer to this last situation as a *meeting* and co-operative activities may take place in ad hoc meetings, with the members coming together only for one occasion. Meetings can however also be part of the activities of a team.

The groupness dimension also implies that the context of a group can vary. A tightly knit project team develops its own structure and is clearly segregated from its environment. Its culture can be quite different from the surrounding organisational culture or from other group cultures, as is sharply illustrated by the well-known differences in values between groups in marketing, production and R&D departments. In loosely coupled social networks however it is often almost impossible to speak of a clear group structure or group culture.

Summarising, various types of groups should be distinguished, from tightly knit task teams to very loosely coupled social networks or reference groups. One can find groups such as committees, working closely together for a common purpose, but only during infrequent meetings and for a relatively short period. Other groups such as certain electronic discussion groups, hardly have a common goal but share some common interest and therefore exchange information now and then. What is called teamwork may in fact consist of combinations of more and of less strongly coupled activities.

Conclusion: Three types of groupings
Several structures of (work)interactions and various processes in these structures have been distinguished in the previous sections. The concept of groupness implies theoretically an almost infinite number of structures. For simplicity's sake three *types of co-operative (work) settings* can be distinguished:

- *Collections:* loosely coupled individuals that exchange information on an ad hoc basis. Membership and commonality of interests may be rather vague. Vast numbers of people can be involved, such as the thousands of users of an Intranet in a large companies.
- *Communities*: a group of people, that have a common interest and therefore interact over a period of time. Many newsgroups on the Internet are formed around common hobbies or other interests. Some companies stimulate the creation of *communities of practice*, i.e. distributed groups of professionals, belonging to separate departments that have a common field of work for which they exchange or develop knowledge.
- *Teams* including task forces, committees: a group of people with a common goal, formality and interdependence, co-operating during a clearly delineated time period.

Teams and communities are particularly interesting in relation to collaboration technology. Communities and particularly organisational Communities of Practice will be discussed in Section 6.8. In the following sections characteristics of teams and the implications for collaboration technology will be explored.

6.4.2 Team Effectiveness

What are the characteristics of effective teams? Before answering this question one has to know what effectiveness is. Various authors (McGrath, 1984; Hackman, 1987) distinguish three functions (or outcomes) of groups, which provide three clusters of criteria for team effectiveness:

- the *production* function: performing a task and producing certain products; effectiveness is the degree to which the productive output meets or exceeds the performance standards set by the clients, e.g. the organisation, in terms of criteria such as product quality, product quantity, efficiency or innovativeness.
- the *group wellbeing* function: effectiveness in this sense is the degree to which the attractiveness and vitality of the group is strengthened.
- the *member support* function: effectiveness in this sense is the degree to which participating in the group results in rewards for the individual group members; criteria are satisfaction, learning new knowledge, payment, feeling of belonging etc.

The production function and the member support function usually dominate in ad hoc teams. The group well-being function is also important in teams with higher duration and groupness (see previous section).

How can these criteria be achieved? What group characteristics are required for an effective team? Many studies have been performed to identify those determinants (see Appendix 2). The main clusters of team characteristics identified are the following:

- *Aspects of the relation with the environment,* such as managerial support, autonomy, recognition, training and supportive physical environment.
- *Group characteristics*, particularly clear common goals and tasks, clear roles and accountability, good leadership, competent and motivated team members, a composition that matches the goal and tasks, team spirit, shared values, and shared knowledge.
- *Group Processes*, above all motivated effort expenditure, intensive communication and information sharing, co-ordination, skilful collaboration according to adequate performance strategies, participation and conflict management.
- *Material resources*, such as technical tools.

If collaboration technology tools are introduced in a group they should support or at least not hinder the central processes, and fit to the input factors, such as member competencies and task. The five central processes and the potential role of collaboration technology will be explored further in Section 6.4 to 6.8.

All these factors are often brought together in models that are variants of a general input-process-output model. The above mentioned conditions imply the model show in Figure 6.3.

Hackman (1987) focuses on three of the above mentioned task related processes, i.e. collective *effort expenditure*, application of *knowledge and skills*, and using the appropriate *performance strategies*. These central processes are, according to Hackman, difficult to change through direct intervention. They are however strongly determined by certain input factors that can be manipulated more easily. *Motivated effort expenditure* is a function of high quality tasks, e.g. autonomous tasks requiring high-level skills, challenging objectives, a group reward system and shared commitment. *Application of knowledge and skills* is a function of group composition, i.e. membership must be moderately diverse, while members have the appropriate mix of task and social skills, of availability of training and expertise, and of fostering of collective learning. *Using appropriate performance strategies* is a function of group norms that support self-regulation and reflection, innovation orientation and an information system that provides adequate input and performance information. These aspects will also be present in the model presented in Chapter 8.

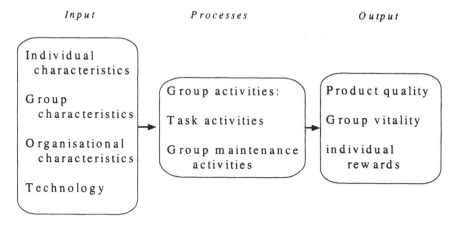

Figure 6.3 Basic input-process-output model

Sundstrom, DeMeuse and Futrell (1990) lay a particularly heavy emphasis on the group's relations with the environment and on boundary-spanning processes. It is, in the perspective of the authors, not environment factors as such but the interaction with and reaction to the context that is of dominant influence. *Boundaries* simultaneously separate a group from its environment and link the group together, they are important for the *group identity*. Boundaries play a role in the *specialisation*, i.e. independence and autonomy of a work team, in relation to other work units, but also in the *co-ordination* and synchronisation with the environment, i.e. with managers, other teams, suppliers, customers. Autonomy from, and synchronisation with, the environment are the factors that differentiate between the four basic types of groups that Sundstrom et al. distinguish (see Section 5.3). One of the major reasons why team development interventions can fail is that they often focus only on internal team processes.

The emphasis of Sundstrom et al. on the external environment matches certain observations e.g. by Ancona and Caldwell (1990). These authors point to the fact that developing a tool that is specific for and only accessible by a group can be detrimental for group effectiveness, because it hinders interaction with the environment. Leede (1997) likewise concludes from his empirical studies that effective coupling with the environment is a major condition for product- and process innovation of autonomous groups.

6.4.3 Group Evolution

In the previous sections we have dealt with group processes, without considering the history of the groups. When people start working together, however, it takes some time before they are welded into a smoothly running team. Small group researchers have distinguished certain *life stages* in this process, without claiming that these stages always follow a neat sequence. A well-known stage model is that of Tuckman (Tuckman, 1965; Tuckman and Jensen, 1977). In this model, which has become quite popular in group dynamics and team training, five stages are distinguished:

- *forming*: coming together, first orientation
- *storming*: struggling over the goal and the tasks to do
- *norming*: developing common ideas and norms about how to do the task
- *performing*: executing the tasks
- *adjourning*: dissolving the team

The longer and more closely a team works together, the more specific the task definition, norms and roles can become, even to such an extent that it hinders innovation. The concept of *groupthink* (Janis, 1982) refers to the phenomenon where high cohesion, high performance norms and limited external influence result in a situation where a group disregards new, critical information for the sake of internal consensus.

The neat sequence of these five stages is seldom found in practice. Gersick (1989) concluded from empirical research that groups "...*progress through long periods of inertia, punctuated by concentrated, revolutionary periods of quantum changes*". McGrath (1990) prefers to speak of *modes* instead of stages, since groups do not always follow the expected stages sequentially. Moreover, groups can be simultaneously in more than one stage. According to McGrath's view each task team has to deal with certain developmental issues, which he calls *orientation* (=forming), *means choice* (= norming), *conflict solution* (= storming) and *execution* (= performing). *Healthy team development requires that the group has to go through all four modes*. In practice the order of precedence of the modes depends on the circumstances.

The earlier mentioned three group functions (see Section 6.2.2), i.e. the production, group well being and individual reward function, can to a certain degree be realised in each of the four modes or stages (see Table 6.1). In some situations groups may follow only the modes "preparation" (Mode I) and "execution" (Mode IV) for the production function: the group comes together, agrees on what to produce and then produces it. This may be sufficient for a short meeting of an ad hoc group. A team of people however, working together for a longer time on a range of tasks, probably passes at one time or the other almost all the twelve modes presented in Table 6.1. The actual sequences, or *time-activities paths*, may vary considerably. This is called the Time, Interaction, Performance (TIP) Theory. It is clear that TIP Theory puts considerable emphasis on temporal aspects of groups, and that this model is much more sophisticated than, although related to, the simple four or five stage models such as that of Tuckman. The evolution of groups is also reflected in the redefinition of tasks, appropriation of technology and changing membership.

McGrath poses further the hypothesis that co-ordination using collaboration technology in earlier stages is much more difficult than in later stages. This hypothesis was not supported by Velden (1995), who found no differences in tool use between the stages. One may hypothesise however that the difficulty of co-ordinating using collaboration technology is related to the organisational setting of the task. Task teams in this respect have much stronger co-ordination requirements than loosely coupled social networks that interact only for the exchange of certain information.

Table 6.1 Group functions and modes (Source: McGrath, A. J. E. and Hollingshead, A. B. *Groups Interacting with Technology. Ideas, Evidence, Issues and an Agenda*, pp. 64, © 1991. Sage Publication. Reprinted by Permission of Sage Publications Inc.)

Functions:→ Modes:	**Production**	**Member Support**	**Well being**
Mode I **Inception**	Project selection / Assignment	Member participation choice	Group interaction choice
Mode II **Problem Solving**	Technical problem solving	Position / Status attainments	Role network definition
Mode III **Conflict Resolution**	Policy conflict resolution	Contribution / payoff relations	Power / Payoff distribution
Mode IV **Execution**	Performance	Participation	Interaction

The four modes are related to McGrath's (1994) classification presented in his *group task circumplex* (see Sections 5.3 and 6.4). Some tasks are mainly creative, i.e. brainstorming, some are of the problem solving and decision making type, a third type consists of conflict resolution and the fourth category is the (manual) execution of activities. *TIP Theory states that the four tasks are not only separate types, but also form a logical sequence in the lives of teams.*

McGrath and Hollingshead (1994) have related this model to the use of collaboration technology. Group interaction and outcomes are "...*a joint function of a number of features (of groups, tasks, situations) in interaction with a given form of technology*" (p70). Here the model is combined with Media Richness Theory (see Section 5.2): tasks and media should fit, in terms of required and provided media richness. TIP Theory can interpret some of the findings concerning computer-mediated communication. An exclusive focus on the task, excluding group maintenance activities, is more often found in computer-mediated groups than in face-to-face groups. According to TIP Theory this reflects an over-concentration on the simple productivity function, often on the *default path* (Mode I followed by Mode IV), as a consequence of the social distance in distributed groups.

In TIP Theory, groups are considered to be very dynamic systems, dynamic in several ways. First of all, natural groups are involved in many projects, with many sometimes simultaneous activities. Secondly, groups mature by passing through various stages and learning phases, which change the characteristics of the group, and those of the technology. Thirdly, the membership of natural groups often changes, as do their tasks or tools, both because the group may choose so, i.e.

redefining tools and tasks, and because the external environment may force the group to change.

Box 6.7 *Central points of attention from group dynamics*
1. The difference between three group related effectiveness criteria: product quality, group viability and individual rewards
2. The importance of organisational characteristics and the interaction of teams with their environment
3. The specification of group composition, and of characteristics of culture and structure
4. The role of new tools in supporting or hindering group cohesion and group identification
5. The stages in the life cycle of a group and the role of new tools in supporting or hindering the rites of passage
6. Groups are dynamic in various ways: changing tasks, changing stages, changing membership

---

Conclusion. Apart from team development five central processes of group functioning have been identified: communication, co-operation, co-ordination, group maintenance and collective learning. Collaboration technology tools have been presented in Table 1.1, in terms of the group processes they are intended to support. The question is however to what degree they can indeed support or at least not hinder teams in performing these processes. The five processes and the potential role of collaboration technology will be discussed briefly in the following sections.

6.5 Interpersonal Communication

Co-operative task behaviour and social interactions can only occur through communication between people. Communication is the basic process in interaction, and technology for channelling this communication may have profound effects on interaction. It was shown in Section 2.4 that various effects of mediated communication have been discovered. Some basics of communication processes will be presented and implications for mediated communication will be discussed in this section.

6.5.1 Mediated Communication

The phenomenon of communication has been approached from the information transmission side and from the interpersonal communication side. As far as the first is concerned, Shannon and Weaver developed the technical information theory, which is not concerned with the meaning of messages but with their transmission and reception (Littlejohn, 1989, p44). The theory poses that information from a source is encoded by a transmitter into a signal that is sent through a channel, decoded through a receiver and brought to its destination. The transfer through the channel can be distorted by noise. To decrease the distortion, the causes of noise may be attacked or the message may be made richer through redundancy of information. Talking face-to-face can be represented in this model: a speaker, the source, encodes his thoughts and produces words, the signals are sound waves, transferred through the air, and received by a hearer, who decodes the words into understandable thoughts.

This model has been criticised in theories of interpersonal communication and changed according to the following lines of reasoning. Interpersonal communication is not simply the transfer of information, but the transfer of meaning and interpretation: when I, a native Dutch speaker, hear a Chinese person talking there is information exchange, because I hear him uttering certain sounds, but there is no communication since I do not understand the verbal code being used. Or, when I think I understand what colleagues are saying, I may misunderstand them, when they are from a different culture and may use the same words with different intentions and meanings. Distortion is therefore not only a function of noise, disturbing the transfer of signals, but also of the extent to which the participants in the communication have a common frame of reference, i.e. a common language, common world view or common way of communicating. This frame of reference is strongly determined by education, culture, scientific discipline and daily experiences, but it is also developed continually during communication. Interpersonal communication therefore requires a two way process. Weick (1979) speaks of *double interacts,* meaning that A's message to B requires a reaction by B, so that A can conclude that he has been understood. An ongoing process of interaction is needed to reduce ambiguity and to create shared meanings, a shared interpretation of the situation and shared intentions (see Figure 6.4).

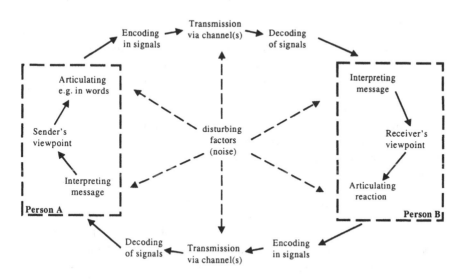

Figure 6.4 Model for interpersonal communication

In the case of mediated communication the encoding and transmission processes are composite processes in which on the one hand physical encoding and decoding occur and on the other hand psychological encoding and decoding (interpretation) take place. The implications for our discussions of collaboration technology are obvious. Communication channels may be distorted by noise. Firstly there is the technical aspect of this distortion. The traditional telephone is quite reliable, but video connections, particularly through the Internet, are still very vulnerable to channel distortion or small bandwidth. Required channel capacity is high and often not available. Signal compression techniques may help to alleviate this problem, but in practice desktop video conferencing is still rarely perfect and smoothly running.

Secondly there is the interpersonal interaction issue. Distortion through differences in background, culture, knowledge or other factors, is bound to play a significant role in mediated communication. The first reason is that mediated communication by its very existence promotes communication over boundaries, i.e. between persons from different organisations, disciplines or countries. In these cases the probabilities are much larger that communication takes pace between people who are not familiar with each other, i.e. who do not share common meanings. The second reason is more directly related to the nature of the collaboration technology tools and to the fact that the richness of face-to-face communication is reduced and that non-verbal cues are lacking. This issue is discussed in the following section.

6.5.2 Interpersonal Communication Processes

A group of researchers called the Palo Alto group developed in the sixties a theory of interpersonal communication, that is still considered fundamental to many other theories (Watzlawick, Beavin and Jackson, 1967, see also in Littlejohn, 1988). According to the Palo Alto group, rules of relationships emerge from the interaction between people. *"People set up interaction rules, which govern their communicative behaviours. By obeying the rules, behaving appropriately, the participants sanction the defined relationship... . A status relationship in an organisation may be observed in a subordinate's non-verbal behaviour. The subordinate, for example, may pause at the supervisor's door to await an invitation to enter"*. Signals can be either verbal (words), para-linguistic (the intonation of the words, or sounds such as humming) non-verbal (facial expressions, posture, clothing) or signs (pictures, symbols). Five basic axioms govern communication, of which we present the first three:

1. *One cannot not communicate*, i.e. any behaviour in interaction somehow communicates a message, even the deliberate attempt not to communicate.
2. *Every communication has a content and a relationship aspect.* The relationship aspect provides meta-communication, i.e. it gives information on the way the content and the relationship between the speakers has to be understood.
3. *Interactions form interrelated sets*, they cannot be understood as a string of isolated elements. To make sense they must be grouped systematically. This means that strings of actions and reactions belong together and their meaning depends on the earlier elements of that string. This is taken care of in advanced e-mail systems by grouping messages in *threads*, i.e. in sequences of responses.

6.5.3 Achieving Common Ground and Awareness

It has been made clear in the previous section that communication has two sides, i.e. the content side, often transferred by the words and texts, and the relational side, often transferred by non-verbal signals. This relational side has two functions (Clark and Brennan, 1991; Whittaker and Conaill, 1997):

1. *co-ordination of process*, i.e. the conversation is managed through communication. Certain signals, such as looking, raising a hand, bending forward, help proper turn taking in conversations. This is desirable since in many, though not all, societies people do not like talking at the same time, and prefer conversations to have only very minimal overlap.
2. *co-ordination of content*, i.e. through communication it is possible:
   - to identify the objects and events people jointly want to talk about.
   - to inform each other of the common ground.
   - to inform each other about emotional stance, motivation, and affect.

According to Clark and Brennan (1991) these two processes cannot take place "*...without assuming a vast amount of shared information or common ground – that is shared knowledge, beliefs and assumptions*". This common ground requires a continuous process of *grounding*, i.e. using mechanisms to ensure that A's utterances are understood by B and to inform A about this understanding. Many mechanisms are used in conversation for this purpose, such as:

- acknowledgement: uh huh, yeh, mm etc.
- relevant next turn: B gives a reaction that shows his/her understanding
- attention: looking at the sender
- indicative gestures: pointing by B at the object A is referring to
- verbatim repetition or spelling in the case of transferring numbers or names

Usage of these mechanisms is governed by the *principle of least collaborative effort*: participants in conversation try to minimise their collaborative effort for communication. This minimising is related to the purpose of the contact. For social chat this minimising is quite different from that used for formal instruction. The grounding mechanisms should also be related to the characteristics of the medium used: during a telephone call it is possible to check on understandability by sending and receiving acknowledgements, but this is not possible when e-mailing. The characteristics that Clark and Brennan consider relevant for grounding, and the differential costs of media, are presented in Section 5.1. Three types of information may be used to support these processes:

- *Non-verbal information*. The non-verbal signals, such as gaze, intonation, gestures, emoticons [e.g. :-) or :-( ], and facial expressions can give information both on the order of the conversation and on the emotions and feelings: leaning forward, or coughing means that one wants to say something, while facial expressions or certain emoticons may imply joy.
- *Object information*. The objects of the interaction, such as documents, pictures, commercial products or the body of a patient on an operation table.

- *Context awareness.* The situation, i.e. the physical background and the setting in which the participants are communicating, may convey information about who does or does not participate in the interaction, about the work context or about the status of the participants.

It appears that people generally prefer to have these three types of information, because it reduces the uncertainty of the interaction setting. In mediated communication many of these types of cues are lacking. Mediated communication has therefore certain disadvantages compared to face-to-face encounters. Nevertheless, experiments (e.g. Velden, 1995) show that groups under various conditions, face-to-face or mediated, may have the same final results, but that it takes mediated groups longer and they need more structured communication processes because the relational information is limited. This is related to Walther's findings (1992) that adequate impressions of other people can be formed even with very "lean" media, but that this process takes more time and is therefore not found in experimental short-lived groups or in superficial task oriented contacts.

During interaction of some duration people appear to develop ways and means to achieve positive interpersonal relations over time. Walther (1992) concludes from his studies that the negative effects may be limited to the initial phase of mediated interaction. If sufficient time is available and sufficient messages are exchanged, users adapt their remaining cues, i.e. language and textual display, to the process of relation management. Walther proposes a social information processing perspective: certain motivations prompt communicators to "..*develop distinctive impressions of other interacting people by decoding text-based cues, and they derive psychological-level knowledge about other actors from computer mediated interaction. As this occurs they manage relational changes and encode relational signals in their messages*".

Despite the above mentioned adaptation to situations of limited communication means, face-to-face settings appear to be preferred for many contacts. In distributed organisations this is, however, often not possible and many people expect that a video-channel may provide more or less the same cues. Using a video monitor one may see the non-verbal signs, relevant objects and the environment of the participants. As has been discussed in Section 2.4 the results of empirical research in this field, however, has not always been very positive (Finn, Sellen and Wilbur, 1997).

- *Providing non-verbal information.* This issue has been studied intensively. Few task outcome and process differences have been found between audio and video enhanced communications. Communication process aspects such as turn taking appear to depend heavily on good audio, and are not improved markedly by video. So disrupting audio to include video appears to be detrimental for the process of co-ordination. These conclusions are, however, specific for problem solving tasks, where even face-to-face contact is often not better than speech only, and even high quality video will not provide extra cues. Video can be used to provide support for tasks that require access to affective information, i.e. tasks such as bargaining and conflict resolution, and members of groups that use video tend to like each other more than members of other groups. Since communication through a video-channel requires extra effort, however, people do prefer to come together face-to-face for conflict resolution and for emotional interactions.

- *Object information.* Video can provide dynamic visual information about objects and events, which is important for certain collaborative tasks. Actually this application of a video channel is becoming the most frequent. Some examples of this use of video are presented in Section 2.4.
- *Context awareness.* Video may provide visible information about the environment and about the presence of other people. Although the technical problems of camera setting and limited monitors are still considerable, the issue of context awareness is very popular in Computer Supported Co-operative Work discussions, since it appears to be highly appreciated by people. Various types of awareness can be distinguished, i.e. awareness concerning the state of affairs of the task, about who is communicating with whom, about what the workspace looks like, and about what the group feelings are (e.g. Totter, Gross and Stay, 1998).

Summarising, video links are not the ideal that people expected. Although performance improvements have seldom been reported, in many cases users appear to prefer having a video link over an audio-only connection. The reason may be found in the ability to achieve common ground easier through this medium (Fussel, Kraut and Siegel, 2000).

Steinfield, Jang and Pfaff (1999) expand the notion of awareness to knowledge about a project as a whole. They define awareness as occurring "...*when group members possess knowledge about the current status and actions of the various components (including people) in a collaborative system*". They distinguish five types of awareness:

1. activity awareness: knowledge about project related activities of group members, both during and between meetings; activities between meetings may be found reported in asynchronous groupware such as BSCW (see Section 1.3.2).
2. availability awareness: knowing the physical availability of group members; e.g. through active badges, certain features of video systems or of chat box systems.
3. process awareness: knowing the state of affairs of the primary work process, for instance through a workflow management system.
4. environment awareness: knowledge about outside events that may have implications for the group.
5. perspective awareness: knowing background information to make sense of other people's actions.

Tasks differ in the extent to which they require mutual awareness, and CSCW systems in the extent to which they support this awareness (Dourish et al. 1996; Velden, 1995; Totter et al. 1998).

Awareness is related to what others call "shared cognition" or "team knowledge" (Cannon-Bowers and Salas, 2001). The value of these concepts seems to be high, but measuring the extent of shared knowledge is difficult (see Cooke, Salas, Cannon-Bowers and Stout, 2000 for a clear review of the state of the art). Two aspects of team knowledge/shared cognition are distinguished i.e. "team mental model" and "team situation model" (see reference in Cooke, Salas, Cannon-Bowers and Stout, 2000). The first contains the relatively static information that team members bring to the actual task situation, i.e. information about the team members, such as skills and roles, and about the task and task strategies. This is comparable to the above mentioned awareness type 5, perspective awareness. The second is the team's collective understanding of the ongoing task performance situation, which develops during the task execution. This is comparable to awareness types 1 to 4. Support for sharing these two types of knowledge probably requires different types of CT-tools.

Box 6.8 *Central points of attention derived from Communication theories*
1. The interactive nature of communication
2. The distinction between content and relational aspects of communication and the role of non-verbal communication, particularly in co-ordinating conversation
3. The role of noise factors, such as group/cultural differences in disturbing co-operation
4. The role of the visual channel and of video-connections for non-verbal signals, for object information and for situational awareness
5. The role of new tools for supporting situational awareness

---

6.6 Co-operation and Competition

Social psychologists and sociologists have studied processes of co-operation for a long time. Deutsch (1949, 1990) presented an early formulation of central notions in this area. He argues that the level and type of interaction between people is strongly related to the extent people believe that their goals are connected. If they believe that their goals are positively linked they tend to co-operate, while belief in negative links results in competition. A co-operative process *both induces and is induced* by perceived similarity of beliefs, sensitivity to common interest, and a climate of helpfulness, openness in communication and trust. So the conditions, which give rise to a constructive process, are the same as the consequences of such a process.

As a result group productivity is expected to be higher and qualitatively better in co-operative groups. This is contrary to the common notion that competition results in better outcomes. Empirical analysis indicates, however, that co-operation induces higher performance than competition, particularly in complex tasks. Tjosvold (1996) explored the nature of this productive interaction and expanded Deutsch's theory, by developing the Theory of *Constructive Controversy*. Tjosvold's theory "...*proposes that open discussions of opposing views are most critical for making co-operative situations productive. It is under competitive and individualistic conditions that people are more likely to avoid conflict and, if that proves too impractical, to try to win the fight or dissolve the relationship*" (p89). Empirical research supports this argument. Competition and independence implies distrust, restricted information exchange, distorted communication, and may also lead to increasing conflicts, frustrations and stress.

Co-operation does not prevent conflict. Research has shown that, ceteris paribus, the more communication and participation, the higher the opportunities for conflict (e.g. Easterbrook, 1993). One reason for this, perhaps unexpected, phenomenon is the fact that with open participation, differences in viewpoints and interests come to the fore. The Theory of Constructive Controversy states however that in a co-operative context, information will be exchanged and opposing views will be revealed and discussed. Despite possible conflicting discussions, in the end the group will be more creative and effective.

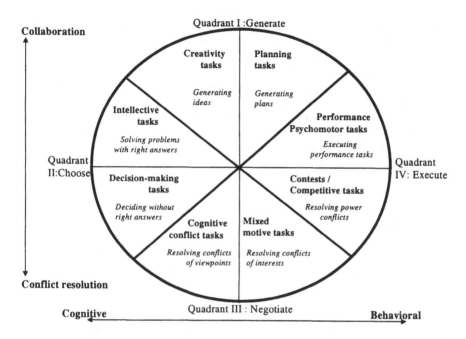

Figure 6.5 Circumplex of group tasks (Source: McGrath, A.J.E. and Hollingshead, A.B. *Groups Interacting with Technology. Ideas, Evidence, Issues and an Agenda*, pp. 67, © 1994. Sage Publication. Reprinted with Permission of Sage Publications, Inc.)

What types of co-operative activities can we distinguish? McGrath (1984) has developed a well-known classification of *co-operative tasks*, on the basis of social psychological theories. It is called the group task circumplex (see Figure 6.5). The group task circumplex is based on the combination of two dimensions along which tasks can differ, i.e. *co-operation versus competition* and *cognitive versus behavioural activities*. The following four (times two sub-) tasks are distinguished: *creative* tasks (brainstorming), *problem solving and decision making*, *conflict resolution*, and *execution* of activities. The set of tasks a team has to perform, together McGrath calls them their "project", is a mixture of most or all of these (sub)tasks. In Section 5.2, (Figure 5.1) the expected fit between these tasks and collaboration technology tools is presented. The more a task has elements of conflict resolution (downwards), the more difficult it is to communicate using collaboration technology.

6.7 Co-ordination

A third basic group process is *co-ordination*. Co-ordination processes can be found at various levels of interaction: interpersonal conversations, group work and organisational processes. Co-ordinating distributed work is difficult and collaboration technology tools are being developed to support this. Understanding co-ordination processes may improve the design and evaluation of CT-tools.

The two basic characteristics of groups and organisations are *differentiation* and *co-ordination*. Organisations are characterised by a division of the work between specialists, groups, departments, i.e. by *differentiation* of task activities. The more the work is divided over people or groups, the more *co-ordination* is required to adjust the activities to the common goals.

Co-ordination can be defined in many ways. Malone and Crowston (1990) use the following definition: *"Co-ordination is the act of management of interdependencies between activities performed to achieve a goal"*. The expression "the act of management" could be interpreted to mean that co-ordination is only being carried out in interpersonal interaction. However, impersonal mechanisms such as the use of assembly lines or formal rules and prescriptions can also play an important role in co-ordination. Schmidt and Bannon (1992) add to Malone's definition: "... *involving the allocation, planning and integration of the tasks of individual group members"*. Since co-ordination does not only take place in a specific group, a more general definition should imply this wider context. I have therefore combined and adapted the two formulations to give the following definition:

> *Co-ordination is the use of mechanisms to manage interdependencies between activities performed to achieve a goal, involving the allocation, planning and integration of tasks of individuals or groups.*

It is clear from this definition that co-ordination implies actors working in the framework of a common goal. This common goal does not exclude that the individuals involved may also have different goals and/or conflicts. If, however, there is no commonality whatsoever, co-ordination is not needed.

Commonality of goals implies interdependency of activities. This notion of interdependence is very central to co-ordination. *Degree of task interdependence* refers to the degree to which individuals or groups must rely on one another to perform their tasks effectively. The higher the task interdependence, the higher the need for co-ordination. According to Thompson (1967) it is not only the degree of task interdependence, but also the *type of task-interdependence* in a group or organisation that determines the way the group or organisation should be co-ordinated. Thompson distinguishes three types of interdependence:

- *pooled interdependence*, where the members of a group each make a contribution to the group output, without the need for direct individual interaction, e.g. a group of typists; a co-ordinator (boss) may be responsible for adjusting the contribution of each member's output to the task of the group.
- *sequential interdependence*, where the output of one is the input for the other, e.g. work on an assembly line.

- *mutual (or reciprocal) interdependence,* where people exchange products or information for a common goal; the group members generally have different but prescribed roles and perform different parts of the task in a flexible order, e.g. a surgical team.

Van de Ven et al. (1976) defined a fourth category, *team interdependence,* where group members, without having separate roles, jointly diagnose and solve problems, and co-operate to complete a task; generally the group autonomously decides on its course of action, e.g. a design team. Some call the third type of interaction *collaboration* and the fourth type *co-operation* (Bair, 1989).

Types of co-ordination. The discussion about co-ordination can be found in various communities, i.e. of communication scientists, of work psychologists and of organisation theorists. The discussion can be ordered in three levels:

- Co-ordination of interpersonal communication
- Co-ordination of tasks
- Co-ordination of organisational processes

Co-ordination of interpersonal communication

Co-ordination of interpersonal communication has been touched upon in Section 6.4.3. Conversation in face-to-face meetings often takes place through non-verbal signals: participants can be aware of each other's activities and intentions through gestures and postures. In mediated communication this *mutual awareness* is less easily achieved and *floor control* is therefore an important topic in the CSCW field. The notion of co-ordination through language is developed strongly by linguists and theorists in the area of Speech Act Theory. Central in this approach is the idea that all social actions are basically co-ordinated by the structure of *communicative acts* or *speech acts.* Human conversation has a specific structure and consists of a limited number of utterance-types, which govern interpersonal interaction and thereby also organisational processes (see Section 6.4).

Co-ordination of tasks

Many types of mechanisms for co-ordinating tasks have been identified. Mintzberg (1979, 1989) expanding on earlier views (March and Simon, 1958) has grouped them into six categories (see Table 6.2). In ongoing organisational work several of these mechanisms may be used concurrently. The last two co-ordination mechanisms are very important, particularly in modern organisations, where traditional authority, routine and physical proximity are limited. This applies within teams, but also refers to the role of teams in organisations. One of the major functions of teams is indeed that they function as co-ordination mechanisms in decentralised organisations. Several interesting question can be formulated. How to coordinate teams that are distributed geographically?. In which way can the various types of coordination mechanisms be supported by ICT applications? Will the fact that teams are distributed in itself result in the use of different coordination mechanisms?

Table 6.2 Six categories of co-ordination mechanisms (Table constructed on the basis of text in Mintzberg, 1979, 1989)

- *Direct supervision*: by a person with authority, who instructs and monitors the activities and the results.
  Collaboration technology support could be through video-camera's for remote supervision.
- *Standardisation of tasks*: the work situation is structured in such a way that the workers can only do the tasks in a co-ordinated way; structure can be induced by machinery, e.g. assembly line, and by rules, e.g. precise task descriptions, standard working procedures, international standards.
  Workflow management systems are CT-tools for co-ordination in this sense. Collaboration technology can also simply provide support for work procedures, by making them available, e.g. through a company Intranet.
- *Standardisation of skills*: the way the work has to be performed is learned through training; this is the case with professionals such as physicians, teachers and consultants who have been trained in such a way that they can often work together without much instruction or mutual adjustment.
  Collaboration technology can aid the training by providing computer supported teaching or Intranet supported training courses.
- *Standardisation of output*: specification and measurement of the characteristics of the products and "management by objectives".
  Collaboration Technology is very powerful for this purpose; computers and networks can register products of information processing work like the number of letters produced, policies processed or (electronic) contacts with customers.
- *Mutual adjustment*: co-ordination by mutual consultation and discussion, in meetings, teams, workgroups, or through liaison officers.
  Many collaboration technology systems listed in Table 1.1 are relevant: asynchronous, e.g. e-mail, synchronous, e.g. video conferencing, and meeting support systems.
- *Standardisation of norms and values*: a culture of shared visions, meanings and behaviour, of trust and commitment, supports the adjustment of behaviour to common goals. Malone and Crowston (1990), moreover, point to the importance of a common language and of communication channels.

Leadership and control. One of the six co-ordination categories mentioned in Table 6.2 is *direct supervision*. Supervision is only part of the activity of a leader. Managers above the direct supervisory level usually spend their time dealing with affairs that are only indirectly related to supervising group members. Writing reports, administration, telephone calling, maintaining relations with suppliers or customers, and meetings with colleagues all appear to take up much of the managers' time. Potentially collaboration technology can support many of these activities. Asynchronous and synchronous communication and message systems can provide support for networking and communication, while meeting support systems may support certain decision-making activities. A change in work arrangements and information and communication technology, however, can have two other roles: requiring different styles of leadership, or even substituting leadership.

A different style of leadership is required where distant relations replace face-to-face relations. The well-known example is telework. Traditional ways of motivating and supporting employees become less easy to maintain when the employees are working at home or at the client's office. Managing people at a distance requires managing by objectives, i.e. by their products, instead of by keeping a constant eye on them. Experience with tele-homework shows that many managers find it difficult to change their style of leadership.

Substitutes of leadership have been studied by Kerr and his colleagues (Kerr and Jermier, 1978). Their concept of "leadership substitutes" arises from the observation that situational factors may provide so much structure and personal support that group members can derive all their work guidelines and their motivation and job satisfaction from these factors alone. It is an interesting question to which extent collaboration technology can provide substitutes for leadership or at least for certain leadership functions. Traditional and modern forms of automation can provide such leadership functions as task clarity, work assignment, procedure specification, information support and task feedback. Lee and Guinan (1991) showed that even intrinsic motivation can be improved by the use of challenging and interesting computer tasks. Their study showed that IT tools can systematically support planning and control of workgroups and also the self-control of the group members. Both the leader and the workgroup members used IT tools successfully for (self)control purposes.

Co-ordination of organisational processes in the value chain

Co-ordination of processes in the value chain of production is a major issue of organisation theory. More and more forms of externalisation of work are found. Externalisation refers to the fact that certain organisational functions are redistributed both internally and externally (Huws, 1988). Within organisations, local departments are increasingly performing functions that previously were executed at central headquarters. Other functions are subcontracted to freelance employees, e.g. clerical work to homeworkers, to newly constituted, often small, enterprises, or to existing outside companies. These issues are part of more general changes in the boundaries between organisational functions, which are dealt with by the *Transaction Costs Theory,* developed by Williamson (1975).

Ouchi (1979) has expanded the original Transaction Cost Theory to include *three* types of arranging transactions: *markets, bureaucratic organisations* and *clans.* The balance between production costs and co-ordination costs explains why in some cases the transactions between certain production stages are found *within* one organisation, while in other cases these transactions take place in different organisations and are exchanged in an open market. Production costs include the costs, financial and all others, of creating and distributing goods or services. Co-ordination costs include the costs of the information process necessary to co-ordinate the activities of the people and machines involved in the production process. Certain conditions determine the choice between the three arrangements (Ciborra, 1987, p.259). None of the three arrangements will be found in a pure form. In most cases a combination has developed, with one of the three dominating.

The role of *Information and Communication Technology* in this discussion is central. Information exchange is a very crucial process for the co-ordination of transactions, and ICT can support the processes substantially. Rochart and Short (1989) synthesise various findings and theories concerning this issue, on the basis of an extensive research project. They confirm that the most important role of information technology is to manage interdependence, i.e. to serve as a mechanism for horizontal and vertical integration of organisational processes. They distinguish several organisational contexts in which this integration is particularly important, i.e. *value chain integration,* to integrate the product development chain, product delivery chain and customer service chain, *functional integration* of comparable departments through centralised information systems, and *planning and control* through the use of a central executive support system. On top of these co-ordinating information systems they note the growth of systems for team support, i.e. collaboration technology tools. In the thirteen years since their 1989 article the role of these systems has grown impressively.

It is expected that ICT will reduce the costs of co-ordination activities, and will therefore lead to an overall shift toward proportionately greater use of markets, rather than hierarchies, to co-ordinate economic activities. This is indeed what one can see all around, i.e. decentralisation, outsourcing and the growth of networks of more or less independent companies who co-operate in the value chain. The wide availability of information networks has also resulted in certain companies losing their position, since their role in the transfer of information is no longer required. As an example, connections to the large scale information networks of transport companies have enabled travel agencies to take over information processing concerning the availability of hotel rooms and booking of holiday tours from tour operators.

Within companies, information technology may have a centralising effect because it provides higher echelons with systematic information about lower levels (Galbraith, 1973). Yet lateral communication mechanisms tend to have a decentralising effect. According to Keen (1988) coping effectively with external turbulence implies networking processes, in which individuals, groups and departments have easy access to information bases, to each other and to the clients. Communication structures and processes in such circumstances have to be horizontal, boundary spanning and short lived. In such structures rapid information exchange and mutual adjustment between professionals is required. Communication of this type can only be realised when supported by new media.

Box 6.9 *Central points of attention from co-ordination theories*
1. Three types of co-ordination levels
2. Several mechanisms for co-ordination at each level
3. Role of ICT-tools in support of these mechanisms

6.8 Group Maintenance: Trust and Cohesion

Social psychologists have often made the distinction between two functions of groups, i.e. task performance and group maintenance. *Group maintenance* refers to processes that are not directly task oriented but have the objective of fostering the vitality, attractiveness and continuity of the group, through strengthening of the co-operative climate. Central issues in this context are the development of trust (Section 6.6.1), cohesion and group identity (Section 6.6.2). Effectiveness in longstanding groups is supposed to depend on these factors. Recently, the importance of these aspects of groups and organisations were brought forward strongly, in terms of the "emotional intelligence" of groups (Druskat and Wolff, 2000) and "social capital" in organisations (Prusak and Cohen, 2001).

6.8.1 Trust

Trust is a major condition for effective interaction (e.g. Lane and Bachman, 1998). It may not be obvious how crucial trust is, because in our western society it is implicit and inherent in many relationships. Confrontations with other societies may reveal, however, how much we take the existence of trust for granted (see Box 6.10).

Trust is conceived of as a psychological state, based on a general expectancy concerning the behaviour of other people and social systems in general (Kramer, 1999). It may involve both calculative and social orientations. Trust can lead to three types of outcomes, i.e. the reduction of transaction costs within organisations, to spontaneous sociability, and appropriate deference to organisational authorities (Kramer, 1999). Technical barriers such as mediated communication may hinder the development of trust.

It is no surprise that trust has become a buzzword in an age when traditional binding forces of society and organisations are disappearing, such as knowing each other through long co-located interaction, meeting each other face-to-face, and sharing strong local norms and values. Physical separation and technological mediation tend to prevent or slow down the articulation of ideas and the development of trust. This finding is an important warning for distributed groups and for technical support. In these groups openness and trust should be guarded explicitly. The theory of co-operation and of constructive controversy (see Section 5.5) requires that collaboration technology in groups should not restrict information exchange and distort communication. It also suggests that collaboration technology tools for the exchange of information and sharing of views will not be very successful in competitive groups.

Other theoretical domains also point to the importance of trust for adequate interaction. According to innovation diffusion theory (see Section 7.1), knowledge and opinions are not so much changed on the basis of information, but on the basis of trust in the opinions of others. When mediated communication implies that information is anonymous, the effect of that information will probably be rather limited.

So far in this discussion the focus has been on trust in people. Trust in tools is another relevant issue. Modern automatisation and the use of complicated information and communication technology require that people trust the reliability of the technology. Muir (1994) developed a model that is applicable to trust in both people and machines.

Starting from earlier theories she identified three aspects of trust, reflected in the definition of trust in work situations: *"Trust is the expectation of a member of a system of the persistence of the natural and moral social orders, and of technically competent performance and of fiduciary responsibility, from a member of the system..."* (Muir, 1994, p1911).

A system can have both human and non-human members, so the definition is applicable to trust in colleagues as well as to trust in machines and software.

Box 6.10 *Basic Trust*

Shortly after the changes in Russia, a Dutch software company set up a team of programmers in Russia. In one of the university cities many academicians with high grades in computer science had become jobless. They were recruited by the Dutch company and as a team made responsible for certain parts of software development. The person with the longest experience was made co-ordinator of the group. Telephone and e-mail were available to keep contacts with the partners in the Netherlands. Although the Russians were very expert, the performance of the team was disappointing. Solving problems in the assignments almost always required the intervention of the Dutch colleagues. Competition within the group seemed to be high. A thorough investigation revealed that the culture within the group was in line with what other researchers looking at eastern European work relations have found. In these countries basic trust is often lacking and it is in many cases quite uncommon to share creative ideas with others, because you can be certain that they will try to take advantage of it. You keep bright ideas to yourself as long as possible, until you have profited personally from them. In this case profit could only be found through contacts with the Dutch counterparts. The Russians could only function as a co-operating group after they had stayed in the Netherlands for a long period and experienced the benefits of trust and collaborative work.

The dynamics of trust are reflected in the *three levels* that trust may pass through (Muir, 1994). Early in a relationship a person's trust in another or in a tool is based on *predictability* of (desired) behaviour. After a period of predictable interaction, trust becomes based on a general feeling of stable characteristics, i.e. on *dependability*. A last stage of trust, encompassing the earlier ones is one of *faith*, i.e. expectation that in future situations the person or machine will continue to behave like before.

This model has hardly been tested empirically, but it contains concepts that are implicitly associated with the notion of trust. Adopting and using collaboration technology systems is indeed to some extent related to expectation of reliable performance, which is commonly lacking. Despite this, many information and communication technology tools are used, regardless of the fact that the users know that they may break down and indeed regularly do.

6.8.2 Cohesion and Social Identity

Cohesion is the extent to which group members perceive and feel attracted to their group. The more a team is interconnected in terms of the five groupness aspects (see Section 5.3), the higher the probability that cohesion develops. This cohesion is an important element in the group maintenance function of teams, i.e. in processes to prevent destructive conflicts and power struggles. It has become a challenging question under what conditions a loosely coupled community can develop sufficient cohesion to keep exchanging and sharing knowledge. Although not yet widely identified, some people fear that the introduction of ICT in organisations may result in a decrease in physical interaction between people and therefore in cohesion of the group.

Cohesion is sometimes defined in terms of *interpersonal attraction between team members*. This may be applicable to small task oriented groups, but is less useful for much larger and also for more loosely coupled groups. Hogg (1992) defines cohesion not in terms of attraction to group members as persons but in terms of commonality of tasks or other characteristics. He speaks of *social attraction* that is based on a person's perceptions of a certain common membership. Social attraction is based on so-called self categorisation, i.e. on a process of identifying with a group on the basis of certain factors such as propinquity, shared experiences and similarity.

In electronic co-operation and in anonymous newsgroups, these determinants may be limited. The findings concerning loss of social cues in computer mediated communication, of flaming and equalising of participation in distributed groups (see Section 2.5) have invited social psychologists to develop appropriate theories. Some (e.g. Kiesler, Siegel and McGuire, 1984) explain these phenomena in terms of lack of social norms in anonymous groups. The absence of social feedback on one's behaviour and of consensus about acceptable conduct is assumed to result in normless and unconstrained behaviour. The argument follows that, as in huge crowds, people lose some of their recognisable identity, and a process of *de-individuation* takes place. Computer mediated communication is therefore assumed to be inferior to face-to-face communication, as fewer controls exist to control participants' behaviour.

Spears and Lea (1992) and Postmes (1997) attack this line of reasoning. They argue that visual anonymity, either through being a member in a crowd or by physical isolation, leads to decreased attention to individual differences and increased attention to the social context. If persons are anonymous but identify themselves with a group, the de-individuation process results in a strong identification with that group. Anonymity in such cases makes the differences between group members invisible. This results in even stronger attention to common characteristics of the group and thereby in stronger cohesion and adherence to group norms. The authors acknowledge that anonymity in computer mediated groups potentially provides greater freedom for the group member. This freedom can be realised in deviating from the group norms or even leaving the group, but people have a need to belong and therefore often prefer to maintain their relationship within their communication group. Since anonymity in mediated groups to a certain extent prevents individual prominence, the dominance of group norms may therefore even be greater than in face-to-face groups, of course always under the condition that the person prefers to identify with the group.

Using literature research and empirical studies Postmes (1997) has found support for this theory. In a field study of students communicating by e-mail it was found that e-mail messages within groups tended to converge as a result of social influence. It appeared that norms for group communication and for communication with the university staff developed slowly but surely. Postmes concludes first that, under the condition of anonymity and group identification, de-individuation does not induce anti-social behaviour but socially regulated behaviour. Behaviour is influenced by the cognitive representation of the group, i.e. what people expect and think of the group. The second major conclusion is that the bandwidth of communication media has no direct effect on the level of social influence. Studies of videoconferencing suggest that under certain conditions a reversed effect can occur: people often dislike a video channel, while being positive about leaner media. This is explained by the hypothesis that the relative influence of the social context increases as the bandwidth decreases.

According to the above mentioned researchers flaming is not a symptom of normless behaviour but of adhering to the norms of the computer mediated groups. In those groups emotions are allowed and a form of expression is found, e.g. in using so-called "emoticons", such as :-) for joy and $#@(&# for anger. This anger is often not reflected in uncontrolled use of bad language but in very controlled use of certain specific emoticons.

6.9 Knowledge Sharing and Learning

The fifth basic group process to be discussed is knowledge sharing. Management of knowledge processes and learning by organisations are some of the most discussed subjects in recent organisation science. The growth of information and communication technology has lured many organisations into believing that sophisticated ICT-tools are the answer to questions concerning the acquisition, preservation, distribution, exchange and application of knowledge. All these information processes were considered to benefit enormously from investing millions of dollars in knowledge technologies. Procedures to elicit tacit knowledge from employees, to convert it into explicit knowledge and store it in expert systems and company wide repositories are the core activities of what is labelled the *codification strategy* of knowledge management (Hansen et al., 1999).

This approach has been successful to the extent that information systems can store and handle the large amount of data that is generated and used in organisations today. The approach however has seen many failures, particularly since organisations have tried to store and make accessible real *knowledge*. Knowledge consists of information that is contextualised and embedded in personal experiences, values and attitudes. Strictly speaking knowledge stored in an impersonal (technical) system is no longer knowledge, it has become information. Several studies show that people are often incapable or unwilling to explicate personal knowledge and to store it in systems (Huysman and De Wit, 2002). Moreover, there may also be resistance to retrieving other people's knowledge from such systems, since the knowledge is not expected to be sufficiently relevant for one's own situation.

A second way of dealing with sharing, applying and developing knowledge is what Hansen et al. (1999) call the *personalisation strategy*. In this strategy the focus is on people meeting each other, on interpersonal knowledge sharing, on master-apprenticeship relationship and on what is called *communities of practice* (see below). The role of ICT applications is limited to supporting the communication between people and e.g. to a yellow pages system, containing information concerning the expertise of organisation members and on where to find them. The authors argue that a codification strategy is called for in organisations or departments where the information processes are routinised, such as certain consultancies with more or less standard methods. A personalisation strategy is appropriate for organisations or departments with non-standardised, non-routine production processes.

The personalisation strategy is quite in line with the focus of organisational learning. Various learning and knowledge processes that are distinguished in the literature are brought together in Figure 6.6 (expanded from Huysman and De Wit, 2000).

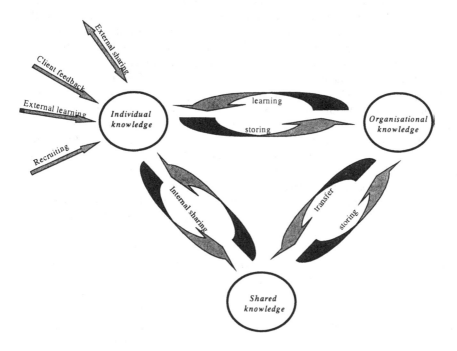

Figure 6.6 Knowledge processes in organisations (Expanded from an original figure by Huysman and de Wit. © 2000. Reproduced by permission of Koninklijke Van Gorcum)

It points to the fact that learning takes place at the individual, group and organisational level. At each level one can find tacit and explicit knowledge, and both can be exchanged, the explicit knowledge e.g. through documents, training or presentations, the tacit knowledge by socialisation. Individuals learn from external and internal sources, such as task performance and errors. When individuals share their knowledge with others, this may result in group learning. Shared knowledge, however, has to be accepted by the organisation, to become organisational knowledge, which is then available to be distributed to individuals or groups. Both individuals and groups may store knowledge in explicit and digital organisational repositories, or in the implicit norms, values and culture of the organisation.

Communities of Practice (CoPs) are expected to play an important role in the interaction between individuals, resulting in shared knowledge. CoPs form a framework by which both explicit and tacit knowledge can be shared, both for solving individual or common problems, and for developing new knowledge.

Of course, communities are not the only vehicles for this transfer of knowledge. Ad hoc meetings, encounters and presentations may also realise this objective. But modern organisations feel themselves heavily dependent on knowledge sharing, since the short life cycle of project teams, the geographic distribution of expertise and rapid employee turnover may easily result in losing valuable knowledge. Connecting employees in more or less permanent communities may solve this problem to some degree. This should be complemented by integrating knowledge generated in the communities into the organisation as a whole.

Researchers such as Lave and Wenger (1991) developed the first ideas about CoPs. They showed that proper learning often occurs as a function of the activity, context and culture in which it occurs, i.e. not in formal training, but on the job. Thus, much learning is situated learning, where social interaction is critical.

Central in all these ideas is the concept of *practices*, around which communities build, acquire, and create their knowledge. This is not theoretical knowledge, but knowledge related to a common practice such as a professional discipline, a skill or a topic. Sharing knowledge in a community will build or enrich a (set of) common practice(s). A community builds capability in its practice by developing shared action repertoires and resources such as tools, documents, routines, vocabulary, stories, symbols, artefacts, heroes, etc., that embody the accumulated knowledge of the community. This shared repertoire serves as a foundation for future learning (Allee, 2000).

The idea of communities as breeding grounds for sharing experiences and particularly for developing innovative concepts has found a receptive audience in modern organisations, looking for ways and means of strengthening their most important assets, the knowledge embedded in their employees, who are often distributed world-wide. Instead of referring to processes of knowledge transfer to newcomers in small groups of co-located craftsmen, the concept of communities of practice has become linked to groups of professionals, generally from different organisational units that share a common interest in a certain knowledge domain. McDermott (2000) defines CoPs as "... *loosely knit groups driven by the value they provide to members, defined by the opportunities to learn and share what they discover and bounded by a sense of collective identity*".

CoPs can be distinguished from teams in the sense that teams are formally institutionalised groups with the objective of achieving a certain product within a certain period of time. A CoP is a loosely coupled, often, but not always, a spontaneously grown group, brought together to provide their members with opportunities for sharing experiences and learning. Teams progress by moving through a work-plan, while communities develop by discovering new areas to share current knowledge and develop new knowledge around the practice. This is why managing these two groups is a very different job. Managing a team consists of co-ordinating interdependent tasks. Managing a CoP is making connections between members and keeping the topics of the community fresh and valuable (McDermott, 2000).

The practice and literature on CoPs show a wide variety of forms. The discussion is complicated by the fact that different names can be found for concepts or constellations, which are similar to CoPs, such as virtual communities, knowledge communities, and occupational communities. Virtual communities can be found in organisations but also on the Internet, focusing on a hobby, on political issues, or on social issues, such as a patients' group. Many communities in organisations prefer a certain degree of face-to-face meeting, but the *degree of virtuality* can differ widely. ICT facilitation is central in the study of virtual communities (Kimble, Hildreth and Wright, 2000).

Communication and co-operation, and also document exchange and information retrieval in geographically distributed groups may be supported by ICT. Despite many studies however, little is yet known about the role collaboration technology can fulfil in support of effective teamwork, let alone for communities. In practice one can find both extremes as to the value of ICT support for CoPs (see box below).

Providing considerable ICT support and expecting that a group will function optimally *just because* this support is available may be detrimental to the success of a group. This is valid for teams, but may be even more valid for CoPs, since such a group has no strong common task that pushes for interaction. Whether to provide a CoP with few or many ICT-tools may therefore be a real dilemma. Another dilemma concerning ICT is the choice between customisation and uniformisation. The application offered to a group should match the needs of this group.

Box 6.11

At BP Amoco a sophisticated set of tools is used to support its communities, while at Shell the IT use is quite limited. The most frequently used tool in Shell is a discussion group facility on which everyone can post a request or question for help. Currently, there appears to be no need for a storage-system, since it is quicker to ask a (highly specific) question repeatedly than to search for answers in a database, which is probably too generic anyway. The communities of BP and Shell both communicate mainly via communication tools, while the communities of Unilever appear to communicate mainly via face-to-face meetings held once or twice a year, with limited IC facilitated communication between these meetings.

So in the most ideal case the CoP should decide which ICT application it wants to use and how to customise that tool. Yet uniform platforms and applications make it possible to communicate and share applications between different locations and with other parts of an organisation.

6.10 Conclusions

In this chapter groups and collaboration processes have been analysed from various angles. Major issues can be summarised as follows:

- Co-operation is not always the best solution. Some tasks can better be done individually. Process losses (Steiner, 1972) such as co-ordination problems and social loafing may prevent optimal performance if done in a group setting.
- Group work is also individual work. Group work is a mixture of co-operative activities and individual or subgroup task performance.
- *Groupness* is a dimension. The more a collection of individuals have a common task, the longer and more often they interact, the longer and more formal their group membership and the smaller the number of members, the more such a collection group is considered to be a group or even a task oriented team.

- Groups develop. These developments proceed not necessarily through a fixed set of stages, but by interaction and external influences which result in changes in setting and processes.
- Co-operative groups can be very uncooperative. Groups are considered to exchange information freely to communicate openly, to co-ordinate their interactions, build trust and cohesion and are open to the environment. But members often (also) withhold information, have conflicts, play power and status games and are closed to external influence.
- Groups have five basic group processes: communication, which is basic to the others, co-operation, co-ordination, knowledge sharing and social interaction. Groups differ as to the processes that are the purpose, the raison d'être, of their existence. For teams co-operation is central, in friendship groups social interaction and in communities of practice knowledge sharing is most important.
- Favourable conditions have to be developed for effective group performance, related to goals and characteristics of the members, the group, the tools the setting and the environment (see Chapters 4 and 5).
- For groupware to support group work adequately it has to fit to the other conditions and support, or at least not hinder, the group processes and the attainment of the outcomes.

Chapter 7. Innovation and Implementation

7.1 Introduction

Theories concerning ongoing work processes and the use of collaboration technology in context have been presented in previous chapters. Technical tools, however, do not fall from heaven. New technologies and new tools are brought into the market after research and development and they are slowly adopted and implemented by organisations. Organisations can also design and develop their own version of a technical system. After being implemented, socio-technical systems may evolve into various directions, and new ways of working and of using the tools may emerge, partly intended, partly unintended and emerging from a multitude of interacting factors. Experiences in some organisations will be fed back to developers and contribute to new versions of the tools. The use and effects of tools are therefore also determined by the way they are designed and introduced.

In these cycles of invention, adoption, use and renewal, three large developmental processes interact:

- *diffusion processes* of new technologies in society and the adoption by organisations.
- strategic *design and change* processes within organisations.
- processes of *appropriation,* i.e. of mutual adaptation of users and technology, through emergent processes of knowledge exchange and learning.

In the following sections the three processes will be discussed.

7.2 Diffusion and Adoption of New Technologies

Diffusion is the process by which an innovation is transferred to members of a social system via certain channels and during a certain period (Rogers, 1995). If a particular organisation, more or less intentionally, decides to introduce an innovation, it is called "adoption". The purpose of theories concerning these processes is to describe and to explain, firstly, how the diffusion of an innovation to potential users, i.e. individuals, organisations or sectors, proceeds. Secondly the theories focus on the question why some users/organisations are quicker than others to adopt certain innovations. The emphasis in these theories is on the relationships between organisations and environment.

Traditionally the view is held that diffusion of a new technology follows an S curve: during a long introduction period only a few organisations or individuals adopt the innovation. After this time more and more mainstream users adopt the new idea/technology in a relatively short time (see Box 7.1). In a third period the "laggards" finally take up the innovation. Rogers (1995) distinguished five categories of adopters: innovators, early adopters, early majority, late majority, and laggards. Many reasons for early or late up-take, from financial costs to individual dispositions to social pressure, have been discussed in Chapter 4.

Box 7.1
The telephone was available in the Netherlands in 1880. In 1945 about 5% of the population, had adopted the innovation. Between 1945 and 1970 the majority of the households and companies bought a telephone. After that time the penetration rate slowed down, leaving today 1% to 2% of the population without a connection (Wit, 1998)

Not every organisation has to strive to be an early adopter. The criterion of success is whether an organisation is sufficiently open and informed about technical developments, i.e. that it can discover new opportunities in time.

Analysing the development of video telephony and a few other ICT innovations, Ortt (1998) developed an extended diffusion model. He distinguishes three diffusion phases:

- *The innovation phase*, the period from invention of the technology to the market introduction of a product incorporating the technology. During the innovation phase market potential can only be assessed through analysis of necessary conditions: expected performance quality and unique functionality of the new product, available infrastructure and available application areas.
- *The market adaptation phase*, a period of introduction, decline and re-introduction of various versions of products incorporating the technology. During this market adaptation phase, market potential can be assessed through the study of supply factors, e.g. advantage for the supplying companies, entry barriers, willingness of market parties to co-operate, demand factors, i.e. potential customers, and conditional factors such as governmental strategy. In this phase several little S-curves for different forms of the new technology may be found.
- *The market stabilisation phase*, in which dominant product forms penetrate the actual market. Only in this third phase will the normal S-curve be encountered. Analysis of consumer segments and consumer demands can predict adoption and use, at the beginning of the market stabilisation phase. In this phase user(organisation)s adopt innovations on the basis of perceived characteristics, such as relative advantage, compatibility with existing values and habits, complexity, triability and communicability (see Section 4.7). Once an innovation becomes available on the market, organisations may adopt, or develop their own version of that innovation.

> **Box 7.2**
>
> Analysis of the development of video-telephony (Ortt, 1998) shows that it still in the market adaptation phase, since a dominant product form and application has not yet been found. Market structure analysis for video-telephony in the Netherlands, based on the judgement of 10 experts came to the conclusion that video-telephony has a relatively large market potential for tele-entertainment, tele-health, hearing impaired and family applications, but *not* for distant education, teleshopping, telework and telebanking.

Adoption processes within organisations can be approached from different disciplines. Firstly one can find (information) *systems development models,* which distinguish stages such as: information planning, definition study, global design, detailed design, implementation, installation, operation and control. Secondly, there are *decision making models* with stages concerning organisation planning, such as objective setting, strategic programming, budgeting, monitoring, establishing rewards. Finally there are *organisational change stages* such as unfreezing, moving, refreezing (Lewin, 1947).

The models are of course different, but most of them have a sequence of activities in common, which can be summarised as follows:

- an *initiation* phase consisting of all activities concerning the experiencing of a problem and gathering and evaluating information about possible solutions, resulting in the decision to choose a certain solution.
- an *implementation* phase consisting of all activities regarding the design or modification of the innovation and the organisation, and regarding the introduction in the organisation and to the individual users.
- an *incorporation* phase, in which the system is incorporated operationally in the work processes.

The following remarks can be made concerning this model:

Linear or chaotic. The model suggests a simple linear sequence of stages, which is based on a rational view of decision-makers. Studies of actual innovations and studies of decision making in general (e.g. Mintzberg, 1973; The Minnesota Innovation Research Program, Schroeder et al., 1986) have shown that reality is different. Decision making and innovation processes appear to be quite complex and characterised by regression to earlier phases, iteration of sub-cycles, or the execution of various activities simultaneously. An initial innovative idea tends to proliferate into several ideas, initial ideas tend to develop into various separate decision making processes, unpredictable setbacks and surprises are inevitable, and as innovations develop the old and the new become slowly linked.

Innovations mix. In the field of collaboration technology, several categories of innovations play a simultaneous role. Many organisations face a complex mix of innovations, i.e. of infrastructures, services, e.g. the Internet, and specific applications. For each of these the stages model applies, partly interdependent, partly independent. The research and development stages of the various technologies can to some extent proceed separately, but for individual users or organisations the adoption and implementation of telecommunication infrastructures, terminals, or network services are often only relevant in relation to certain applications.

Three settings. The diffusion and adoption processes are different for the following (organisational) settings:

a. *Individuals and groups of very small organisations,* such as farmers, physicians or small transportation companies. In small organisations the speed and success of diffusion, adoption and implementation processes often depend on the existence of organised networks and of central (professional) organisations that can play the part of initiator, advisor and manager.
b. *Medium sized organisations,* have some resources to manage the introduction and have some power to resist too great a dependence on other organisations.
c. *Large organisations.* In some aspects they resemble the medium-sized organisations, in other aspects a group of small organisations. The model can become complicated for two reasons. Firstly, large companies often have laboratories for research and development of systems to be used in their organisation. This implies that the whole innovation process may take place within the same organisation. Secondly, an innovation, implemented and incorporated in one part of the organisation, sometimes passes through an erratic diffusion process on its way to other parts of that same organisation.

Networks. Crucial to all telematic systems and services is the notion of *networks*. This is probably the most important distinguishing aspect of electronic communication systems in comparison to other innovations. There is always an interconnection between several users. Depending on the application, the network is *intra-organisational, inter-organisational* or *extra-organisational.* Intra-organisational networks may be simple e-mail networks, but have recently been extended into Intranets. Intranets are meant to be comparable to the Internet with its databases, but used by organisation members only. Inter-organisational networks are for example EDI networks for a specific group of organisations. Inter-organisational networks of the Internet type, for the exclusive use of a relatively small group of organisations, are called Extranets. The Internet is the best known inter-organisational network.

All networks, but particularly inter-organisational networks, increase the interdependency of organisations. Systems for electronic data interchange may have some implications which companies do not always realise: the companies involved have to co-operate intensively to standardise data, using one system may cause a company to be sometimes excluded from relations with companies that use other systems. Companies become more open to the prying eyes of the other network members, and they are more vulnerable to failures of the other network members. Decision making in individual organisations thereby becomes increasingly determined by other organisations. The implication is that adoption may be a *two stage adoption process:* adoption by a cluster of organisations, which become interconnected through the electronic network, and adoption by individual organisations.

Strategic choice? The introduction of networking technology is propagated as a strategic choice to gain competitive advantage. Telecommunications can be harnessed as a major new force for organisational design and redesign, and organisations are urged to exploit the strategic opportunities it opens up. Collaboration technology, however, is rarely regarded as such by its potential adopters, which may be responsible for its limited use and success.

Box 7.3

Among the organisations studied by Veen (1993) several had introduced e-mail as an add-on to other communication systems. In these cases use and success of the e-mail system was limited, and depended partly on geographical distribution, task interdependency, critical mass and adequate integration with other computer tasks. Where networking technology was introduced for strategic reasons, e-mail use was quite intensive. In an international trading company the e-mail network between its agencies all over the world had become the very backbone of the company and widely used and appreciated.

Summarising, the diffusion of an innovation depends on many factors, such as the characteristics of the innovation (see also Section 4.4.3), of the market and of the organisation. The main groups of characteristics determining the success of adoption, implementation and incorporation of innovations are summarised in Figure 7.1. Not all groups of conditions are equally important in all stages.

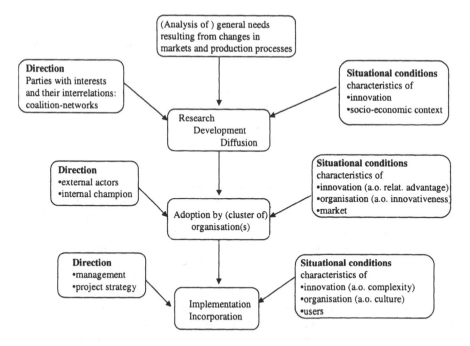

Figure 7.1 Determinants of the innovation processes (Source: Andriessen, J.H.E. (1994a). Telematics and Innovation. Conditions for Adoption, Implementation and Incorporation of Electronic Communication Systems. In J.H.E. Andriessen and R.A. Roe (Eds.), *Telematics and Work*. © 1994. Reproduced with permission by Lawrence Erlbaum Associates)

The following statements appear to hold (Andriessen, 1994a):

- *diffusion* of an innovation is a function of the characteristics of the innovation, of the interaction of major societal stakeholders and of socio-economic context.
- *adoption* of an innovation by an organisation is particularly contingent on characteristics of the innovation, e.g. relative advantage, of the environment, i.e. market conditions, and of the organisation, e.g. innovativeness.
- *implementation* of an innovation is particularly contingent on characteristics of the innovation, e.g. triability, and of the organisation, e.g. change strategy.
- *incorporation* of an innovation is particularly contingent on characteristics of the innovation, e.g. complexity, of the organisation, e.g. culture, and of the individual users, e.g. innovation orientation.

7.3 Design and Introduction Processes

Some innovations are not adopted from outside the organisation, but developed within the organisation. The literature concerning ICT-systems design and system development methods is immense. In the last two decades an increasing number of publications (see below) argue that particularly in the area of collaboration technology systems design should take account of the social and organisational aspects of the situation during (almost) all the phases of design and introduction. It is argued that design and introduction of a technological innovation are more successful if three rules are followed:

- the people concerned should be involved in the various stages of the process.
- the wider context is taken into account in the sense that tools and organisational context have to match.
- the organisation should be adapted at the same time: technical innovation cannot operate without organisational innovation.

An implementation process should have the objectives of *developing* a new system in line with the existing organisational structure, culture and processes, of *learning* to work with and to manage the new system, and of developing *acceptance* of the innovation, thereby preventing or reducing resistance to changes.

Several models aiming at this form of integrative design have been developed. These models tend to converge towards an approach that is *process oriented*, versus solely product oriented, *evolutionary*, versus at the start developing a final blueprint, *participative*, versus top down, and *iterative*, versus linear. Apart from these characteristics successful implementation processes require adequate project management. This includes finding competent people, i.e. strong sponsors and champions, experts and involved users, and setting up adequate project structures.

Participative design. Traditional design methods have been criticised for several reasons. One is that they are often heavily dominated by the designer's ideas about what is an adequate system. In reaction, design methods with a user centred orientation have been developed (Nielsen, 1992a; Nielsen and Mack, 1994;

Lindgaard, 1994). The *user-centred approach* tries to gauge the reactions of end-users by trying out different prototypes. This method however, does not account for other relevant parties involved in system design, such as developers, managers, support engineers, or even evaluators. These parties or stakeholders are of relevance since they can potentially provide requirements and evaluation criteria. Stakeholders can be defined as those actors (individuals or groups) that have an interest in the design, development and implementation of the new system.

The next phase in the development of a design methodology is the step from passive single stakeholder involvement into active multiple stakeholder involvement. This is called *participative design* or *co-operative design* (Ehn, 1988; Greenbaum and Kyng, 1991; Muller and Kuhn, 1993). The basic tenet of this approach is that all stakeholder-groups should be actively involved in the design of the systems they subsequently will use. Participative design does not necessarily imply consensus. The stakeholder model of system development recognises that different people can have different interests and stakes. Even then, however, "...*a project will only succeed completely if and only if you make winners of all the critical stakeholders*". (Egyedi and Boehm, 1998). Congruence between tools and work settings requires that designers and users develop a common understanding of tasks and work processes.

Linear or iterative. User centred participative design is iterative. In the traditional waterfall model of design, progression at each design stage can be checked to ensure that the design of a system conforms to the client's requirements. The waterfall model supports project leaders in effectively managing the development of a system. There are however prominent disadvantages. For instance, it is impossible to completely understand and express user requirements until a fair amount of design has been undertaken. Only then can a user get a clear view of the future system. This model ignores also the organisational changes and different parties that are involved in different phases of the model. Models such as the *spiral design model* (Boehm, 1988), which promote an iterative design process, are an alternative to the linear waterfall model.

The life cycle design approach (Nielsen, 1992b) takes the idea of active stakeholder involvement and iterative design of system prototyping and system evaluation further. It recognises that ICT systems follow an ongoing process of *design–operational use–redesign*. Rapid prototyping and incremental developments are central in this process. System development alternates between (top-down) design and (bottom-up) feedback. Evaluation is prominent and takes place during the whole design process. The traditional distinction between formative evaluation, i.e. contributing to the redesign of the system, and summative evaluation, i.e. considering the system for purchase and operational design, is often difficult to maintain. Evaluation has to be seen as (Stern, in Sommerlad, 1992) "... *any activity that throughout the planning and delivery of innovative programmes enables those involved to learn and make judgements about the starting assumptions, about the implementation processes and about the outcomes of the innovation concerned*".

Scenario construction. Evaluation of prototypes by future users in an iterative fashion is one way of approaching a desired future system state. The nature and implications of new systems, however, particularly of advanced multimedia systems, are often difficult to foresee. Constructing scenarios which describe in a systematic manner the future usage of a system, is one way to overcome this problem (Carroll, 1995; Anker and Lichtveld, 1999). A (future) usage scenario is a description of the application environment that is expected when the new system is implemented. Constructing a scenario involves firstly identification of the stakeholders and their responsibilities, and secondly a prediction of how each stakeholder will be affected by the new application or service. After the construction of various scenarios, it is possible to identify the potential benefits or negative impacts that a new system will bring to each stakeholder. These benefits can then be used as the criteria against which to evaluate the success of the new system.

   To summarise the above notions it is concluded that particularly in the case of collaboration technology tools:

- design should be iterative and stakeholder centred.
- stakeholders should participate in the evaluation process and their critical success factors should be established.
- evaluation should be integrated in the design process from the beginning.
- future usage scenarios can support the identification of design requirements and evaluation criteria.

According to the socio-technical perspectives, design and evaluation should not be merely restricted to a technical application, but should also take into account the social and organisational context. A new system should be developed in such a way that the existing organisational context and the new system can be adjusted to each other.

Introducing a new system. The design process further implies the development of prototypes and the, possibly experimental and limited, tryout of operational systems in which people learn to work with and to manage a new system. This process of learning and adaptation may be supported by the appointment of "user advocates" (Pankoke-Babatz and Syri, 1997) or intermediaries, i.e. user-representatives that act as change agents between users and designers, during development of a system and during the first period of introduction. This approach is applicable to technical systems and organisational arrangements.

Conditions for strategy choice. It has been argued that a participative and iterative design strategy is not needed or possible in all situations. The choice of a design strategy, including participation of stakeholders, should be contingent on various conditions (Algera et al., 1989; Leonard-Barton, 1988; van Offenbeek, 1993), and particularly on *organisational complexity*. Innovations that involve many persons, tasks, and organisational units are more difficult to implement successfully than simple innovations. Dealing with complexity can be done in two ways, i.e. by reducing or by managing the complexity (Galbraith, 1977). Reduction of complexity can be achieved by dividing the innovation process into small steps. Managing complexity requires the use of integrating mechanisms such as sophisticated process strategies.

   Several researchers have concluded that complexity of the situation should also determine the level of involvement of the users (Van Offenbeek, 1993). Leonard-Barton (1988) argued that the higher the complexity, i.e. the number of people and number of different organisational units affected, the more implementation success depends on user involvement, although user involvement may then be more difficult (Algera et al., 1989).

Choice and success of implementation strategy may not only be contingent on the organisational setting, it may also depend on the kind of technology being introduced (Orlikowski and Hofman, 1997). Concerning the match between technology and change strategy, a
traditional planned change process may well be effective, if a fixed technology is implemented, which leaves very little room for adaptation by its users, or when the impacts of a technology are well understood. For the case of new and customisable technologies, however, such as collaboration technology, Orlikowski and Hofman advise using an "improvisational strategy", providing the organisation is sufficiently flexible.

An improvisational strategy is characterised by an ongoing process rather than an event with an end point, and opportunity based changes, i.e. deliberate changes are introduced during the change process in response to an unexpected event; opportunity based changes can be part of a process which also includes stages of planned change and emergent change.

Finally, according to the above mentioned authors the change strategy and the technology should also fit the organisational culture. A flexible change strategy, such as their improvisational strategy, is more suited to an informal co-operative organisation than to a bureaucratic one, and for groupware to succeed, a team-oriented culture within the organisation is required.

Box 7.4 *Central points of attention from Diffusion and Change theories*
1.   The role of diffusion and adoption of new tools
2.   The role of characteristics of the change process in the adoption and incorporation of new tools and systems
3.   The importance of iterative and user oriented design

7.4 Appropriation and Adaptive Structuration Theory

Despite carefully planned design and introduction processes new systems will be adapted to local situations, may be used differently from the way the designers intended, in short, the new systems will be appropriated into the social setting. This issue of adaptation and appropriation, of learning and of mutual adjustment of technology and social setting (co-evolution, Rogers, 1994) has been discussed from various perspectives in earlier chapters. The strategic choice approach (see Section 3.3) views the conscious and rational choices of managers as all-determining, assuming insight into and unlimited choice over technological options and their effects. Certain change theories are related to this perspective by assuming that the development of adequate socio-technical systems can be planned in detailed ways. This perspective ignores the role of other actors and of social and economic processes that make developments anything but transparent. The emergent structures perspective focuses on evolving and unpredicted processes and on the creative abilities of users to interpret and use tools in novel ways. These theories emphasise adaptation, learning and appropriation (Orlikowski, 1996; Ngwenyama, 1998; Hettinga, 2002). They hold that the uses and consequences of information technology may emerge rather unpredictably from complex social interactions. The influence of unexpected external influences, the interaction of people with different backgrounds, interests and interpretations, the discovery of possibilities to use a tool in unintended ways, all make the outcome of the introduction of a new technology unpredictable. The development of new technologies and of new social structures is therefore not a matter of grand strategies of planned change but rather a combination of planned strategies and a series of actions in reaction to unplanned developments. Orlikowski (1996) speaks of *situated change*, Hutchins (1991) of *local adaptation and local design*.

Adaptive Structuration Theory (AST) tries to account for some of the unintended consequences of the introduction of a new technology. AST (see Figure 7.2) is a specification of Structuration Theory, developed to account for differences in the way certain advanced information technologies, particularly meeting support systems, are used (Poole and DeSanctis, 1990, 1994).

> *The assumption is that groups draw on social structures as rules and resources for interaction. Examples of social structure are the rules governing turn-taking in speech, the norm of deference to a leader or other influential person, discussing topics according to agenda, or specific decision making procedures that have been learned in the past or are currently available. These social structures come from general cultural values and experiences in group-interaction, as well as from management philosophies or procedures within the particular organisation.*
> (DeSanctis et al. 1993, p3)

The technology and the procedures of advanced information systems such as Meeting support Systems provide other social structures. They provide rules, e.g. voting rules, and resources, e.g. databases, the use of which determine the way the group interact. However, "*... no matter what features are designed into a system, users mediate technological effect, adapting the systems to their needs, resisting them, or refusing to use them at all*" (Poole and DeSanctis (1990). The rules and procedures described here provide the structures of interpretation, domination and legitimisation that are presented in Structuration Theory (Section 3.5).

The social structures provided by advanced information technologies can be described in two ways. Firstly, a technological application has *structural features*: the specific functionalities, rules, resources of the system, and the degree of sophistication, restrictiveness and comprehensiveness. Secondly, there is what is called the *spirit* of the features, i.e. "*... the general intent with regard to values and goals underlying a given set of structural variables....(it supplies a) normative frame with regard to the behaviours that are appropriate in the context of a technology*" (Poole and DeSanctis, 1994, p126). As an example, the spirit of a certain GDSS may be the expectation of consensus decision making, structured interaction, efficiency and informal interaction.

The concept of *spirit* is related to what is sometimes called *script*, referring to usage patterns and task divisions that are, as it were, embedded in and "prescribed by" the technology. These scripts may unintentionally provoke, encourage or constrain certain behaviours, such as a huge office desk that forces a hierarchical relation between the person that sits behind it and another that comes to stand in front of it. While scripts are considered to be characteristics of the technology, spirit may change through the changing usage patters of the owner/user.

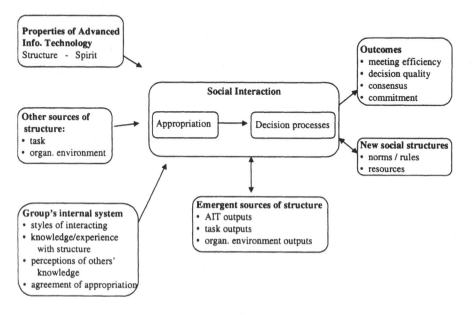

Figure 7.2 Adaptive Structuration Theory (Source: DeSanctis and Poole, 1994. Reproduced with permission of *Organization Science)*

The use of advanced information technology depends on the features and spirit of the tool and also on structures provided by the task and the environment. Moreover, when a technology is used, its output, e.g. proposals, new ideas, but also emerging ways of using the technology in interaction, becomes in its turn new sources of structure. This is the process of *structuration*, i.e. the production and reproduction of emergent social structures. When emergent rules or behaviours are accepted over time they become institutionalised and will determine subsequent behaviour. It is not only new emergent but also existing structures that become appropriated, such as existing rules and norms, roles and meanings and other institutional systems.

The institutionalisation of meanings and rules in a group or of the use and social structure of a technology is called "appropriation". It is defined as "... *the mode or fashion in which a group uses, adapts and reproduces a structure*" (Poole and DeSanctis, 1990). It happens when a group makes a tool its own. It is a combination of users adapting to a technology, and of the adaptation of the technology to the group. The example in Box 7.5 shows that patterns of interaction and groupware use may be established in the very beginning of a process and can then endure for a long time.

Box 7.5

A study is described in Box 2.4 (Section 2.4) concerning mechanical engineering students from two universities, in the Netherlands and the USA, who co-operated for three months in a design project (Huysman et al., forthcoming). An in depth analysis was made of the appropriation process. The evolving use of the CSCW tools, and group processes such as role differentiation, the forming of routines and temporal work planning were analysed. One USA/NL team used a videoconferencing facility regularly while another team used it only a few times during two months of co-operation. This second team had a much sharper division of roles and appeared to be exclusively concerned with the end product, while the first team also cared much for the process aspects of social interaction. These choices were decided upon during the first videoconferences. The first USA/NL team decided to meet at least once a week using videoconferencing. The three USA members of the second team indicated at the end of the first videoconference that e-mail would probably be sufficient to co-ordinate the work. The two Dutch students accepted this. The teams went on to develop a different use of the set of tools available based on these first decisions.

According to AST, appropriation is a process in which four elements or aspects can be distinguished:

- intensity of appropriation moves: using the structure, relating it to other structures, constraining the use, and making judgements about it.
- using the technology faithfully or unfaithfully, degree to which the user adheres closely to the letter of described procedures.
- whether the system is used for purposes such as domination.
- having more or less confidence in, comfort with and respect for the system.

The appropriation process is ideal when all types of appropriation moves are made, when it is used in the sense of the original spirit of the tool, when the features of the tool are used for task purposes rather than for power games, and when the attitudes towards appropriation are positive.

Why is appropriation of a technology in one group nearer to the ideal than in another group? Poole and DeSanctis relate this to characteristics of the group and its members, i.e. their interaction style, their knowledge and experience, their perception of other's acceptance of the structures and the degree to which members agree on which structures should be appropriated. They make, amongst others, the following predictions (concerning GDSSs):

- the more structured the design of the tool, or the better group members' knowledge of its intended purposes, the more faithful the appropriation will be, and there will be fewer conflicts about the appropriation.
- faithful appropriation of the tool will depend on the willingness of the group leader to act in accordance with the purposes of the system.
- the more faithful the group's appropriation process, the more predictable the outcomes of the use of the tool will be.

DeSanctis et al. (1993) use AST successfully to explain the differences in results between three teams using a GDSS over a long period.

AST may be viewed as a contingency approach to the question of the determinants of effective technologies, i.e. the effects depend on certain situational conditions, but the difference with traditional contingency approaches is the emphasis on the emergent sources of structure. Poole and DeSanctis formulate the following summarising proposition: *"Given Advanced Information Technology and other sources of social structure and ideal appropriation processes, and decision processes that fit the task at hand, then desired outcomes of AIT use will result."*

The study of appropriation processes is usually done using in-depth case studies in which analysis of speech acts and participative observation play a dominant role (e.g. Ciborra, 1996).

Conclusion. Comparing Figure 6.3 and 7.2 it becomes clear that Adaptive Structuration Theory has in a certain sense similarities with earlier mentioned input-process-output models. It is however less deterministic and focuses on processes of structuration and appropriation. This brings our attention to feedback loops of emergent structures that change in their turn the input social structures and technology. Structuration Theory and Adaptive Structuration Theory are particularly relevant because of their focus on processes of mutual adaptation of systems and users during the implementation of a system, and on emergent structures that change input characteristics. In this conceptualisation AST can integrate group dynamic and organisational processes. The theory gives explanations for the different ways of technical systems are appropriated, but these causal mechanisms have to be elaborated in more depth.

AST does not provide clear guidelines for design. This is not strange since it grew out of Structuration Theory, which is a theory of societal processes on a high abstraction level. Moreover, AST's main focus is on the analysis of the way *existing* technologies are taken up by groups and evolve in their role during the appropriation process. Dourish (2002) identifies certain aspects of appropriation that may be used to derive design principles for collaboration technology.

Box 7.6 *Central points of attention from Adaptive StructurationTheory (see also Structuration Theory, Section 3.5):*
1.   The role of appropriation processes with regard to technical tools
2.   Specific characteristics of ideal appropriation
3.   The role of both features and spirit of new tools / systems
4.   Specific characteristics of social structures and outcomes

Chapter 8. Integration for Evaluation

8.1 Introduction

The various strands of the previous chapters will be brought together in this chapter. The concepts and theories presented will be integrated into a set of three models with the objective of providing a framework for evaluation. The models are developed in Sections 8.1 and 8.2, while in 8.3 and 8.4 an explanation is given of how collaboration technology tools, and the setting in which they are used, can be evaluated systematically, using the models.

8.2 Theories and Heuristic Models

The models presented in this chapter are a mixture of theory and heuristic models. A *theory* or theoretical model can contribute to the *explanation*, and sometimes *prediction*, of certain phenomena. In the preceding chapters many theories have been discussed that can contribute to the explanation of the role of collaboration technology in group work. A *heuristic model* in its barest form only brings together the many variables that appear to be relevant.

The relevance of a theory depends on the type of questions asked in a certain context. Answering questions such as *when is groupware useful* or *under what conditions are video-connections effective* requires a theory concerning interpersonal communication. The question *how is the introduction of a particular groupware in our organisation best organised* requires insight into organisational change processes. Solving the problem *why so many Collaboration technology applications fail to be used adequately,* requires insights based on technology acceptance and media match theories. Cognitive psychology and human computer interaction models deal with the issues of learnability and mental load.

In the previous chapters four grand and many small theories were presented. The four theories, Action Theory, Activity Theory, Structuration Theory and Adaptive Structuration Theory, provide each a general perspective for conceptualising the behaviour of people. They focus on three levels of aggregation, i.e. on individual goal directed behaviour and cognitive processes (Action Theory, Activity Theory) on interpersonal and group processes (Activity Theory and Adaptive Structuration Theory) and on macro-social processes (Structuration Theory). None of these theories gives an exclusive representation of reality. Like a map a theory is an instrument for a certain purpose. Certain features are enlarged and others omitted. A map for sailors shows details of rocks, rivers, bridges and harbours but hardly any details of roads or towns. A map for drivers gives details of roads or towns, but almost nothing about coastal waters for example. The value of a theory is not found in whether it presents reality adequately, but in whether it is useful for a certain purpose. Morgan (1996) has discussed several organisation theories and has shown that they reflect certain perspectives on organisations and are therefore better called metaphors. These metaphors reflect ways in which organisations can be viewed, e.g. as machines, or as organisms. Theories, like metaphors may be more or less useful, depending on the purpose for which they are needed. In the same way the theories presented in the preceding chapters can be seen as different spectacles, through which to view different aspects of reality.

Each of the grand theories is quite rich but also quite general. All four incorporate many notions that separately can be found in other theories. Each is a kind of umbrella theory, or rather perspective, sensitising a researcher and designer towards an integrated whole of potentially important elements and processes. Other theories however – middle range theories – are needed to distinguish specific factors and processes, to explain certain phenomena and to identify relevant individual, group and organisational characteristics. These other theories, many of which are presented in previous chapters, may be more precise in predicting behaviour or success and failure of collaboration technology. Some of these other theories are also more suitable for deriving design guidelines. Together they point at the potential relevance of a large number of factors.

Heuristic models satisfy the need for ordering the many factors that are potentially relevant. Such a model is often not much more than a useful visualisation of several categories of variables that have been found to be of importance. It is used as a framework that points to the potential relevance of certain issues and its justification depends on the purpose it has to serve. In this case the heuristic model presented is the basis for identifying the issues that may be relevant in a user oriented evaluation and design of tools for computer supported co-operation. It also includes diverse theories that are relevant in explaining the relations between the elements in the model.

The basis for heuristic models concerning group processes is often a simple input-process-output schema (see Figure 6.3). The field of social and organisational psychology has produced several sophisticated versions (McGrath, 1984; Hackman, 1987). In overviews of the findings in this field the basic model has been "filled" with many variables (e.g. Kraemer and Pinsonneault, 1990; DeSanctis and Gallupe, 1987; McGrath and Hollingshead, 1994). In recent empirical studies this model has been specified further (e.g. Hooff, 1997; Hinssen, 1998).

McGrath and Hollingshead (1994, p95) and Hollingshead and McGrath (1995) present models that seem to present a fourth set of factors, called "organising concepts" and "conditions under which group x does task y", such as anonymity, time pressure, change in division of labour. However, the organising concepts are "... *summaries or reflections of the combination of input conditions*" (p101), i.e. they are metaphors that focus on specific functions of groups and the conditions are more or less similar to what is called 'context' in other publications. So, this model is basically still the same input-throughput-output model, but with emphasis on special interactions.

Many of the models are limited. They suggest a linear and one-directional causal relation: the characteristics of the input determine the processes which then determine the outcomes. It is clear, however, from experience and reflected in theories such as (Adaptive) Structuration Theory or group stage models, that human action and group interaction change the social structures, which means that they have feedback effects on group characteristics, task definition and tool use. These feedback effects can be explicitly planned, but unforeseen events will often result in the unplanned emergence of new settings and processes. For this reason the term *context-of-use* is adopted in this book, instead of the term input factors, which suggests to indicate the starting moment only.

Behind some of the models lies the contingency-idea, that the context-of-use factors must fit, i.e. must match to produce the best processes and output. The models are in this sense quite static in nature. However, several theories point to the fact that characteristics of tasks, tools and context are perceived and subjectively re-interpreted. Moreover, learning and adaptation processes take place through which input elements are constantly adapted to each other. Nevertheless one cannot count on an automatic adaptation process when introducing a new tool or a new setting. The larger the gap between existing and new settings the more energy has to be directed to the introduction processes.

Many models focus on the level of group task interaction and pay less attention to aspects of individual human computer interaction and task performance or to organisational functioning. As has been argued earlier, co-operative group work contains much individual task performance, and computer mediated group work implies individual tool use and issues of human computer interaction. Cognitive theories point to the fact that when designing and evaluating ICT-tools from a user perspective, one has to take into account the question of whether they fit the action mechanisms, the human motivation and the self-image of the potential users.

The models presented in the following sections try to take into account these criticisms. The models are a combination of the input-process-output model, with elements of Activity Theory, Adaptive Structuration Theory and several group dynamic theories combined.

8.3 Integrated Models

The theories and notions discussed in the previous chapters are integrated in three steps, i.e. from the individual user perspective, the co-operative group perspective and from the organisational tool adoption perspective.

8.3.1 The Individual User Perspective

The acceptance, adoption, choice and use of ICT-tools and media appear to be processes in which many factors plays a role (see Chapter 4). The constituting elements are on the one hand the goals and tasks set by the *environment*, the social and physical *setting* and the *tools and other artefacts*, and on the other hand the *actor* involved. The actor has properties such as knowledge, skills, and attitudes, based on dispositions, roles and demographic characteristics. It is the interaction of these two sets of factors which forms the determinants of individual action. People perceive, or better: construct, the setting in their own way. They define their own personal goals, their view on the task, on the social roles, norms and constraints, and particularly on the tools and artefacts they use. This results in a certain perceived usefulness and perceived ease of use of the tools, which determines the acceptance, adoption, choice and use of tools/media (see Figure 8.1).

The context-of-use factors and their interpretation results in motivation to use the tools and perform the task. Individual abilities have a double role. First people interpret their own abilities in relation to the task and goals, which influences motivation. Secondly tool use and task performance is determined by an interaction of motivation and actual abilities to do so. Task performance then results in certain outcomes, both for the organisation, such as quality of products, and for the person, e.g. satisfaction and rewards. The perception of the context-of-use and the motivation is also determined by the implementation process and by feedback from performance experiences.

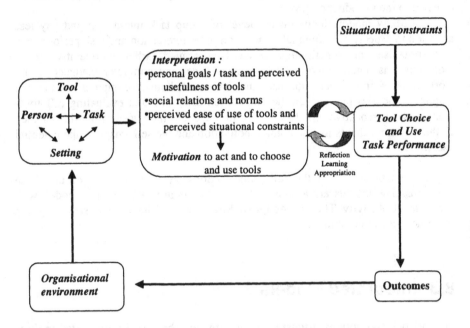

Figure 8.1 The individual tool choice and use model

This model reflects the elements and processes in relation to individual behaviour. Group work implies interaction of several individuals, which results in new elements and processes. The individual perspective model is embedded in the group perspective model, discussed in the next section.

8.3.2 The Co-operative Work Perspective

The purpose of introducing collaboration technology is to support the interaction of several people interacting in a certain way. Introduction of new systems implies changes in ways of working, in the use of tools and in group interaction. At the end of Chapter 6 the basic principles of group interaction have been summarised. The *Dynamic Group Interaction Model* (DGIn model, see Figure 8.2) is based on these principles and on the integration of group dynamic and other theories. These theories have a long tradition and are supported by many empirical studies. Figure 8.1 is contained within in this figure

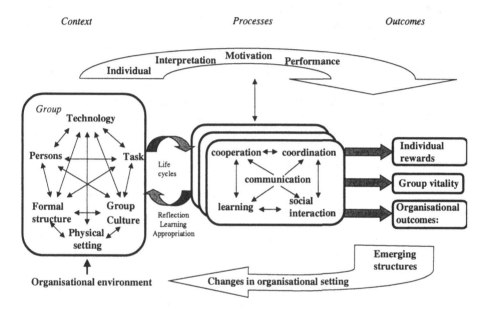

Figure 8.2 The Dynamic Group Interaction Model (DGIn -model)

The model has the following basic tenets:

- The effectiveness of a group depends on the quality of five group processes, which in their turn depend on the extent to which six types of conditions (aspects of the context-of-use) support them and on the interaction with the environment.
- The five processes have to fit to each other.
- The six aspects of the context-of-use have to fit to each other.
- The effectiveness of a (groupware) tool depends therefore on:
  a. the characteristics of the tool
  b. the fit to the other conditions
  c. the extent to which it in practice supports (or at least does not hinder) the group processes and the attainment of the outcomes
- Groups develop and tools become adopted and adapted to, through interaction processes and feedback.

The DGIn model is constructed along three dimensions. A specification of the variables involved can be found in Table 8.1 and Appendix 1.

Dimension 1. Three levels of interaction: individual, group and organisation
Individual tool use and task performance is part of group interaction which in its turn is nested in organisational activities, influenced by wider environmental forces. In this book the focus is on the co-operative and group processes, which therefore are central in this model. However, many aspects of a group, such as its task, its membership, its resources etc. may come from the environment. Moreover, groups constantly interact with the environment.

Dimension 2. Context-of-use (input) – processes – output
Social systems can be described in terms of three types of elements: context-of-use characteristics, processes and outcomes:

a. The *context-of-use* refers to the characteristics of the tools, of the tasks, of the individuals, of the group (structure and culture), of its physical setting and of the (organisational) environment. These characteristics may change gradually as a result of the processes taking place (see dimension 3). Systems theory states that the context-of-use characteristics have to match each other. In the case of the development and introduction of collaboration tools this implies that new tools have to match the existing context aspects.

b. *Processes*. The context-of-use factors are determinants of, but also changed by, certain processes and activities. The following processes can be distinguished:

• Individual activities (see Chapter 4):
    1. *Perception, interpretation and motivation* concerning the context-of-use elements, as a basis for:
    2. *Motivated effort expenditure in task oriented activities* and *exploration.*
• Group interaction processes (see Chapter 6). The major activities in co-operative settings can be ordered into *basic categories of interaction*. The basic interaction types are task- and group oriented processes, which are both based on communication:

    1. *Communication*: This process is of a different nature than the other processes. Communication refers to the exchange of signals, to the issue of verbal and non-verbal interaction. It is basic to and part of information sharing, co-ordination, co-operation and social interaction.
    2. *Task-oriented processes*:

        • *Information sharing and learning*, i.e. exchanging (sharing) and developing information, views, knowledge.
        • *Co-operation*, i.e. working together, applying one's knowledge and skills and using appropriate performance strategies in e.g. decision making, designing a new system or organising a conference.
        • *Co-ordination*, i.e. adjusting the work of the group members to each other and to the goals of the group.

3.   *Group-maintenance oriented* processes or *Social Interaction*. This refers to team building to develop trust and cohesion, to power oriented behaviour and to reflection on team activities and team development.

c.   *Outcomes*. The interaction processes result in *outcomes*, i.e. *final outcomes* and *feedback effects*. *Feedback effects* are discussed below (Dimension 3).
     Final outcomes are of three types:

- Organisational outcomes, i.e. products related to the task performance and task effectiveness and innovation.
- Group related outcomes, such as group rewards and group vitality.
- Individual rewards such as insights, satisfaction, salary, stress.

Dimension 3. Feedback, appropriation and reflection
Both the interaction processes and the outcomes result in feedback processes, by which the original context-of-use factors are changed. Groups build cohesion and trust, shared knowledge and new task definitions through interaction. Tools will be appropriated and adapted, new ways of interaction are developed. This feedback takes place *directly* as a result of the interaction processes, or *indirectly* via the route of outcomes and their effect on organisational processes. They can *emerge unplanned*, develop slowly in daily practice, or they can be the result of *explicit reflection* of the group on its functioning and explicit change (see sections 7.2 and 7.3).

      This implicit or explicit reflection is the result of *contradictions* between the elements in the model (see Activity Theory, Section 6.3). One source of contradiction is the difference between the goals of the subject and the actual results. According to Bardram's model (Section 6.3) contradictions may be reflected in breakdowns, i.e. in moments when tools or procedures do not function properly and become the object of attention. Then two types of reflection may take place, i.e. simple reflection to find a direct solution to the problem at hand and secondary reflection to set up new rules, change norms or other aspects of the context-of-use. One may even say that unless the context-of-use changes, collaboration technology tools have not had their full potential innovative impact.

      An important characteristic of the model is related to these feedback, learning and group development effects. They imply that the context-of-use characteristics are both input and output of the processes. They may both be depicted at the left side of Figure 8.2 and also at the right side. While interacting, trust and cohesion develop or deteriorate, group members develop new skills, task get redefined and the group structure may change.

8.3.3 The Organisational Tool Adoption Perspective

The introduction of collaboration technology tools and services is part of a larger process of technology development and diffusion, and of introduction and appropriation. This is partly a general process of technology diffusion in society and partly a user-organisation based process of implementing specific applications. Notions from diffusion – adoption theory, planned change and appropriation theory are combined in Figure 8.3.

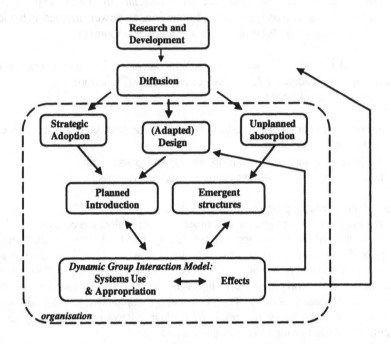

Figure 8.3 Model of technology development and adoption

The models in Figure 8.1 and 8.2 are related to the model given in Figure 8.3, where they form the specifications of the lowest box. In the case of collaboration technology organisations can follow three courses of action. Firstly, they can officially adopt and buy a new system off-the-shelf, introducing it through a systematic course of strategic adoption and a planned change programme. Secondly, an organisation-specific system can be designed and developed. This system is often an adaptation from a generic system. Finally, the introduction can follow a process of unplanned up-take by certain individuals and low profile absorption by the organisation, resulting in the emergence of new ways of working and interacting. In some cases the unplanned penetration comes first and is then followed by the strategic adoption and planned introduction in the entire organisation. This happens when management discovers its potential value, or simply wants to prevent chaotic proliferation of new systems.

In all cases however, new systems are used, interaction processes and the new system are adapted to each other, and effects become visible. The life cycle design approach is represented by the feedback loops. More or less systematic evaluation can result in a change in system requirements, which are then introduced in a new version of the system.

8.4 Design Requirements and Evaluation Criteria

From the previous chapters, visualised in Figures 8.1, 8.2 and 8.3 seven groups of issues and questions can be derived for the design and therefore for the evaluation of CT-tools (Table 8.1). Since these tools are part of a socio-technical setting, i.e. used by (groups of) people for certain tasks in a physical and organisational context, design is not (only) a matter of tool design but (also) of socio-technical system design. Evaluating the effectiveness of a tool, i.e. *tool evaluation*, is therefore one step, but ideally it should be complemented with evaluating the effectiveness of the total (new) work arrangement in which the tool is functioning, i.e. *socio-technical system evaluation*. The term "system" in Table 8.1 can therefore refer both to technical tools and to group settings.

Table 8.1 Design and evaluation parameters following from the DGIn -model

1. **Technical efficacy:** Tools should have the basic technical quality properties, such as *functionality, reliability / robustness, portability, maintainability, infrastructural efficiency.*
2. **Context match: Fitting the users**: Systems have to be easy to use and attractive (=usability). Relevant theory: Action Theory (Section 4.2).
3. **Context match: Matching the task.** Systems have to have the functionalities that are needed for the task. Groupware tools do not necessarily have to support all tasks of the group, but designers should be aware of the following issues: • group members have not only co-operative tasks but also individual tasks   • groups can have multiple tasks and work methods, synchronously and over time; they may redefine their tasks and methods as a result of experiences and external influences.   Relevant theories: Technology acceptance model (Section 4.4). Media Match theories (Section 5).
4. **Context match: Matching the social and physical setting.** Systems should match group structure, composition and culture, be compatible with the physical setting and open to interaction with the environment. Relevant theories: Social Psychological and Group Dynamic theories.
5. **Interaction process support**. Systems should support the intended processes adequately and not hinder other processes. The processes are: individual and co-operative task performance, communication, sharing information and knowledge (learning), co-ordination, and social interaction. Relevant theories: Communication theories, Theories of group dynamics and team effectiveness; Activity Theory.
6. **Outcome support**. The degree to which use of the tool contributes to intended outcomes, does not hinder other outcomes and contributes to the development of new practices. This includes the criteria related to task outcomes (products), individual user outcomes, group outcomes and organisational outcomes. Relevant theories: Theories concerning quality of work, of group dynamics and of organisational effectiveness.
7. **Introduction, adaptation and group development.** Tools and groups should be adaptable to each other and to the environment. Tools should be tailorable and open to appropriation. Groups should be reflective and open to team building. Relevant theories: Adaptive Structuration Theory (Section 4.8), Change theories (Chapter 7).

In summary, the value of a tool is related to the extent to which it has appropriate characteristics (including usability) and functionalities, the degree to which it fits the context-of-use and to which it supports (or at least does not hinder) group processes and the attainment of outcomes. These design requirements are translatable into evaluation criteria.

Measuring and analysing these issues has been dealt with in various research communities and disciplines (Andriessen, 1996):

a. *Analysis of human computer interaction* in the HCI community: analysis of the extent to which the system-interface influences e.g. mental load and the way individuals use the system. This type of analysis is not specific to distributed interaction, but applicable to all kinds of (individual) computer use. Performance measurement, observational methods, psycho-physiological indicators and questionnaire methods for evaluation have been developed (e.g. Howard and Murray, 1987; Nielsen, 1992a; Houwing et al., 1993).

b. *Analysis of conversations and communication behaviour* by researchers in the area of communication sciences and CSCW, i.e. analysis of the extent to which a system influences the way people interact and exchange information (e.g. Sellen, 1994). Three approaches can be found at this level of analysis:

  - Analysis of *conversational structure* (number or length of utterances, of interruptions or overlaps, pause length) or of (non-verbal) *communicative behaviour* such as glances (Tang and Isaacs, 1993) or breakdowns (Urquijo et al, 1993).
  - Analysis of *conversation content*. Many coding schemas exist.
  - *Questionnaire ratings*, particularly of social presence and of awareness of the setting of the other participant(s).

c. *Media choice and media role*. In a third tradition, particularly among communication scientists, the choices between several media and the determinants of the choices have been studied. In these studies attention is focused on organizational processes and the role media can play in making the organization more efficient or effective (e.g. Fulk and Steinfield, 1990; Van Veen, 1993). Within the CSCW community this focus is also penetrating (Sellen, 1994; Kraut et.al., 1994). This type of research is most often done through questionnaires and interview, sometimes supported by logging media use.

d. *Social interaction analysis*, particularly by social psychologists and sociologists; they study co-operative tasks and group processes and the effect of media use thereupon. This type of analysis is based on observation and registration techniques and on data from questionnaires.

  - *Activity registration*, (continuous or retrospective) by participants themselves (e.g. of time, medium and partner of communication), or automatic logging by the system. Social network analysis can be performed on the basis of this type of data, resulting in patterns of interactions.
  - *Interaction-content coding*, based on observation techniques and event marking. Bales and Cohen (1979) have developed a comprehensive observation schema for group discussions.
  - *Questionnaires* concerning aspects of group interaction in general have been developed. Quick-and-dirty scales abound for evaluating distributed interaction, but instruments with tested psychometric properties are not widely available.

8.5   A Design Oriented Evaluation Process

The *what* of evaluation is discussed in the previous section, i.e. the issues that are relevant to study when evaluating a new tool or new socio-technical system. The question *when* and *how* evaluation can be performed is answered in this last section. The approach presented here can be characterised as "design oriented evaluation". It is inspired by the approaches presented in Section 7.2 and based upon work done in the framework of a European Union sponsored project (the MEGATAQ project, Andriessen et al. 1997). During this project a general approach was developed, and also a set of specific tools to support the evaluation processes. It is based on the following principles:

- Evaluation should be integrated in the design process from the very beginning.
- The design and the evaluation process should be iterative and stakeholder centred; critical success factors of stakeholders should be formulated.
- Future usage scenarios can support the identification of design requirements and evaluation criteria.
- Evaluation can take place at three periods in the design life cycle: before, during and after designing the new system, i.e. through "concept evaluation", "prototype evaluation" and "operational evaluation" (see also Eason and Olpert, 1996).

   a. Concept evaluation. An analysis of stakeholder success-criteria and of the, quality of work and organisational efficiency are at stake. The potential impacts of the new (socio-technical) system can be made on the basis of one or more future scenarios, i.e. ideas about future settings,. This analysis will contribute to (re)orientation on the design, and to the (re)formulation of design requirements. Design requirements and other results from scenario discussions may form the basis for formulating criteria against which the impacts of the new system will be assessed.

   b. Prototype evaluation: When a prototype of a new system is developed, tests can be applied. This is often limited to the question of whether the application or new work setting function as they were planned and whether human interfaces are user friendly. Such tests are often qualitative and informal in nature and performed in a usability lab, where all user reactions can be registered and analysed systematically. Speed of performance, errors and subjectively appreciated usability aspects may be relevant criteria.

   c. Operational assessment: The impact on the functioning of the work unit can be evaluated when a new work setting has settled and a technical system has been in operational use for a certain period of time. Issues of communication, social interaction, quality of work and organisational efficiency are at stake. The choice of the evaluation approach, i.e. of the aspects and methods, of the moments and samples for data collection, depends on the type of questions that have to be answered, and on the time, money and expertise available.

The iterative and stakeholder oriented design process is presented in Figure 8.4.

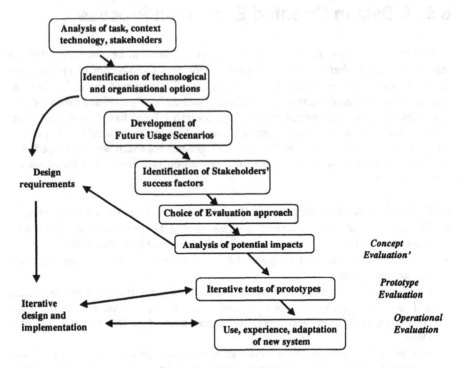

Figure 8.4 Evaluation and Design Model

The design oriented evaluation approach has the following steps:

Situational analysis
In this stage the current situation is the subject of study. This step in the process should result in information concerning the following aspects:

- existing problems and intended solutions.
- characteristics of users, task, context and of the workflow.
- stakeholders and their goals and interests.
- existing norms (e.g. ISO standards) and conditions.
- technological developments: relevant existing and expected technologies, platforms, tools, and applications.

Tools for the analysis of several of these elements are available (e.g. Beyer and Holtzblatt, 1966).

Future usage scenario construction
A (future) *usage scenario* is a description of an (as yet imaginary) setting that is expected to become reality when the new system is implemented. It involves identifying the *users* who will be involved and their required characteristics, the *tasks* that these users will have to complete and their *responsibilities*, the new *application* or service and its expected use, the various types of *potential*

interactions and *outcomes*, and the *context* in which the new application or service will be used (Anker, 2002).

The construction of (a) scenario(s) may help to identify both the explicit success criteria of the stakeholders and other, less intended potential benefits or negative impacts of the new setting. These potential positive and negative consequences can then be used for the formulation of design requirements and the criteria against which to evaluate the potential success of the new system.

Identification of stakeholder success criteria
Stakeholder success criteria are the criteria on the basis of which a stakeholder will decide that the new system or situation is a success. For example, for management of a hospital one of the success criteria for a new patient administration system will be that it delivers bills faster to the patients than the existing system.

Selection of evaluation approach, methods and tools
At this stage the type of research design is chosen, e.g. experiment, survey or case study. Also the methods for data collection are chosen and the evaluation plan developed, including number of users, time and place for data collection.

Systematic analysis of potential impacts: Concept evaluation
When a scenario is chosen as the to-be-designed future, it is possible to identify the explicit success criteria of the various stakeholders for the new system and also other potential impacts (see Box 8.1).

Box 8.1

Problem oriented teaching is a modern type of higher education method, applied in several Dutch universities and academies. At one of the universities a groupware tool has been developed to support the co-operation of students in the periods between the weekly meetings. It will enable students to search in libraries, to co-author a document and to exchange messages. By applying the scenario approach it was discovered that the designers had not fully appreciated the role of a co-ordinator and the relationship with other communication media such as the telephone and meetings at the coffee shop. Via discussions with several stakeholders new criteria for evaluation were identified.

So this *concept evaluation* consists of a systematic discussion of the potential impact of the new system on the aspects of Table 8.1.

Actual evaluation and analysis: Prototype evaluation and Operational evaluation
This phase can consist of many steps, from alpha tests in the laboratory (early evaluation) to analysis of the operational use of the system in an organisation.

Analysis and report of results
Evaluation can be done in many different ways ranging from very simple and informal to very sophisticated. The choice depends on the situation, i.e. on the research questions and on the money and time available for the project, and the existing expertise (Box 8.2.). In some cases the methods have to be tailor-made. In the field of human computer interaction several methods have already been developed and can be used as they are or with small adaptations. Appendix 2

contains some examples of evaluation methods collected in the framework of the
MEGATAQ research project (Andriessen et al. 1998).

Box 8.2

The objective of Project X was the evaluation and improvement of a multimedia
tool for group co-operation. Several types of evaluation data were collected. First a
standardised questionnaire to measure the usability of the tool was presented to two
user groups. This questionnaire contains questions concerning the perceived
satisfaction, learnability, helpfulness and efficiency of a multimedia system. The
reactions to the questionnaire showed that the users were reasonably positive about
the system. However, to be able to derive more specific recommendations, and
requirements for system adaptation, specific *semi-structured interviews* with the
same user groups were held. Through a separate and *tailor made questionnaire* the
desirability of certain new features of the next release was gauged. Finally the *log
files* containing data on the messages exchanged were analysed to discover the
frequency with which the system functions were used. Specific recommendations
concerning the new release of the system could be made on the basis of these data.

8.6 Ten Guidelines

The previous chapters have discussed all kinds of issues that have to be taken into
account when developing a co-operative setting that is supported by groupware.
The major ones can be summarised in the following guidelines:

1. Groupware is part of a social system. Design not for a tool as such but for a new
   socio-technical setting.
2. Design for several levels of interaction, i.e. for user friendly human computer
   interaction, adequate interpersonal communication, group co-operation and
   organisational functioning.
3. Design in a participative way, i.e. users and possibly other stakeholders should
   be part of the design process from the beginning.
4. Analyse carefully the situation of the users. Success of collaboration technology
   depends on the use and the users, not on the technology. Introduction should
   match their skills and abilities, and also their attitudes, otherwise resistance is
   inevitable.
5. Analyse carefully the context, since success of collaboration technology
   depends on the fit to that context. The more a new setting deviates from the
   existing one the more time, energy and other resources should be mobilised to
   make it a success.
6. Introduce the new system carefully. Apply proper project management, find a
   champion, try a pilot, inform people intensively.
7. Train and support end-users extensively.
8. Measure success conditions and success criteria before, during and after the
   development process. Only in this way you can learn for future developments.
9. Plan for a long process of introduction, incorporation, evaluation and adaptation.
   Groupware is not a quick fix.

10. Despite careful preparations groupware is appropriated and adapted in unforeseen ways. Keep options open for new ways of working with the groupware, because this may result in creative and innovative processes.

Appendix 1. Evaluation Issues

1. **Technical efficacy:** Tools should have the basic quality properties, partly (1-5) specified in the ISO standard ISO/IEC9126:

1. *Functionalities:* the tool should be able to do what it is promised to do.
2. *Reliability / robustness:* degree of vulnerability against crashes, errors made etc.
3. *Portability (technical compatibility):* degree to which the tool fits to other technical systems, to different platforms; is system web based and available from everywhere.
4. *Maintainability:* degree to which a tool can be maintained despite new versions.
5. *Infrastructural efficiency:* relatively low costs of infrastructure and other equipment needed for optimal performance of the tool.
6. *Network performance:* adequate speed of information exchange and communication, adequate bandwidth, good audio quality.
7. *Adaptability:* degree to which tool can be adapted to task requirements or user's preferences.
8. *Costs:* of purchase, maintenance, implementation of peripherals and infrastructure, plus training of users.
9. *Security and Privacy.*

2. **Context Match: Fitting the users**: The extent to which the interface of the tool is easy to use and attractive (usability issues). The following criteria can be specified:

1. *Adaptation to user's characteristics:*

   - Capacities, including handicaps.
   - Language and cultural differences.
   - Knowledge, skills and values, with regard to performing the task, handling the tools, co-operation (including "communication competence").
   - Attitudes towards tools in general.

2. *Simple way of operation, easy to use.*
3. *Consistency in operation.*
4. *Support of action preparation and action modification* (see Action Theory).
5. *Efficiency:* degree to which the user is able to achieve the objectives of the interaction with the application with minimal effort (see action facilitation concept in Action Theory).

6. *Control:* degree to which the user feels he/she is in control of what happens (and not the application); one way to achieve this is through *giving sufficient feedback* about activities and position.
7. *Affect / Excitement:* degree to which using the application is exciting and fun for the user.
8. *Support:* degree to which the application provides assistance to the user.
9. *Learnability:* the ease with which a user can get started and learn new features.

3. **Context Match: Fitting task, group and setting.** The degree to which the objective and subjective characteristics of a tool matches the characteristics of the goal and tasks, group culture and structure, physical resources and organisational characteristics.

1. *Required functionalities:* degree to which the tool has the functionalities that are required for the tasks and by the user(s), i.e. adequate for:

- Task modes: e.g. idea generation, problem solving decision making, negotiation, execution.
- Task dimensions: complexity, interdependence.
- Task quality: variety, autonomy, task identity, task significance, and task feedback (see 4.4.2).

2. Providing *adequate information:* accurate, reliable, up-to-date information.
3. *Perceived usefulness and relative advantage:* the extent to which the tools are perceived by the individuals as useful and better than (existing) alternatives.
4. *Media richness:* degree to which a communication tool has the bandwidth that is required by task and users.
5. *Fitting the group (social compatibility):* the degree to which (using) an innovation is perceived as being consistent with:

- *Group structure:* e.g. composition and task/role distribution (incl. leader).
- *Group culture:* trust, cohesion, norms and values; shared knowledge.

6. Fitting the *organisational context:* financial resources, organisation culture, and critical mass.
7. Fitting the *physical context:* noise/light/temperature, geographical distance, accessibility of tools.

4. **Interaction support.** Degree to which the tool supports adequately the intended processes and does not hinder other processes. Quality of the support (and non-hindrance) can be analysed in terms of frequency of tool usage, speed of performance, ease of use, mental load, and errors.
    Availability of support depends on the existing functionalities. Examples of systems that are intended to support the various interaction types below are given in Table 1.1 (Types of collaboration technologies).

1. *Individual task performance:*

- Support for individual, private, task performance.

2. *Co-operative task performance:*

- Support for required activities: e.g. idea generation, problem solving, group decision making, negotiation, execution; execution may imply: co-drawing, co-creating documents, co-Web browsing, etc.
- Speed and quality of collaboration.

3. *Communication:*

- Support of synchronous and asynchronous communication within the group.
- Support of communication with environment.
- Support for awareness:
  Member activity awareness
  Member availability awareness
  Process awareness
  Environmental awareness
  Member Background awareness
- Effect on type, quantity and quality of interpersonal conversation, on exchange of non-verbal signals.

4. *Sharing information and knowledge (learning):*

- Adequate support for shared storing and retrieving information (sufficient storage capacity).
- Support for learning processes.

5. *Co-ordination:*

- Support for assigning roles and tasks.
- Support for planning, scheduling.
- Support for various co-ordination mechanism (see Section 6.7).

6. *Social interaction:*

- Building trust and cohesion.
- Ease of informal interaction.
- Equalised participation.
- Power gaming / conflict handling.

5.   Outcome effects. Degree to which use of the tool contributes to intended outcomes, does not hinder other outcomes and contributes to the development of new practices.

1. *Feedback effects on Input factors:*

- Changed task structure.
- Changed quality of work.
- New individual capacities and attitudes required.

- New group characteristics required.

2. *Product outcomes:*

- Effectiveness: volume, quality, flexibility of products/service.
- Efficiency: costs, speed of delivery.
- Innovation: new products.

3. *User outcomes:*

- Satisfaction with using the tool (fun), with the interaction and work processes and with outcomes.
- Information overload, stress.
- Privacy, behaviour control.
- Individual rewards: learning, status, social contacts.

4. *Group vitality:*

- Cohesion, identity
- Life span

5. *Organisational effects:*

- Market position: efficiency, effectiveness and innovation with regard to product delivery (speed), (Hammer and Mangurian, 1987).
- Effects on wider community.

6. **Introduction and adaptation.** The degree to which the conditions are favourable for an adequate process of development, adoption and adaptation of the tool:

1. *Involvement* of users and other stakeholders.
2. *Training and support.*
3. *Triability:* the degree to which the tool may be experimented with before adoption.
4. *Image:* the degree to which use of the tool is perceived to enhance one's image or status in one's social system (social approval).
5. *Voluntariness of use:* the degree to which the use of the tool is perceived as being voluntary.
6. *Tailorability:* the degree to which the tool can be changed and adapted to the user's preferences.

In the framework of a European Union sponsored project (the MEGATAQ project, Andriessen et al. 1997), extended checklists concerning these issues were developed and calibrated instruments to assess certain factors collected (see Appendix 3).

Appendix 2. Effective Teams

Important overviews and meta-analyses of characteristics of effective and innovative teams can be found in the following literature: Anderson and West, 1992; Campion et al., 1996; Guzzo and Dickson, 1996; Hackman, 1987; Larson and Defasto, 1989; McGrath, 1984; McGrath, 1990; McIntyre and Salas, 1996; Tjosvold, 1992. The main clusters of conditions for group effectiveness are aspects of the environment, group characteristics and group processes:

A. Environmental aspects

- organisational and physical context
- mission clarity
- autonomy
- strong managerial support
- adequate feedback
- group-oriented rewards system, including adequate recognition
- training and consultation
- supportive physical environment and material resources

B. Group characteristics

- Goals: clear common goals, standards of excellence, results driven.
- Group Structure (composition): clear roles and accountabilities (e.g. facilitator or leader), size, limited power/status relations, competent team members, sufficient diversity in composition (Guzzo and Dickson, 1996).
- Group Culture: trust, team spirit, mutual social support, single team identity, shared values, norms, meanings and knowledge.

The various aspects of culture are to some extent related, giving rise to certain specific group cultures or organisational cultures. Many taxonomies of organisational cultures can be found. According to Quin's Competing Values Approach (Quin and Rohrbach 1983) four types can be distinguished:
- *Supportive:* characterised by co-operation, mutual trust, commitment, individual growth and informal communication.
- *Innovative*: creative, experimenting, with informal and lateral communication.
- *Goal orientation and competition*: achievement oriented; competitive (internal and external).

- *Rules orientation (bureaucratic)*: formalised, hierarchical, respect for authority, rational procedures, and vertical formal communication.

C. Group Processes

- Intensive and adequate communication.
- Co-operation: workload sharing, intensive interaction.
- Adequate co-ordination and leadership.
- Effective relational behaviour: participation, conflict management.
- Adequate information sharing and learning.
- Adequate reflection on performance (West, 1996), resulting in effective team development.

Appendix 3: Examples of Assessment Tools

In the European Union sponsored MEGATAQ project (Andriessen et al. 1998) many methods and tools for the assessment of the quality of ICT applications and ICT supported cooperation were collected. The methods and tools are clustered in seven groups. From each cluster one or a few examples are given. Between brackets the total number of tools per cluster.

1. Inspection methods (8)	
• Heuristic Evaluation	Heuristic evaluation incorporates usability expert studies to identify any potential weaknesses in the design of an interface.
2. Performance analysis(2)	
• Human Reliability Analysis	HRA is used to measure the reliability of the interaction between man and machines by analysing errors.
3. Behaviour analysis (3)	
• Diagnostic Recorder for Usability Measurement (DRUM)	DRUM is a software tool that provides assistance throughout the process of usability evaluation, by recording various aspects of user performance, such as the duration of task activities and the occurrence of errors.
4. Effort and satisfaction (6)	
• NASA-Task Load IndeX (NASA-TLX)	The TLX provides an indication of cognitive workload, based on a weighted average of ratings on six sub-scales.
• Measuring the Usability of Multi-Media Systems (MUMMS)	The MUMMS is a questionnaire, concerned with the users' perception of and satisfaction with six usability-aspects of Multi-Media applications: helpfulness, learnability, efficiency, control, affect and excitement.
• MultiMedia Communication Questionnaire (MMCQ)	The MMCQ is a questionnaire for assessing the quality of on-line communication such as video-conferencing.

5. *Task aspects and relations(2)*	
• Extended Delft Measurement Kit	The EDMK or Quality of Working Life Questionnaire contains a set of well-tested questionnaire modules used to measure aspects of work and organisation such as task characteristics, relationships, conditions and terms of employment, characteristics of work behaviour and expenditure of effort.
6. *Network performance (11)*	
• NetPerf	NetPerf is a software tool that can measure aspects of tele-communication network performance, such as speed of transmission and CPU time.
7. *System usage and interaction registration (5)*	
• Computer logging	Automatic registration of the use of the system and of separate functionalities.
• Coding schemes for communication content	Analytical schemes for coding the type of words or expressions in computer mediated communication.

References

Ajzen, I. (1991). The Theory of Planned Behaviour. *Organisational Behaviour and Human Decision Processes, 50*, pp. 179-211.

Alderfer, C. P. (1972). *Existence, relatedness and growth.* New York: Free Press.

Algera, J.A., Koopman, P.L. & Vijlbrief, H.P.J., (1989). Management strategies in introducing computer-based information systems. *Applied Psychology: An international review, 38(1)*, pp. 87-103.

Allee, V. (2000). *Knowledge Networks and Communities of Practice.* Available: http://www.odnetwork.org/odponline/vol32n4/knowledgenets.html.

Allen, T. J. (1977). *Managing the flow of technology.* Cambridge MA: MIT Press.

Ancona, D. G., & Caldwell, D. F. (1990). Information Technology and work groups: the case of new product teams. In J. Galegher, R. E. Kraut & C. Egido (Eds.), *Intellectual Teamwork: Social and technological foundations of co-operative work.* Hillsdale, NJ: Lawrence Erlbaum Publ.

Anderson, N. R., & West, M. A. (1992). *Climate for workgroup innovation.*

Andriessen, J. H. E. (1990). *Computer supported consultation or conversation. The case of digital image networks in hospitals.* Paper presented at the International Conference Computer, Man and Organisation II, Nivelles, Belgium.

Andriessen, J. H. E. (1991). Mediated communication and new organisational forms. In C.L.Cooper & I.T.Robinson (Eds.), *International Review of Industrial and Organizational Psychology*: New York: John Wiley.

Andriessen, J. H. E. (1994a). Telematics and Innovation. Conditions for adoption, implementation and incorporation of electronic communication systems. In J. H. E. Andriessen & R. A. Roe (Eds.), *Telematics and work.* Hove, Sussex (UK): Lawrence Erlbaum.

Andriessen, J.H.E. (1994b). The introduction of networking technology in organizations. Increasing freedom and control. Contribution for the KNAW/KLI Symposium. Amsterdam, June 1994.

Andriessen, J. H. E. (1996). The why, how and what to evaluate of interaction technology: A review and proposed integration. In P.Thomas (Ed.), *CSCW requirements and evaluation.* London: Springer.Verlag

Andriessen, J. H. E., & Roe, R. A. (1994). *Telematics and Work.* Hove, Sussex: Lawrence Erlbaum.

Andriessen, J. H. E., & Velden, J. M. van der (1993). Teamwork supported by interaction technology. The beginning of an integrated theory. *The European Work and Organizational Psychologist, 3*, pp. 129-144.

Andriessen, J. H. E., Koorn, R., Arnold, A. G., Anderson, A., Fleming, A., McLeod, J. J., & Mullin, J. (1997). *Assessing user aspects of telematics applications. The Megataq approach with Provisional Guidelines for Assessment Tools.* Report for the European Union Telematics Applications Project MEGATAQ, TE 2007, deliverable 4.2.

Anker, F. v. d. (2002). *Mobile Multimedia Communications: The development and evaluation of scenarios for co-operative work.* PhD Thesis. Delft, The Netherlands.

Anker, & van den Lichtveld, R. A. (1999). Early evaluation of new technologies: The case of mobile multimedia communications for emergency medicine. In C. Vincent & B. de Mol (Eds.), *Risk and safety in medicine: From human error to organisational learning.* Oxford: Elsevier Science.

Applebaum, E., & Blatt, R. (1994). *The new American Workplace.* Ithaca, NY: ILR.

Arnold, A. G., & van der Velden, J. (1992). A user centred evaluation of an on line library system for (re)design purposes. In H. Kragt (Ed.), *Enhancing industrial performance: experiences of integrating the human factor.* London-Washington DC: Taylor Francis.

Arnold, A. G. (1998). *Action facilitation and interface evaluation. A work psychological approach to the development of usable software.* Delft, The Netherlands: Delft University Press,.

Aydin, C., & Rice, R. E. (1989). *Social worlds, implementation, and individual differences: predicting attitudes toward a medical information system.* Paper presented at the Technology and Innovation Management Division of Academy of Management Annual Conference, Washington, D.C.

Bair, J. H. (1989). *Supporting co-operative work with computers: addressing meeting mania.* Paper presented at the 34th IEEE Computer society international conference - COMPCON, San Francisco.

Bair, J. H. (1991). A layered model of organizations: Communication processes and performance. *Journal of Organizational Computing, 1*, pp. 187-203.

Bajaj, A., & Nidumolu, S. R. (1998). A feedback model to understand information system usage. *Information and Management, 33*, pp. 213-224.

Bales, R. F., & Cohen, S. P. (1979). *Symlog: a system for the Multiple Level Observation of Groups.* New York: Free Press.

Bannon, L. J., & Schmidt, K. (1989). *CSCW: Four characters in Search of a Context. Proceedings of First European Conference on CSCW - E CSCW 89*, London.

Bardram, J. E. (1997). Plans as situated action: An activity theory approach to workflow systems. In J. Hughes & W. Prinz & K. Schmidt & T. Rodden (Eds.), *ECSCW '97. Proceedings of the Fifth European Conference on Computer Supported Cooperative Work.* Dordrecht: Kluwer.

Bardram, J. (1998). Designing for the dynamics of co-operative work activities. *CSCW' 98. Proceedings of the conference on Computer supported cooperative work.* New York: ACM.

Barley, S. R. (1986). Technology as an occasion for structuring: Evidence from observations of CT scanners and the social order of radiology departments. *Administrative Science Quarterly, 31*, pp. 78-108.

Benford, S., Greenhalgh, C., Rodden, T., & Pycock, J. (2001). Collaborative virtual environments. *Communications of the ACM, 44, 7*, pp. 79-85.

Benbasat, I., & Lim, L. H. (1993). The effects of group, task, context and technology variables on the usefulness of group support systems: a meta analysis of experimental studies. *Small Group Research, 24*(4), pp. 430-462.

Beyer, H. & Holtzblatt, K. (1998). *Contextual design: Defining Customer-centered Systems.* San Francisco: Morgan Kaufmann, 1998.

Bismarck, W. v., Bungard, W., Maslo, J., & Held, M. (2000). Developing a system to support informal communication. In M. Vartiainen & F. Avalone & N. Anderson (Eds.), *Innovative theories, tools and practices in work and Organisational Psychology.* Seattle: Hogrefe & Huber.

Björn-Andersen, N., Eason, K., & Robey, D. (1986). *Managing Computer Input. An international study.* Norwood N.Y: Able.

Blackler, F. (1995). Activity theory, CSCW and organizations. In A. F. Monk & N. Gilbert (Eds.), *Perspectives on HCI. Diverse approaches.* London: Academic Press.

Blau, P. M. (1970). *On the nature of organisations.* New York: John Wiley.

Bly, S., Harrison, S. R., & Irwin, S. (1993). Media Spaces: bringing people together in a video, audio and computing environment. *Communications of the ACM, 36*(1), pp. 28-47.

Boehm, B. (1988). A spiral model of software development enhancement. *IEEE Computer, 21*, pp. 61-72.

Bullen, C., & Bennet, J. (1990). Learning from user experience with groupware. *CSCW'90. Proceedings of the conference on Computer supported cooperative work.* New York: ACM.

Busch, E., Hamalainen, M., Suh, Y., Whinston, A., & Holsapple, D. (1991). Issues and obstacles in the development of team support systems. *Journal of Organizational Computing, 1*, pp. 161-186.

Campion, M. A., Papper, E., & Medsger, G. (1996). Relations between work team characteristics and effectiveness: a replication and extension. *Personnel Psychology, 49*, p429-451.

Cannon-Bowers, J. A., & Salas, E. S. (2001). Reflections on shared cognition. *Journal of Organizational Behavior, 22*, p195-202.

Cannon-Bowers, J. A., Tannenbaum, S. I., Salas, E., & Volpe, C. A. (1995). Defining competencies and establishing team training requirements. In R. A. Guzzo & E. Salas & Associates (Eds.), *Team effectiveness and decision making in organizations.* San Francisco: Jossey-Bass Publishers.

Carroll, J. M. (1995). *Scenario-based design. Envisioning work and technology in systems development.* New York: John Wiley.

Chapanis, A., Ochsman, R.B., Parrish, R.N. & Weeks, G.D. (1972). Studies in interactive communication: I The effects of four communication modes on the behaviour of teams during cooperative problem solving. *Human Factors, 14*, pp. 487-509.

Ciborra, C. U. (1987). Research agenda for a transactions costs approach to information systems. In R. J. Boland & R. A. Hirschheim (Eds.), *Critical issues in information systems research.* London: John Wiley.

Ciborra, C.U. (1996). *Groupware and Teamwork, Invisible Aid or Technical Hindrance?* New York: John Wiley & Sons.

Ciborra, C. U., & Lanzara, G. F. (1994). Designing networks in action. Formative contexts and post-modern systems development. In J. H. E. Andriessen & R. A. Roe (Eds.), *Telematics and work..* Hove, Sussex (UK): Lawrence Erlbaum

Clark, H. H., & Brennan, S. E. (1991). Grounding in Communication. In L. B. Resnick & J. M. Levine & S. D. Teasley (Eds.), *Perspectives on Socially Shared Cognition* (pp. 127-149). Washington: American Psychological Association.

Coleman, D. (Ed.). (1997). *Groupware: Collaborative Strategies for corporate LANs and Intranets*. Englewoods Cliff, NJ: Prentice Hall.

Cooke, N. J., Salas, E., Cannon-Bowers, J. A., & Stout, R. J. (2000). Measuring team knowledge. *Human Factors, 42*(1), pp. 151-173.

Culnan, M. J. (1985). The dimensions of perceived accessibility to information: implications for the delivery of information systems and services. *Journal of the American Society of Information Systems, 36*(5), pp. 302-308.

Daft, R. D., & Lengel, R. H. (1984). Information richness: a new approach to managerial behavior and organizational design. In B. Staw & L. L. Cummings (Eds.), *Research in organizational behavior, 6*, pp. 191-233. Greenwich, CT: JAI Press.

Davis, D. D. (1995). Form, function and strategy in boundaryless organizations. In A. Howard (Ed.), *The changing nature of work*. San Francisco: Jossey-Bass.

Davis, F. D. (1989). Perceived Usefulness, Perceived Ease of Use, and User Acceptance of Information Technology. *MIS Quarterly*(September), pp. 319-340.

Davis, F. D. (1993). User acceptance of information technology: system characterisics, user perceptions and behavioral impact. *International Journal of Man-Machine studies, 38*, pp. 475-487.

Dennis, A. R., Valacich, J. S., Speier, C., & Morris, M. G. (1998). Beyond media richness: An empirical test of media synchronicity theory. *Proceedings of the 31st Hawaii International Conference on System Sciences (HICSS'98)*.

DeSanctis, G., & Gallupe, R. B. (1987). A foundation for the study of group decision support systems. *Management Science, 33*(5), pp. 589-609.

DeSanctis, G., & Poole, M. S. (1994). Capturing the Complexity in Advanced Technology Use: Adaptive Structuration Theory. *Organization Science, 5*(2), pp. 121-147.

DeSanctis, G., Poole, M. S., Dickson, G. W., & Jackson, B. M. (1993). Interpretative analysis of team use of group technologies. *Journal of Organizational Computing, 3*(1), pp. 1-29.

Deutsch, M. (1949). A theory of co-operation and competition. *Human Relations, 2*, pp. 129-152.

Deutsch, M. (1990). Sixty years of conflict. *International Journal of Conflict Management, 1*, pp. 237-263.

Donaldson, L. (1996). The normal science of Structural Contingency Theory. In S. R. Clegg & C. Hardy & W. Nord (Eds.), *Handbook of Organization Studies*. London: Sage Publications.

Dourish, P., Adler, A., Belotti, V. & Henderson, A. (1996). Your place or mine? Learning from long-term use of audio-video communication. *Computer Supported Cooperative Work: The Journal of Collaborative Computing, 5*, pp. 33-62.

Dourish, P. (forthcoming). The Appropriation of Interactive Technologies: Some

Lessons from Placeless Documents. *Computer Supported Co-operative Work. An International Journal (in press).*

Druskat, V. U., & Wolff, S. B. (2000). Building the emotional intelligence of groups. *Harvard Business Review, May/June.*

Dubé, L., Paré, G. (2001). Global virtual teams. *Communications of the ACM, 44*(12), pp. 71-73.

Dutton, W., Fulk, J., & Steinfield, C. (1982). Utilization of videoconferencing *Telecommunications Policy, 6*, pp. 164-178.

Eason, K. & Harker, S. (1994). Developing teleinformatics systems to meet organizational requirements. In: J.H.E. Andriessen and R.A. Roe (Eds.) *Telematics and work*, Hove, Sussex (UK): Lawrence Erlbaum.

Eason, K., & Olpert, W. (1996). Early Evaluation of the Organisational Implications of CSCW Systems. In P.Thomas (Ed.), *CSCW requirements and evaluation*: London: Springer Verlag.

Easterbrook, S. (1993). *CSCW: Co-operation or conflict?* London: Springer Verlag.

Egido, C. (1988). Video Conferencing as a Technology to Support Group Work: A Review of its Failures. *Proceedings ACM Conference on Computer-Supported Cooperative Work, CSCW'88*, Portland, OR, pp.13-24.

Egyedi, A., & Boehm, B. (1998). Telecooperation experience with the win win system. *Proceedings of the XV IFIP World Computer Congress. Section on Telecooperation*, Vienna/Austria.

Ehn, P. (1988). *Work-oriented design of computer artefacts*. Hillsdale, NJ: Lawrence Erlbaum.

Ellis, C. A., Gibbs, S. J., & Rein, G. L. (1991). Groupware: some issues and experiences. *Communications of the ACM, 34*(1), pp. 38-58.

Ellis, C. A., & Wainer, J. (1994). Goal based models of collaboration. *Collaborative Computing, 1*, pp. 61-86.

Engeström, Y. (1990). *Learning by expanding*. Helsinki: Orienta-konsultit.

Engeström, Y., & Middleton, D. (1996). *Cognition and communication at work*. Cambridge: Cambridge University Press.

Engeström, Y., Brown, K., Christoper, L., & Gregory, J. (1997). Co-ordination, Co-operation and Communication in the courts. In M. Cole, Y. Engeström & O. Vasquez (Eds.), *Mind, Culture and Activity*. Cambridge: Cambridge University Press.

European Foundation for the Improvement of Living and Working Conditions (1997). *Second European survey on working conditions*. Dublin. ISBN 92-828-0541-7.

Fenech, T. (1998). Using perceived ease of use and perceived usefulness to predict acceptance of the World Wide Web. *Computer Networks and ISDN Systems, 30*, pp. 629-630.

Finholt, T., Sproull, L., & Kiesler, S. (1990). Communication and performance in ad hoc task groups. In J. Galegher, R. E. Kraut & C. Egido (Eds.), *Intellectual Teamwork: Social and technological foundations of co-operative work*. Hillsdale, NJ: Lawrence Erlbaum Publ.

Finn, K.E., Sellen A.J. & Wilbur, S.B. (Eds.) (1997). *Video-mediated communication*. Mahwah, NJ: Lawrence Erlbaum.

Frese, M., & Zapf, D. (1994). Action at the core of work psychology: A German approach. In H. C. Triandis & M. D. Dunnette & L. M. Hough (Eds.),

Handbook of Industrial and Organizational Psychology. Palo Alto: Consulting Psychologists Press.

Fulk, J. (1993). Social construction of communication technology. *Academy of Management Journal, 36*(5), pp. 921-950.

Fulk, J., Steinfield, C. W., Schmitz, J., & Power, J. G. (1987). A social information processing model of media use in organizations. *Communications Research, 14*(5), pp. 529-552.

Fulk, J., & Ryu, D. (1990). *Perceiving electronic mail systems: a partial test of social information processing model of communication media in organizations.* Paper presented at the ICA Annual Convention, Dublin.

Fulk, J., & DeSanctis, G. (1995). Electronic communication and changing organisational work. *Organisational Science, 6*(4), pp. 337-339.

Fulk, J., & Steinfield, C. W. (1990). *Organizations and communication technology.* Newbury Park, CA: Sage Publications

Fussel, S. R., Kraut, R. E., Lerch, F. J., Scherlis, W. L., McNally, M. M., & Cadiz, J. J. (1998). Co-ordination overload and team performance: Effects of team communication strategies, *Proceedings of the CSCW' 98. Proceedings of the Conference on Computer supported cooperative work.* New York: ACM.

Fussel, S. R., Kraut, R.E., Siegel, J. (2000). *Coordination of communication: Effects of shared visual context on collaborative work.* Proceedings of the CSCW'00, Philadelphia, PA, USA.

Galbraith, J. R. (1973). *Designing complex organizations.* Reading, MA: Addison-Wesley.

Galbraith, J. R. (1977). *Organization design.* Reading, MA: Addison-Wesley.

Gammon, D., Sørlie, T., Bergvik, S. & Sørensen, Høifødt T. (1998). Psychotherapy supervision conducted by video-conferencing: A qualitative study of user experiences. *Nordisk Journal of Psychiatry, 52,* pp. 411-421.

Gardner, W. L., & Peluchette, J. V. E. (1991). Computer-mediated communications in organizational settings: A self-presentational perspective. In E. Szewczak & C. Snodgrass & M. Khosrowpour (Eds.), *Managerial impacts of information technology: Perspectives on organizational change and growth.* Harrisburg, PA: Idea Group Publ.

Garton, L., & Wellman, B. (1995). Social impact of electronic mail in organizations: Review of the research literature. *Communication Yearbook, 18,* pp. 434-453.

George, J. F., & King, J. L. (1991). Examining the computing and centralization debate. *Communications of the ACM, 34*(7), pp. 63-72.

Gersick, C. J. G. (1989). Marking time: Predictable transitions in task groups. *Academy of Management Journal, 32,* 2, p274-309.

Giddens, A. (1984). *The Constitution of Society, Outline of the Theory of Structuration.* Berkeley and Los Angeles: University of California Press.

Gill, T. G. (1996). Expert Systems Usage: Task Change and Intrinsic Motivation. *MIS Quarterly, 20*(3), pp. 301-330.

Greenberg, S. (1991). Computer-supported co-operative work and groupware: an introduction to the special issue. *International Journal of Man Machine Studies, 34,* pp. 133-141.

Greenbaum, J. & Kyng, M. (1991). *Design at work.* Hillsdale: Lawrence Erlbaum.

Greif, I. (1988). *Computer Supported Co-operative Work. A book of readings.* San Mateo, CA.: Morgan Kaufmann Publishers.

Grudin, J. (1994). Eight challenges for developers. *Communications of the ACM, 37*(1), pp. 93-105.

Gutek, B. A. (1990). Work group structure and information technology: A structural contingency approach. In J. Galegher, R. E. Kraut & C. Egido (Eds.), *Intellectual Teamwork: Social and technological foundations of co-operative work.* Hillsdale, NJ: Lawrence Erlbaum Publ.

Guzzo, R., & Dickson, M. (1996). Teams in organizations: recent research on performance and effectiveness. In J. Spence & J. Darley & D. Foss (Eds.), *Annual Review of Psychology* (Vol. 47, pp. 307-338).

Hacker, W. (1985). Activity: A fruitful concept in industrial psychology. In M. Frese & J. Sabini (Eds.), *Goal directed behaviour: the concept of action psychology.* Hillsdale NJ: Lawrence Erlbaum.

Hackman, J. R. (1987). The design of workteams. In J.W.Lorsch (Ed.), *Handbook of organizational behaviour* (pp. p315-342). Englewood Cliffs, NJ: Prentice Hall.

Hackman, J. R., & Oldham, G. R. (1976). Motivation through the design of work. *Organizational Behaviour and Human Performance, 16*, pp. 250-279.

Hackman, J. R., & Oldham, G. R. (1980). *Work redesign.* Reading, MA: Addison Wesley.

Hage, J. (1995). Post industrial lives: New demands, new prescriptions. In A. Howard (Ed.), *The changing nature of work.* San Francisco: Jossey Bass.

Halper, M. (1998). It's not just for meetings anymore. *CIO-Section 1*, June. http://www.cio.com.

Hammer, M., & Mangurian, G. E. (1987). The changing value of communications technology. *Sloan Management Review, 28*(2), pp. 65-71.

Hansen, M. T., Nohria, N. & Tierney, T. (1999). What's your strategy for managing knowledge. *Harvard Business Review,* (March-April).

Heath, C and Luff, P. (1992). Collaboration and control; crisis management and multimedia technology in London Underground line control rooms. *Computer Supported Cooperative Work, 1*, pp. 69-94.

Heeren, E. (1996). *Technology support for collaborative distance learning.* PhD Thesis. Centre for Telematics and Information Technology, Enschede.

Herik, K.J. van den (1998). *Group support for policy making.* Delft, The Netherlands: Delft University of Technology. PhD Thesis

Hettinga, M. (2002). *Understanding evolutionary use of groupware.* Delft, the Netherlands: Delft University of Technology. PhD-thesis

Hildreth, P., Kimble, C., & Wright, P. (2000). Communities of Practice in the distributed international environment. *Journal of Knowledge Management, 4*(1), pp. 27-38.

Hiltz, S. R. (1988). Productivity enhancement from computer-mediated communication: a systems contingency approach. *Communications of the ACM, 31*(12), pp. 438-454.

Hiltz, S. R., & Turoff, M. (1985). Structuring computer-mediated communication systems to avoid information overload. *Communications of the ACM, 28*, pp. 680-689.

Hinssen, P. (1998). *What difference does it make? The use of groupware in small groups.* University of Twente, The Netherlands: Telematica Instituut.

Hofte, H. t. (1998). *Working apart together. Foundations for component groupware*. University of Twente, The Netherlands: Telematica Instituut.

Hogg, M. A. (1992). *The social psychology of group cohesiveness: From attraction to social identity*. New York: Harvester Wheatsheaf.

Hollingshead, A. B., & McGrath, J. E. (1995). Computer-assisted groups: a critical review of the empirical findings. In R. A. Guzzo & E. Salas & Associates (Eds.), *Team effectiveness and decision making in organizations*. San Francisco: Jossey-Bass.

Hooff, B. v. d. (1997). *Incorporating Electronic Mail. Adoption, Use and Effects of Electronic Mail in Organizations*. Amsterdam: Otto Cramwinckel.

Houwing, E. M., Wiethoff, M., & Arnold, A. G. (1993). Usability evaluation from users' point of view. In S. Ashlund & K. Mullet & A.Henderson & Hollnagel & T.White (Eds.), *Bridges between worlds: INTERCHI '93* (pp. 197-198). Reading: Addison Wesley.

Howard, A. (1995). *The changing nature of work*. San Francisco: Jossey-Bass.

Howard, S., & Murray, D. M. (1987). A taxonomy of evaluation techniques for HCI. In H. J. Bullinger & B. Shackel (Eds.), *Human Computer Interaction - Interact '87*. Amsterdam: Elsevier.

Howes, A. (1995). An introduction to cognitive modeling in human computer interaction. In A. F. Monk & N. Gilbert (Eds.), *Perspectives on HCI*. London: Academic Press.

Huang, W. W. (1998). *Does GSS favor group task or socio-emotional interaction - An empirical investigation*. Proceedings of the XV. IFIP World Computer Congress. Section on Telecooperation. Vienna, Austria.

Huber, G. P. (1990). A theory of the effects of advanced information technologies on organizational design, intelligence and decision making. *Academy of Management Review, 15*(1), pp. 47-71.

Hutchins, E. (1991). Organizing work by adaptation. *Organization Science, 2*(1), pp. 20-57.

Hutchins, E. (1995). *Cognition in the wild*. Cambridge, MA: MIT Press.

Hutchinson, C. (1999). Virtual teams. In R. Stewart (Ed.), *Handbook of teamworking*. Aldershot, Hampshire, UK: Gower.

Huws, U. (1988). Remote possibilities: some difficulties in the analysis and quantification of telework in the UK. In W. B. Korte & S. Robinson & W. J. Steinle (Eds.), *Telework: Present situation and future development of a new form of work organization*. Amsterdam: North-Holland.

Huysman, M. (1996). *Dynamics of organisational learning*. Amsterdam: Thesis Publishers.

Huysman, M. & Wit, D., de, (2000). Kennisdelen in de praktijk. Van Gorcum.

Huysman, M. & Wit, D., de, (2002). *Knowledge sharing in practice*. Dordrecht, The Netherlands: Kluwer.

Huysman, M., Steinfield, C., Jang, C.-Y., David, K., Huis in 't Veld, M., Poot, J., & Mulder, I. (forthcoming). Virtual Teams and the Appropriation of Communication Technology; Exploring the Concept of Media Stickiness. *Computer Supported Co-operative Work. An International Journal (in press)*.

Introna, L. D. (1998). *Telecooperation as working-together*. Proceedings of the XV. IFIP World Computer Congress. Section on Telecooperation, Vienna, Austria.

Janis, I. L. (1982). *Victims of groupthink (2nd ed.)* Boston: Houghton-Miflin.

Johansen, R. (1988). *Groupware: Computer support for business teams.* New York: The Free Press.

Kaptelinin, V. (1996). Computer-Mediated Activity: Functional Organs in Social and Developmental Contexts. In B. A. Nardi (Ed.), *Context and Consciousness, Activity Theory and HCI* (pp. 45-68). Cambridge, MA: MIT Press.

Katz, J. E., & Aspden, P. (1997). A Nation of Strangers? *Communications of the ACM, 40*(12), pp. 81-86.

Keen, P. (1988). *Competing in time: Using telecommunication for competitive advantage.* Cambridge MA.: Ballinger.

Kelley, H. H., & Thibaut, J. W. (1978). *Interpersonal relations: A theory of interdependence.* New York: John Wiley.

Kerr, S., & Jermier, J. M. (1978). Substitutes for leadership: their meaning and measurement. *Organizational Behaviour and Human Performance, 12,* pp. 62-82.

Khoshafian, S., & Buckiewicz, M. (1995). *Introduction to groupware, workflow and workgroup.* New York: John Wiley.

Kiesler, S., Siegel, J., & McGuire, T. W. (1984). Social psychological aspects of computer-mediated communication. *American Psychologist, 39*(10), pp. 1123-1134.

Kimble, C., Hildreth, P., & Wright, P. (2000). Communities of Practice: Going Virtual. In: *Knowledge Management and Business Model Innovation* (pp. 220-234). London: Idea Group Publishing.

Kinney, S. T., & Panko, R. R. (1998). *The manager's day: Another use of time study.* http://www.cba.hawaii.edu/panko/papers/time/UTstudy.htm.

Kling, R. (1996). Hopes and horrors: technological utopianism and anti-utopianism in narratives of computerization. In R. Kling (Ed.), *Computerization and controversy.* San Diego: Academic Press.

Knights, D., & Willmott, H. (1988). New technology and the labour process. Basingstoke: The MacMillan Press.

Köhler, H. (1994). Potentials of computer conferencing, methodological contributions to the development of good computer support for human communication at work. In: J.H.Erik Andriessen & R.A. Roe (Eds.), *Telematics and work,* Hove, Sussex (UK): Lawrence Erlbaum.

Kramer, R. M. (1999). Trust and distrust in organizations: emerging perspectives, enduring questions. *Annual Review of Psychology, 50,* pp. 569-598.

Kraemer, K. L., & Pinsonneault, A. (1990). Technology and groups: Assessment of the empirical research. In J. Galegher, R. E. Kraut & C. Egido (Eds.), *Intellectual Teamwork: Social and technological foundations of co-operative work.* Hillsdale, NJ: Lawrence Erlbaum Publ..

Kraut, R. E., Egido, C., & Galegher, J. (1990). Patterns of Contact and Communication in Scientific Research Collaboration. In J. Galegher, R. E. Kraut & C. Egido (Eds.), *Intellectual Teamwork: Social and technological foundations of co-operative work.* Hillsdale, NJ: Lawrence Erlbaum Publ.

Kraut, R. E., Cool, C., Rice, R. E., & Fish, R. S. (1994). Life and death of new technology: Task utility and social influences on the use of a communication medium. Proceedings of the Conference on Computer supported cooperative work CSCW94. New York: ACM.

Kraut, R., Patterson, M., Lundmark, V., Kiesler, S., Mukhopadhyay, T., & Scherlis, W. (1998). Internet paradox: A social technology that reduces social involvement and psychological well-being? American Psychologist, 53(9), pp. 1017-1031.

Kuutti, K. (1991). Activity theory and its applications to information systems research and development. In H. E. Nissen & H. K. Klein & R. Hirschheim (Eds.), Information Systems Research: Contemporary approaches and emergent traditions (pp. 529-549). Amsterdam: North Holland.

Kuutti, K. (1996). Activity theory as a potential framework for human computer interaction research. In B. Nardi (Ed.), Context and consciousness. Activity theory and human computer interaction. Cambridge, MA: MIT Press.

Kuutti, K. & Arvonen, T. (1992). Identifying CSCW applications by means of activity theory concepts: a case example. In J. Turner & R. Kraut (Eds.), Sharing perspectives. Proceedings of the CSCW92 conference. Cambridge, Ma: University Press.

Lane, C., & Bachman, R. (Eds.). (1998). Trust within and between organizations. Conceptual and empirical applications. Oxford: Oxford university Press.

LaRose, R., Eastin, M. S., & Gregg, J. (2001). Reformulating the Internet Paradox: Social cognitive explanation of Internet use and depression. Journal of Online Behavior, 1(2), http://www.behavior.net/JOB/v1n2/paradox.html

Larson, C. E., & Defasto, F. M. J. (1989). Teamwork. London: Sage Publications.

Lave, J., & Wenger, E. (1991). Situated Learning. Legitimate Peripheral Participation. Cambridge: University Press.

Lawrence, P.R. & Lorsch, J.W. (1969). Developing organizations: Diagnosis and action. Reading, Mass.: Addison Wesley, Leavitt, H. & Whistler, T. (1958). Management in the 1980's. Harvard Business Review, Nov/Dec. p41-48.

Lee, S., & Guinan, P. J. (1991). The impact of information technology on work group innovation and control. In E. Szewczak & C. Snodgrass & M. Khosrowpour (Eds.), Managerial impacts of information technology: Perspectives on organizational change and growth (pp. 241-272). Harrisburg, PA: Idea Group Publ.

Leede, J. de (1997). Innoveren van onderop. Over de bijdrage van taakgroepen aan product- en procesvernieuwing. Dissertation (Innovating bottom up. The contribution of taskgroups to product and process innovation). Enschede: Universiteit Twente.

Leonard-Barton, D. (1988). Implementation characteristics of organizational innovations. Communication research, 15(5), pp. 603-631.

Leontjev, A. (1978). Activity, consciousness and personality. Englewood Cliffs, NJ: Prentice Hall.

Lewin, K. (1947). Frontiers in group dynamics. Human Relations, 1, pp. 5-41.

Lindgaard, G. (1994). Usability Testing and System Evaluation. London: Chapman and Hall.

Littlejohn, S. W. (1989). Theories of human communication. Belmont CA:

Wadsworth.

Luthans, F. (1992). *Organizational behaviour*. New York: McGraw Hill.

Lyytinen, K. J., & Ngwenyama, O. K. (1992). What does computer support for co-operative work mean? A structurational analysis of computer supported co-operative work. *Accounting, management and information technology* 2(1), pp. 19-37.

Malone, T. W., & Crowston, K. (1990). What is co-ordination theory and how can it help design co-operative work systems? *CSCW' 90. Proceedings of the conference on Computer supported cooperative work.* New York: ACM.

March, J. G., & Simon, H. A. (1958). *Organizations.* New York: John Wiley.

Markus, M. L. (1983). Power, politics and MIS Implementation. *Communication of the ACM, 26,* p430-444.

Markus, M. L. (1987). Toward a "Critical Mass" Theory of interactive media: universal access, interdependence and diffusion. *Communications Research, 14*(5), pp. 491-511.

Markus, M. L., & Robey, D. (1988). Information technology and organizational change: causal structure in theory and research. *Management Science, 34*(5), pp. 583-598.

Maslow, A. H. (1968). *Towards a psychology of being.* New York: Van Nostrand.

Mathieson, K. (1991). Predicting user intentions: Comparing the technology acceptance model with the theory of planned behaviour. *Information Systems Research* (September), pp. 173-191.

McDermott, R. (2000). Knowing in Community: 10 Critical Success Factors in Building Communities of Practice. *IHRIM Journal,* (March), pp. 1-12.

McGrath, J. E. (1984). *Groups: interaction and performance.* New Jersey: Prentice-Hall.

McGrath, J. E. (1990). Time matters in groups. In J. Galegher, R. Kraut & C. Egido (Eds.), *Intellectual Teamwork: Social and technological foundations of co-operative work.* Hillsdale, NJ: Lawrence Erlbaum Publ.

McGrath, A. J. E., & Hollingshead, A. B. (1993). Putting the "group" back in group support systems: some theoretical issues about dynamic processes in groups with technological enhancements. In L. M. Jessup & J. S. Valacich (Eds.), *Group support systems: new perspectives* (pp. 78-96). New York: McMillan.

McGrath, A. J. E., & Hollingshead, A. B. (1994). *Groups Interacting with Technology. Ideas, Evidence, Issues and an Agenda.* London: Sage Publications.

McIntyre, R. M., & Salas, E. (1996). Measuring and managing for team performance: emerging principles from complex environments. In R. A. Guzzo & E. Salas & Associates (Eds.), *Team effectiveness and decision making in organizations.* San Francisco: Jossey-Bass Publishers.

Menneke, B. E., Valacich, J. S., & Wheeler, B. C. (2000). The effects of media and task on user performance: A test of the task media fit hypothesis. *Group Decision and Negotiation, 9,* pp. 507-529.

Mills, K. L. (1999). Introduction to the electronic symposium on computer supported cooperative work. *ACM Computing Surveys,* 31(2), pp. 105-115.

Mintzberg, H. (1973). *The nature of managerial work.* New York: Harper Row.

Mintzberg, H. (1979). *The structuring of organizations.* Englewoods Cliff, NJ:

Prentice Hall.

Mintzberg, H. (1989). *Mintzberg on management: Inside our strange world of organizations*. New York: Free Press.

Mohrman, S. A., Cohen, S. G., & Mohrman, A. M. (1995). *Designing team based organizations; new forms for knowledge work*. San Francisco: Jossey Bass.

Monk, A. F., & Gilbert, N. (1995). *Perspectives on HCI*. London: Academic Press.

Moore, G. C., & Benbasat, I. (1991). Development of an instrument to measure the perceptions of adopting an information technology innovation. *Information Systems Research*, (September), pp. 192-232.

Morgan, G. (1996). *Images of Organization*. London: Sage Publications.

Muir, B. M. (1994). Trust in automatization: Part I. theoretical issues in the study of trust and human intervention in automated systems. *Ergonomics*, *37*(11), pp. 1905-1922.

Muller, M., & Kuhn, S. (1993). Special Issue on Participatory Design, *Communications of the Association for Computing Machinery*, *36*(4), pp. 25-103.

Nardi, B. (1996a). *Context and consciousness. Activity theory and human computer interaction*. Cambridge, MA: MIT Press.

Nardi, B. (1996b). Studying context: A comparison of activity theory, situated action models, and distribute cognition. In B. Nardi (Ed.), *Context and consciousness. Activity theory and human computer interaction.*. Cambridge, MA: MIT Press.

Ngwenyama, O. K. (1998). Groupware, social action and organizational emergence: on the process dynamics of computer mediated distributed work. *Accounting, Management and Information Technologies*, *8(4)*, pp. 123 – 143.

Nielsen, J. (1992a). Finding Usability Problems through Heuristic Evaluation. In P. Bauersfield & J. Bennett & G. Lynch (Eds.), *Human Factors in Computing Systems (CHI'92 Conference Proceedings)* (pp. 373-380). New York: ACM Press.

Nielsen, J. (1992b). The Usability Engineering Life Cycle. *IEEE Computer, 25*(3), pp. 12-22.

Nielsen, J., & Mack, R. L. (1994). *Usability Inspection Methods*. New York: John Wiley.

Nurcan, S. (1998). Main concepts for co-operative work place analysis. *Proceedings of the XV. IFIP World Computer Congress*. Vienna, Austria.

Nunamaker, J. F., Briggs, R. O., & Mittleman, D. D. (1997). *Electronic Meeting Systems: Ten years of lessons learned*. http://www.cmi.arizona.edu/users/bbriggs/grid/decade.html

O'Conaill, B. & Whittaker, S. (1997). Characterizing, predicting and measuring video-mediated communication: A conversational approach. In: K.E. Finn, A.J. Sellen & S.B. Wilbur (Eds.), *Video-mediated communication*. Mahwah, NJ: Lawrence Erlbaum.

Offenbeek, M. van (1993). Van *methode* naar *scenario's. Het afstemmen van situatie en aanpak bij de ontwikkeling van informatiesystemen*. (From method to scenario's. Adjusting situation and approach when designing information systems). PhD Thesis. Groningen, The Netherlands: University Press.

Olson, M. H. (1989). Work at home for computer professionals: current attitudes and future prospects. *ACM Transactions on Office Information Systems, 7*(4), pp. 317-338.

Olson, G. M., & Olson, J. S. (1997). Making sense of the findings: Common vocabulary leads to the synthesis necessary for theory building. In K. E. Finn, A. J. Sellen & S. B. Wilbur (Eds.), *Video-mediated communication*. Mahwah, NJ: Lawrence Erlbaum.

Olson, Judith S., Gary M. Olson, Marianne Storrosten & Mark Carter (1992), "How a Group-Editor Changes the Character of a Design Meeting as well as its Outcome," In Jon Turner & Robert Kraut, eds., Proceedings of the Conference on Computer-Supported Cooperative Work, pp.91-98. New York, NY: ACM Press.

Olson, J. S., Olson, G. M., & Meader, D. K. (1994). *What mix of video and audio is useful for remote real-time work*. Paper presented at the Workshop "Video-mediated communication", at ACM Conference on CSCW '94, Chapel Hill.

Olson, G. M., Olson, J. S., & Finholt, T. (1994). *Workshop on Behavioral Evaluation of CSCW technologies at the ACM Conference on CSCW '94*, Chapel Hill.

Orlikowski, W. J. (1992). The duality of technology: rethinking the concept of technology in organizations. *Organization Science, 3*, pp. 398-427.

Orlikowski, W. J. (1996). Improvising organizational transformation over time: A situated change perspective. *Information Systems Research, 7*(1), pp. 63-92.

Orlikowski, W. J., & Hofman, J. D. (1997). An improvisational model for change management: the case of groupware technologies. *Sloan Management Review* (winter), pp. 11-21.

Orlikowski, W. J., & Robey, D. (1991). Information technology and the structuring of organizations. *Information Systems Research, 2*(2), pp. 143-169.

Ortt, J. R. (1998). *Videotelephony in the consumer market* (ISBN 90-72125-61-4). Den Haag: KPN Research.

Ouchi, W. G. (1979). A conceptual framework for the design of organisational control mechanisms. *Management Science,* (September), pp. 833-848.

Panko, R. R. (1992). Patterns of Managerial Communication. *Journal of Organizational Computing, 2*(1), pp. 95-122.

Pankoke-Babatz, U., & Syri, A. (1997). Collaborative workspaces for time deferred electronic co-operation. In S. C. Hayne & W. Prinz (Eds.), *Proceedings of the Group97 International ACM SIGGROUP Conference on Supporting Group Work - The Integration Challenge; Nov 16-19; Phoenix Arizona* (pp. 187-196). New York: ACM.

Peiro, J. M., & Prieto, F. (1994). Telematics and organizational processes. In J. H. E. Andriessen & R.A.Roe (Eds.), *Telematics and work*. Hove, Sussex: Lawrence Erlbaum.

Pennings, J. M. (1998). Structural contingency theory. In P. J. D. Drenth & H. Thierry & C. J. de Wolff (Eds.), *Handbook of work and organizational psychology*. Second edition. Hove, Sussex: Psychology Press.

Perrow, C. (1967). A framework for the comparative analysis of organizations. *Amarican Sociological Review, 32*, pp. 194-208.

Perrow, C. (1983). The organizational context of human factors engineering. *Administrative Science Quarterly, 28*, pp. 521-541.

Pinch, T. J., & Bijker, W. E. (1987). The social construction of artefacts. In W. E. Bijker & T. P. Hughes & T. J. Pinch (Eds.), *The social construction of technological systems* (pp. 79-108). Beverley Hills, CA: Sage Publications.

Poole, M. S., & DeSanctis, G. (1990). Understanding the Use of Group Decision Support Systems: The Theory of Adaptive Structuration. In J. Fulk & C. Steinfield (Eds.), *Organizations and communication technology* (pp. 173-193). Newbury Park, CA: Sage Publications.

Porter, A. L. (1987). A two factor model of the effects of office automation on employment. *Office: Technology and People, 3*(1), pp. 57-76.

Postmes, T. T. (1997). *Social Influence in computer-mediated groups*. Enschede: Print Partners Ipskamp.

Prusak, L., & Cohen, D. (2001). How to invest in Social Capital. *Harvard Business Review, June*, pp. 86-93.

Quinn, R.E., & Rohrbach, J. (1983). A spatial model of effectiveness criteria: towards a competing values approach to organisational analysis. *Management Science , 29*, pp. 363-377

Qureshi, S., Zigurs, I. (2001). Paradoxes and prerogatives in global virtual collaboration. *Communications of the ACM, 44*(12), 85-88.

Rasmussen, J. (1986). *Information processing and human-machine interaction.* Amsterdam: North Holland.

Rasmussen, J. (1987). Reasons, causes and human error. In: J.Rasmussen, K.Duncan & L Leplat (Eds.), *New technology and human error*. London: John Wiley

Reason, J. (1990). *Human error.* New York: Cambridge University Press.

Rice, R. E. (1987). Computer-mediated communication and organizational innovation. *Journal of Communication, 37*(4), pp. 65-94.

Rice, R. E., Grant, A., Schmitz, J., & Torobin, J. (1990). Individual and network influences on the adoption and perceived outcomes of electronic messaging. *Social networks, 12*(1), pp. 27-55.

Rice, R. E., & Love, G. (1987). Electronic Emotion: Socio-emotional content in a computer-mediated communication network. *Communication Research, 14*(1), pp. 85-105.

Rice, R. E., & Shook, D. E. (1988). Access to, usage of, and outcomes from an electronic messaging system. *ACM Transactions on Office Information Systems, 6*(3), pp. 255-276.

Rice, R. E., & Steinfield, C. W. (1994). New forms of organisational communication via electronic mail and voice messaging. In J. H. E. Andriessen & R. A. Roe (Eds.), *Telematics and work.* Hove, Sussex (UK): Lawrence Erlbaum.

Rice, R. E., & Williams, F. (1984). Theories old and new: the study of new media. In R. Rice & Associates, *The New Media*. Beverly Hills: Sage Publications.

Robinson, M. (1989). Double level languages and cooperative working. *AI and Society, 5*, pp. 34-60.

Robinson, M. (1993). Design for unanticipated use. In G. DeMichelis & C. Simone & K. Schmidt (Eds.), *ECSCW '93. Proceedings of the Third*

European Conference on Computer Supported Cooperative Work. Dordrecht: Kluwer Academic Publishers.

Rockart, J. F., & Short, J. E. (1989). IT in the 1990s: Managing organizational interdependence. *Sloan Management Review*(winter), pp. 7-17.

Roe, R. A. (1988). Acting systems design - an Action Theoretical approach to the design of man-computer systems. In V. de Keyser & T. Qvale & B. Wilpert & S. A. Ruiz Quintanilla (Eds.), *The meaning of work and technical options* (pp. 211-227). Chichester: John Wiley.

Roe, R. A. (1998). Work performance. In P. J. D. Drenth & H. Thierry & C. J. de Wolff (Eds.), *Handbook of work and organizational psychology.* Second edition. Hove, Sussex: Psychology Press.

Rogers, D.M. (1994). Exploring obstacles: integrating CSCW in evolving organisations. In: T. Malone (Ed.), *CSCW '94. Proceedings of the Conference on Computer-Supported Cooperative Work.* New York: ACM.

Rogers, E. M. (1995). Diffusion of innovations (4th ed.). New York: The Free Press.

Salancik, G. R., & Pfeffer, J. (1978). A social information processing approach to job attitudes and task design. *Administrative Science Quarterly, 23*, pp. 224-253.

Scheepers, R., & Damsgaard, J. (1997). Using Internet technology within the organization: a structurational analysis of intranets. *Proceedings of the GROUP 97 Conference,* (pp. 9-18).

Schmidt, K. (1994). Cooperative work and its articulation: Requirements for computer support. *Travail Humain, 57*(4), pp. 345-366.

Schmidt, K. & Bannon, L. (1992). Taking CSCW Seriously: Supporting Articulation Work. *Computer Supported Cooperative Work (CSCW): An International Journal, 1(1),* pp. 7-40.

Schmitz, J., & Fulk, J. (1991). Organizational colleagues, information richness, and electronic mail: A test of the Social Influence Model of Technology Use. *Communication Research, 18*, pp. 487-523.

Schroeder, R. (2002). *The social life of avatars.* London: Springer Verlag.

Schroeder, R., Van de Ven, A., Scudder, G. & Polley, D. (1986). Managing innovation and change processes: Findings from the Minnesota Innovation Research Program. *Agribusiness, 2(4),* pp. 501-523.

Sellen, A. J. (1992). Speech patterns in video mediated conversations., *Proceedings of the CHI'92* Conference (pp. 49-59). New York: ACM.

Sellen, A. J. (1994). *The effects of video-mediation on human interaction.* Paper presented at the Workshop "Video-mediated communication", at ACM Conference on CSCW '94, Chapel Hill.

Sellen, A. J. (1995). Remote conversation: the effects of mediating talk with technology. *Human Computer Interaction, 10*, pp. 401-444.

Shneiderman, B. (2000). Universal usability. *Communications of the ACM, 43*(5), pp. 85-91.

Short, J., Williams, E., & Christie, B. (1976). *The social psychology of telecommunications.* London: John Wiley.

Siegel, J., Dubrowski, V., Kiesler, S., & McGuire, T. W. (1986). Group processes in computer-mediated communication. *Organizational Behavior and Human Decision Processes, 37*, pp. 157-187.

Smith, M. J. (1997). Psychosocial aspects of working with video display terminals (VDTs) and employee physical and mental health. *Ergonomics, 40*(10), pp. 1002-1015.

Sommerlad, E. and members of the Evaluation Development Research Unit, Tavistock Institute of Human Relations (1992). *A Guide to Local Evaluation*. London: Employment Department Evaluation Development Research Unit, Tavistock Institute of Human Relations.

Spears, R., & Lea, M. (1992). Social influence and the influence of the "social" in computer mediated communication. In M. Lea (Ed.), *Contexts of computer mediated communication*. Hemel, Hempstead: Harvester Wheatsheaf.

Sproull, L., & Kiesler, S. (1986). Reducing social context cues: Electronic mail in organizational communication. *Management Science, 32*(11), pp. 1492-1512.

Steiner, I. D. (1972). *Group processes and productivity*. New York: Academic Press.

Steinfield, C. W. (1990). Organizational communication via computer: Electronic mail at the Xerox Corporation. In B. D. Sypher (Ed.), *Case studies in organizational communication*. New York: Guilford.

Steinfield, C. W., & Fulk, J. (1987). On the role of theory in research on information technologies in organizations: an introduction to the special issue. *Communication Research, 14*(5), pp. 479-490.

Steinfield, C., Jang, C.-Y., & Pfaff, B. (1999). *Supporting virtual team collaboration: The SCOPE system*. In: Proceedings of the *GROUP'99 International Conference on Supporting Group Work*, New York: ACM.

Stewart, R. (1999). *Gower handbook of team working*. Aldershot, Hampshire, UK: Gower.

Stone, E. F., & Stone, D. L. (1990). Privacy in organizations: Theoretical issues, Research findings, and protection mechanisms. In G. R. Ferris (Ed.), *Research in personnel and human resources management (8)*. Greenwich, CT: JAI Press.

Strom, J. & Neisser, G. (1998). Re-engineering the Desktop: Taking the Knowledge Base to the User to support Education an City Communities. *Computer Networks and ISDN Systems, 30(16)*, pp. 1649-1656.

Suchman, L. A. (1987). *Plans and situated actions, The problem of human machine communication*. Cambridge, UK: Cambridge University Press.

Sundstrom, E., DeMeuse, K. P., & Futrell, D. (1990). Work Teams. Applications and Effectiveness. *American Psychologist, 45*(2), pp. 120-133.

Swanson, E. B. (1987). Information systems in organization theory: A review. In R. J. Boland & R. A. Hirschheim (Eds.), *Critical issues in information systems research*. New York: John Wiley.

Tang, J. C., & Isaacs, E. (1993). Why do users like video. *Computer Supported Co-operative Work, 1*, pp. 163-196.

Thierry, H. (1998). Motivation and satisfaction. In P. J. D. Drenth & H. Thierry & C. J. d. Wolff (Eds.), *Handbook of work and organizational psychology, second edition*. Hove, East Sussex: Psychology Press.

Thomas, J. B., & Trevino, L. K. (1989). *The strategic implications of media mismatch: coping with uncertainty and equivocality*. Paper presented at the International Communication Association Conference, San Francisco.

Thompson, J. D. (1967). *Organizations in action*. New York: McGraw-Hill.

Tjosvold, D. (1992). *Team Organization. An enduring competitive advantage*: New York: John Wiley.

Tjosvold, D. (1996). Co-operation theory, constructive controversy and effectiveness: Learning from crisis. In R. A. Guzzo & E. Salas & Associates (Eds.), *Team effectiveness and decision making in organizations*. San Francisco: Jossey-Bass

Totter, A., Gross, T., & Stay, C. (1998). Functional versus conscious awareness in CSCW systems. *Proceedings of the XV IFIP World Computer Congress. Section on Telecooperation.* World Computer Congress, Vienna, Austria.

Townsend, A., DeMarie, S., & Hendrickson, A. (1998). Virtual teams: technology and the workplace of the future. *Academy of Management Executive, 12*(3), pp. 17-29.

Trevino, L., Lengel, R., & Daft, R. (1987). Media symbolism, media richness and media choice in organizations. A symbolic interactionist perspective. *Communications Research, 14*(5), pp. 553-574.

Tuckman, B. W. (1965). Developmental sequences in small groups. *Psychological Bulletin, 63*, pp. 384-399.

Tuckman, B. W., & Jensen, M. A. C. (1977). Stages of small group development revisited. *Group and Organizational Studies, 2*, pp. 419-427.

Turkle, S. (1996). Virtuality and its discontents: Searching for community in cyberspace. *The American Prospect, 24*, pp. 50-57.

Urquijo, S. P., Scrivener, S. A. R., & Palmen, H. K. (1993). The use of breakdown analysis in synchronous CSCW system design. In G. DeMichelis & C. Simone & K. Schmidt (Eds.), *ECSCW '93. Proceedings of the Third European Conference on Computer Supported Cooperative Work.* Dordrecht: Kluwer Academic Publishers.

Van de Ven, A.H., Delbecq, A.L. & Koenig, R. (1976). Determinants of coordination modes within organizations. *American Sociological Review, 41*, pp. 322-338.

Veen, J. van (1993). *Toy or tool. The study of electronic mail as an organizational medium*. Free University, Amsterdam.

Veer, G. C. van der (1998). *Analyzing complex systems: only a complex of techniques can do the job*. Paper presented at the Teleco-operation. Proceedings of the XV. IFIP World Computer Congress, Vienna/Austria.

Velden, J. M. van der (1992). Delft WIT-lab; research issues and methods for analysing group behaviour. *ACM Siggraph video review*(87).

Velden, J. M. van der (1995). *Samenwerken op afstand: twee longitudinale laboratoriumstudies naar effecten van mediagebruik op groepsfunctioneren*. Delft: Universitaire Pers.

Venkatraman, N. (1989). The concept of fit in strategy research:toward verbal and statistical correspondence. *Academy of Management Research, 14*(3), pp. 423-444.

Vroom, V. (1964). *Work and motivation*. New York: John Wiley.

Wall, & Jackson. (1995). New manufacturing initiatives and shopfloor job design. In A. Howard (Ed.), *The changing nature of work*. San Francisco: Jossey-Bass.

Walther, J. B. (1992). Interpersonal effects in computer mediated interaction. A relational perspective. *Communication Research, 19*(1), pp. 52-90.

Watzlawick, P., Beavin, J., & Jackson, D. (1967). *Pragmatics of Human Communications: A study of interactional patterns, pathologies and paradoxes.* New York: Norton.

Webster, J. (1998). Desktop videoconferencing: Experiences of complete users, wary users, and non-users. *MIS Quarterly* (sept), pp. 257-285.

Weick, K. E. (1979). *The social psychology of organizing.* Reading: Addison-Wesley.

Weisband, S. P., Schneider, S. K., & Connolloy, T. (1993). Participation, equality and influence: Cues and status in computer supported co-operative groups. In G. DeMichelis & C. Simone & K. Schmidt (Eds.), *ECSCW '93. Proceedings of the Third European Conference on Computer Supported Cooperative Work.* Dordrecht: Kluwer Academic Publishers.

Wellens, A. R. (1989). Effects of telecommunication media upon information sharing and team performance. *IEEE Aerospace and Electronic Systems Magazine, 4*(13-19).

Wellman, B. (1998). Contribution to Panel "An Internet paradox: A social medium that may undermine sociability". Paper presented at the CSCW98, *Conference on Computer-Supported Cooperative Work.* Seattle, USA.

West, M.A. (1996). Reflexivity and work group effectiveness: A conceptual integration. In: M.A. West (Ed.), *Handbook of work group psychology.* Chicester: Wiley.

White, S.A., Gupta, A., Grudin, J., Chesley, H., Kimberly, G. & Sanocki, E. (1998). *A software system for education at a distance: Case study results.* Technical Report MSR-TR-98-61. Microsoft, Redmond USA.

Whittaker, S., & O.Conaill, B. (1997). The role of vision in face-to-face and mediated communication. In K. E. Finn, A. J. Sellen & S. B. Wilbur (Eds.), *Video-mediated communication.* Mahwah, NJ: Lawrence Erlbaum.

Wilbur, S., Lubich, H. P., & Santos, A. (1993). *Multimedia-supported co-operation. Concepts, applications and technical support requirements.* Brussels: COST.

Williamson, O. E. (1975). *Markets and hierarchies: Analysis and antitrust implications.* New York: Free Press.

Winter, S.J., Chudoba, K.M. & Gutek, B.A. (1998). Attitudes toward computers: when do they predict computer use? *Information and Management, 34,* pp. 275-284

Wit, O. de (1998). *Telefonie in Nederland 1877-1940.* (Telephony in the Netherlands 1877-1940). Dissertation. Delft: University of Technology.

Woodward, J. (1965). *Industrial organization: Theory and Practice.* London: Oxford University Press

Zuboff, S. (1988). *In the age of the smart machine. The future of work and power.* New York, NY: Basic Books.

Zigurs, I., & Buckland, B., (1998). A theory of task/technology fit and group support systems effectiveness, *MIS Quarterly, 22*(3), pp. 313-334.

Author Index

A

Ajzen, 64
Alderfer, 63
Algera, 132
Allee, 122
Allen, 5
Ancona, 101
Andersen, 36
Anderson, 159
Andriessen, 19, 24, 33, 35, 36, 98,
    129, 147, 149, 152, 158, 161
Anker, 27, 132, 151
Applebaum, 97
Arnold, 61, 82
Arvonen, 96
Aspden, 25, 38
Aydin, 35, 86

B

Bachman, 117
Bair, 28, 113
Bajaj, 67
Bales, 148
Bannon, 10, 112
Bardram, 92
Bardram's, 94
Barley, 47, 52
Beavin, 106
Belotti, 109
Benbasat, 31, 40
Benford, 14
Bennet, 21
Beyer, 150
Bijker, 51
Bismarck, 15

Blackler, 96
Blatt, 97
Blau, 45
Bly, 11, 14
Boehm, 131
Brennan, 107
Buckiewicz, 11
Buckland, 81
Bullen, 21
Busch, 98

C

Caldwell, 101
Campion, 159
Cannon-Bowers, 68, 109
Carroll, 132
Chapanis, 25
Ciborra, 21, 35, 115, 137
Clark, 107
Cohen, 83, 117, 148
Coleman, 10
Conaill, 107
Cooke, 110
Crowston, 112, 114

D

Daft, 80, 86
Damsgaard, 49, 52
Davis, 32, 66, 67, 69
Defasto, 159
DeMeuse, 83, 101
Dennis, 81
DeSancties, 14
DeSanctis, 52, 134, 135, 137, 140

181

Subject Index

Out of print titles

Dan Diaper and Colston Sanger
CSCW in Practice
3-540-19784-2

Steve Easterbrook (Ed.)
CSCW: Cooperation or Conflict?
3-540-19755-9

John H. Connolly and Ernest A. Edmonds (Eds)
CSCW and Artificial Intelligence
3-540-19816-4

Mike Sharples (Ed.)
Computer Supported Collaborative Writing
3-540-19782-6

Duska Rosenberg and Chris Hutchison (Eds)
Design Issues in CSCW
3-540-19810-5

Peter Thomas (Ed.)
CSCW Requirements and Evaluation
3-540-19963-2

John H. Connolly and Lyn Pemberton (Eds)
Linguistic Concepts and Methods in CSCW
3-540-19984-5

Alan Dix and Russell Beale (Eds)
Remote Cooperation
3-540-76035-0

Stefan Kirn and Gregory O'Hare (Eds)
Cooperative Knowledge Processing
3-540-19951-9

Peter Lloyd and Roger Whitehead (Eds)
Transforming Organisations Through Groupware: Lotus Notes in Action
3-540-19961-6

Reza Hazemi, Stephen Hailes and Steve Wilbur (Eds)
The Digital University: Reinventing the Academy
1-85233-003-1

Alan J. Munro, Kristina Höök and David Benyon (Eds)
Social Navigation of Information Space
1-85233-090-2

Mary Lou Maher, Simeon J. Simoff and Anna Cicognani
Understanding Virtual Design Studios
1-85233-154-2